JOAN
OF ARC
A MILITARY
LEADER

JOAN OF ARC

A MILITARY LEADER

KELLY DEVRIES

SUTTON PUBLISHING

This book was first published in 1999 by
Sutton Publishing Limited · Phoenix Mill
Thrupp · Stroud · Gloucestershire · GL5 2BU

This edition first published in 2003

British Library Cataloguing in Publication Data
A catalogue record for this book is available from the British Library

ISBN 0 7509 2787 9

Typeset in 10/11.5pt Photina.
Typesetting and origination by
Sutton Publishing Limited.
Printed and bound in Great Britain by
J.H. Haynes & Co. Ltd, Sparkford.

Contents

Chronology

1337	Hundred Years War begins.
1340	English naval success at Sluys, but failure at the siege of Tournai.
1346	The English invade France and capture Caen.
	26 August. Battle of Crécy.
1347	Calais falls to the English after a year-long siege.
1348–9	Black Death sweeps Europe.
1356	The Black Prince defeats the French Army at Poitiers.
	John II of France captured by English and imprisoned in the Tower of London.
1360	Treaty of Brétigny.
1369	Charles V regains Aquitaine from the English.
1376	Edward, the Black Prince, dies.
1377	Edward III dies and is succeeded by his grandson Richard II.
1396	Twenty-eight year truce between France and England embodied in the Treaty of Paris.
	Defeat of Anglo-Franco-Burgundian crusade at Nicopolis.
1399	Richard II overthrown by Henry IV.
1407	Louis of Orléans is assassinated in Paris. France is divided between the Burgundians under John the Fearless and the Armagnacs under Louis's son, Charles of Orléans, and Bernard of Armagnac.
1413	Henry V ascends the English throne.
1415	**14 August**. Henry V's invasion force lands at the mouth of the Seine.
	22 August. Harfleur falls to the English.
	25 August. French defeated by the English at the battle of Agincourt.
1418	**29 May**. Paris falls to John the Fearless of Burgundy.
1419	Rouen falls to the English and their conquest of Normandy is complete.
	John the Fearless is murdered.
1420	Treaty of Troyes between Henry V of England, Philip the

Good of Burgundy and Charles VI of France, makes Henry heir to the French throne.

1422 Son born to Henry V and Catherine; he is soon to become Henry VI, king of France and England.

31 August. Henry V dies at Vincennes.

1428 **May**. Joan of Arc meets Robert de Baudricourt, captain of Vaucouleurs, to tell him of her mission for the first time.

12 October. Thomas Montagu, earl of Salisbury, begins the siege of Orléans.

Christmas. By now Jean, the Bastard of Orléans, has arrived at the city with a sizeable French force.

1429 **January**. Joan probably has a second meeting with Baudricourt.

12 February. Battle of the Herrings: the English defeat the French outside Orléans.

12 February. Joan meets Baudricourt for the last time before leaving for Orléans.

11 March. Joan arrives at Poitiers for questioning about her mission by ecclesiastics chosen by the dauphin. The interrogation lasts eleven days.

c. **22 March**. Joan dictates her 'Letter to the English' outlining her mission.

After 21 April. Joan joins the royal army at Blois.

4 May. French soldiers, with Joan, attack and capture the boulevard of Saint Loup at Orléans.

7 May. French capture the Tourelles at Orléans; Joan is wounded but the siege is effectively lifted.

8 May. English leave Orléans.

12 June. With the reinforcements the dauphin has given her, Joan attacks and recaptures Jargeau from the English.

15 June. French army captures the bridge over the Loire at Meung.

17 June. Sir John Fastolf's army arrives at Beaugency while Joan and the French are attacking the town. The English do not fight and Beaugency falls to the French.

18 June. Battle of Patay: another victory for the French.

24 June. French army marches to Gien to join the dauphin.

29 June. French army begins the march to Reims.

2 July. Burgundian-held Auxerre falls to the French without a fight.

5 July. French troops camp outside Burgundian Troyes but the city refuses to capitulate.

8 July. Joan persuades a council of war to begin a siege.

9 July. Troyes surrenders to the French.

12 July. French army leaves for Reims.

17 July. Dauphin crowned Charles VII of France at Reims; Joan is at his side during the ceremony.

Early August. Joan starts to move against Burgundian-held Paris.

28 August. Charles VII signs a truce with Philip the Good of Burgundy without Joan's knowledge.

7 September. Charles VII arrives at Joan's camp at Saint-Denis, outside Paris.

8 September. Joan attacks Paris and is wounded.

9 September. Charles suspends the assault on Paris in the face of protests from Joan and others.

12 September. French army retreats to the Loire.

21 September. Charles dissolves Joan's army and discharges Alençon.

October. Joan is sent to the upper Loire to target the mercenary captain Perrinet Gressart.

By 1 November. Joan begins the siege of Saint-Pierre-le-Moutier.

4 November. Saint-Pierre-le-Moutier taken.

November. Siege of La Charité-sur-Loire begins but is abandoned between **22** and **24 December**.

25 December. Joan returns to Jargeau and receives news that she and her descendants have been ennobled.

1430   **End of March**. Joan moves off, without permission, to help the people of Compiègne, who are planning to resist Burgundian recapture.

29 March. Battle of Lagny; Joan defeats an Anglo-Burgundian force.

14 May. Joan has reached Compiègne.

16 May. Joan and others forced to withdraw from Choisy to Compiègne in the face of Burgundian fire.

By 22 May. Compiègne is surrounded by Anglo-Burgundian forces.

23 May. Joan is captured during a skirmish from Compiègne. She is later tried by the English and convicted of heresy.

1431   **30 May**. Joan is burned at the stake in Rouen marketplace.

1435   Congress of Arras: Philip the Good of Burgundy swaps from the English to the French side in the Hundred Years War.

1450   **April**. Battle of Formigny: French recapture Normandy.

1453   **July**. Last battle of the Hundred Years War is fought at Castillon.

Acknowledgments

Isuppose that I began to write this book in 1994 when I decided to present a paper on Joan of Arc in a session on 'Women in Medieval Warfare' at the Twenty-Eighth International Medieval Congress held at the University of Western Michigan in Kalamazoo. I started my research by reading Régine Pernoud's marvelous *Joan of Arc By Herself and Her Witnesses*, and then, on a long bus ride taking students to the Cloisters, the medieval section of the Metropolitan Museum of Art, by reading almost all of the contemporary narrative sources gathered by Jules Quicherat in his multi-volumed *Procès de condamnation et de réhabilitation de Jeanne d'Arc dite la Pucelle*. After these wonderful experiences, all that I could think of was: what a woman! I must agree with Albert d'Ourches, who said during his testimony in her nullification trial: 'I wished very much to have had a daughter as good as she was.' (As I have two wonderful daughters, I can only encourage them to acquire the same characteristics that Joan exhibited.) The resulting paper from the Kalamazoo conference was published as 'A Woman as Leader of Men: A Reassessment of Joan of Arc's Military Career' in *Fresh Verdicts on Joan of Arc*, edited by C. Wood and B. Wheeler (New York, 1996), pp. 3–18. After that time I continued to read with great interest all I could about Joan. But I was always disappointed to discover that many of the more modern accounts of the Maid forget what she was famous for. Joan was a warrior, a soldier, and a general. All of the late nineteenth-/early twentieth-century French sculptors knew this, but most late twentieth-century historians seem to have forgotten it.

I owe numerous debts of gratitude for assistance that I received while writing this book. I wish to thank Loyola College, especially Dean John Hollwitz, for granting me an eighteen-month sabbatical during which I completed this text, as well as several other projects, and to the Royal Armouries in Leeds, England, and the Dibner Institute for the History of Science and Technology at the Massachusetts Institute of Technology for hosting me during this sabbatical. I particularly wish to thank the staffs of the Royal Armouries Library and Collections Care for putting up with me during the final few weeks as I tried to meet my deadlines, and for their kindness, patience, and assistance. A great deal of gratitude must especially be given to Bob Smith, the Head of Collections Care at the Armouries, not only for his and his wife Ruth Rhynas Brown's friendship, but also for his understanding as I had to push aside the project we were working on together for a couple of weeks while I finished this book. I also appreciate and love the Midgley family, to whom I dedicated my last book, for again housing me in England while I finished writing; England is a beautiful place, and made all the more so because they live in it. Thanks also to Bert Hall, my mentor and good friend; to David Zimmerman, also my friend, and Robert DeVries, my father, for serving as extra pairs of eyes as we visited places of Joan's life during the summer of 1998; to Bonnie Wheeler and Jeremy duQuesnay Adams, for their kind and encouraging words; to Roger Thorpe, past Senior Editor for History at Sutton Publishing, for commissioning this book; to Jane Crompton, current Senior Editor for History for seeing the project through and for forgiving the many times I missed my deadlines; and to medieval military historians everywhere who are diligently and continually changing the field for the better – no other field of medieval history has such innovators. Last, but certainly not least, I owe my greatest debt of gratitude to my wife, Barbara, and kids, Beth, Michael and Catie, for suffering my frequent absences during the writing of this book. All I have accomplished is only because of your love and encouragement.

1

Introduction

On 28 June 1431 English military leaders at Rouen in occupied France sent the following letter in the name of King Henry VI to 'the prelates of the Church, to the dukes, counts and other nobles and to the cities of his kingdom of France':

> . . . it is commonly reported everywhere how the woman who had called herself *Jehanne la Pucelle* (the Maid), a false prophetess, had for more than two years, against divine law and the estate of her sex, dressed in men's clothes, a thing abominable to God, and in that state journeyed to our chief enemy, whom, with others of his party, clergy, nobles and commoners, she often contended that she was sent from God, and presumptuously boasted that she often had personal and visible communication with St Michael and a great host of angels and saints of Paradise, as well as with St Catherine and St Margaret. . . . She dressed herself also in arms worn by knights and squires, raised a standard, and, in very great outrage, pride and presumption, demanded to have and carry the very noble and excellent arms of France, which she entirely obtained, and carried in many conflicts and assaults . . . In such a state she went to the fields and led men-at-arms and commanded great companies to commit and exercise inhuman cruelties in shedding human blood, in causing popular seditions and disturbances, inciting them to perjuries and pernicious rebellions, false and superstitious beliefs, in disturbing all free peace and renewing mortal war, in permitting herself to be worshiped and revered by many as a holy woman, and working other damnable things in many cases too long to describe, which in many places are recognized always to have greatly scandalized almost all of Christianity.[1]

The reason for the release of such a letter was simple: the English wished to restore what had been the military situation but two years previously, when they controlled almost the entirety of northern and southwestern France. At the time of this letter, they no longer controlled that same territory. In fact, during that two-year span of time not only had the English lost the extremely important Loire town of Orléans, which they had been on the very point of capturing in 1429, but they had been deprived of almost all of their other Loire strongholds – Jargeau, Beaugency, Meung, and, further to the south, Saint-Pierre-le-Moutier. They had suffered the capture and imprisonment of two of their military leaders, John Talbot, earl of Shrewsbury, and William de la Pole, earl of Suffolk. And, perhaps most grievous of all because there had been relatively no military action involved, they had seen the surrender of Auxerre, Châlons, Troyes, Soissons, Laon, Senlis, Compiègne, and Reims. At the last town, their enemy, the man whom they saw as the usurper of their lawful French throne, had been crowned as King Charles VII of France.

There was a simple reason for these losses: a peasant girl, that same *Jehanne la Pucelle*, the false prophetess, whose burning had prompted the epistle quoted in part above, had changed the military affairs of the Hundred Years War. Almost alone, Joan of Arc had transfigured a losing French side into one that not only won those aforementioned numerous victories, but would continue to win until, by 1453, it had completely cleared even Normandy and Aquitaine of English soldiers; only Calais on French soil would be left in English hands. How did she do this?

No person in the Middle Ages, male or female, has been the subject of more historical studies than Joan of Arc. Yet, few of these studies have been devoted to her capabilities as a military leader, despite this being the primary reason for her notoriety, whether famous or infamous. Instead, she has been portrayed as a religious figure – saint or heretic, zealot or witch, seer or demented teenager – a proto-feminist 'gender-bender', a class equalizer – Marxist liberator or aristocratic wanna-be – and a French nationalist – a symbol for both the political right and left. Maybe Joan was all of these, even those that seem dichotomous. This should not be seen as a contradiction, though, as Joan represents the quintessential medieval 'fish-out-of-water'.

A religious figure? Joan of Arc was a devoted believer in the Christian God, but not One Who gives a message of general theological significance, rather One Who sends her on a one-sided military mission – to remove the English from France. Theological questions actually seemed to be irritants to her; many of those asked her at her trial she answered incorrectly.[2] A proto-feminist? Joan of Arc was a woman participating in the most harsh, violent, and cruel part of a medieval man's world, seeming to destroy those very gender boundaries. Yet, when confronting another 'holy woman', Catherine de la Rochelle, who wished to aid the king, Charles VII, in his fight against the English by helping him to discover 'hidden treasures', which she had seen in dreams, with which he could purchase the services of soldiers for his war, Joan remarked that she should go home and attend to her family, hardly a feminist comment.[3] A class equalizer? Joan of Arc never claimed any background other than that of a peasant girl from a relatively small village, Domrémy,[4] and asked as a reward for her victories only that the people of that and a neighboring village, Greux, be discharged from paying taxes.[5] But neither did she turn down the ennoblement of herself and her family,[6] and she became accustomed to wearing fine and costly clothes, the latter of which brought the enmity (and, one suspects, also the jealousy) of Regnault of Chartres, the archbishop of Reims.[7] A French nationalist? Joan of Arc had one cause: a unified, unoccupied France. To achieve this, she wanted to see the rift between the king and his cousin, Philip the Good, duke of Burgundy, mended.[8] And she wanted to see the end of English occupation of any area of her homeland. She praised the towns that had withstood English military threat and conquest, and she disdained the many that had surrendered without putting up a valiant and continual fight.[9] She loved the company of men, like Arthur de Richemont and Jean, duke of Alençon, who wished to rid their homeland of the English invaders,[10] while she would threaten with death and destruction any who might seem half-hearted in their patriotism, as witnessed in her initial meetings with Jean, the Bastard of Orléans and later count of Dunois.[11] She especially remembered the French warrior, Bertrand Du Guesclin, whose brave generalship a generation previously had greatly diminished the English occupation of his age.[12] But her politics stopped there. She would obey her 'divine right' king in his every command, and she even facilitated his crowning at Reims, but she was not above being frustrated with him and especially his counselors for not pressing forward quickly enough or with enough strength to win more definitive victories.[13]

All of these definitions of Joan seem to miss the most obvious one. Joan of Arc was a soldier, plain and simple. If that is understood, Joan's other characteristics are also explained. But, what is more, if one can understand Joan's military purpose and character, so too can one understand France's reversal of the Hundred Years War, which can be dated effectively from her military advent in 1429. One can understand that the English began an easy decline from that time, a decline that would eventually lead to the other major events in their defeat in the Hundred Years War: the Congress of Arras in 1435, which would see the abandonment of their side by the Burgundians, the rebellions in and ultimate loss of Normandy, (the latter in 1450) and, finally, the 1453 fall of Gascony.

But, returning to the question that was sidestepped above, how did she do it? How did she turn the tide of the Hundred Years War in only a little more than one year? Joan was sent from God. At least she believed that she had been sent from God, and for our modern historical purposes this was equal to having actually had the divine mission that she asserted. For with it, and by her confident and direct military tactics, combined with her willingness to risk everything, including the lives of an extraordinarily large number of her own countrymen, Joan put military aggressiveness into an army that had been forced into a psychology of defeat, a psychology that had resulted in little confident military action since at least 1415.

The composition of a military biography of any premodern individual is at the best of times a difficult task, especially as most military leaders living in an age of relative illiteracy wrote, or had someone write in their name, so little. Moreover, Joan of Arc's military career was very brief. Despite this latter fact, or some might say because of it, Joan's exploits are written about frequently in narrative histories. Chroniclers from all lands involved directly or indirectly in the Hundred Years War were attracted to her feats in the war and devoted a portion of their histories to recounting her military exploits. Two of these chronicles are devoted in particular to her story, the *Chronique de la Pucelle* and the *Journal du siège d'Orléans*.[14] Both were written in the French vernacular between thirty and forty years after her death and both have survived without authorial attribution, although it seems probable that they were composed in Orléans, the site of her greatest victory. Numerous other pro-French chronicles also exist, almost all of which are extremely favorable to her and sustain her beliefs in her divine mission. Less praiseworthy and less believing in her divine mission are the equally numerous narrative histories of Joan written by Burgundian and English chroniclers. However, they too contain valuable accounts of her exploits as well as indications of attitudes toward her held by her enemies; some did question whether it was in fact possible that she had heard the voice of deity directing her actions, but most rejected her spiritual claims. Finally, there are a few narrative sources written outside of these warring countries. Because of the duration and importance of the Hundred Years War, Joan's accomplishments became quickly publicized as far away as Constantinople. Even Cardinal Aeneas Silvius Piccolomini, not yet Pope Pius II, commented on what had occurred between 1429 and 1431 and pondered Joan's divine call. Many of these foreign narratives are valuable only in noting Joan of Arc's renown throughout Europe, although one or two, such as Antonio Morosini's *Diario*, give even-handed eye-witness reports from foreigners living within the fought-over regions who were concerned with how the Hundred Years War was affecting their own lands – in Morosini's case Venetian trade and commerce.[15]

All of these narrative sources together provide a portrayal of what Joan did and how. They also relate who was among her noble followers and what roles they played in her adventures. These can then be supplemented by a number of letters written at the behest of Joan of Arc. Contemporary records make reference to seventeen letters 'written' by the Maid and what was contained in them. Three still exist which contain her signature: one written to the town of Riom on 9 November 1429, a second sent to Reims on 16 March 1430, with a third also sent to Reims on 28 March 1430. Others exist as original, unsigned letters from her – six in total. Together these form the only relics left by this young saint. (That is if we discount the mostly burned piece of rib bone today found in the Joan of Arc Museum in Chinon Castle, which the placard affixed to it claims was taken from the ashes after her burning.) They also are an extremely invaluable source for Joan's military career as they all contain her thoughts as a leader of the French forces. Even the letter written by Joan to the Hussites on 22 March 1430 and preserved in a contemporary German translation in the Vienna *Reichsregister* shows her confident military leadership as Joan threatens to leave the fighting against the English to direct her military attentions against those heretical Christians fighting in Bohemia at the time.[16] Other documentary sources, muster rolls, etc., also add to the history of this French leader in the Hundred Years War.

But perhaps the most valuable contemporary sources of Joan of

Arc's military career are her trial and nullification trial transcripts. Unprecedented in medieval military history, these records contain an accurate account of Joan's short life from her own mouth (the trial) and the mouths of her neighbors, confederates, followers, friends, and even some of her judges and tormenters (the nullification trial). The trial transcripts, written in French each evening from notes taken during the day's interrogation and later translated into Latin (both the French and Latin versions still exist), are definitely slanted to make Joan appear guilty of heresy, much as the trial was; nevertheless, they seem to record her words accurately.[17] The nullification trial, also called the retrial or rehabilitation trial, took place over a period of four years from 1452 to 1456. King Charles VII commissioned this trial in an effort to review Joan's condemnation, sending notaries and investigators throughout the kingdom to interview those who knew Joan well and could thereby shed light on the justice or injustice of her original trial. Numerous witnesses were interviewed, including many who had served with her during her military campaigns, such as Jean, the Bastard of Orléans, Jean, duke of Alençon, Jean d'Aulon, Joan's squire, and also some of her soldiers. These transcripts form a sort of oral history of Joan's exploits, necessitating the same cautions in using these testimonies which apply to modern use of oral histories.[18] Memories fade, and legendary individuals, like Joan of Arc, grow in proportion over the years; still, what these witnesses to her life add to the chronicles and other narrative histories is priceless.

But, if all of these sources do exist, and if Joan of Arc has been the subject of so many modern authors, what is the need of yet another history? It is true that since the middle of the eighteenth, and especially during the nineteenth and twentieth centuries, there has been an increase in Joan of Arc studies. Indeed, during this time she undoubtedly was the most written about individual of the Middle Ages. French nationalism, especially in the wake of the failed wars of the eighteenth century and the end of the nineteenth century, coupled with a drive for theological authenticity leading to sainthood undoubtedly aided the resurgence of academic interest in this fifteenth-century French hero. Her greatness crossed all political boundaries, it seems, as her image was appropriated by both the political and scholarly right and left. Additionally, the whole process was facilitated by the collection and editing of most of the documents, letters, poems, and chronicles concerning Joan's life, as well as the transcripts of her trial and nullification trial made by Jules-Etienne-Joseph Quicherat in 1841–9. While superseded and updated in some parts by later editors, this work still stands as one of the great editorial collections of medieval history.[19]

After Joan's sanctification in 1920, scholarly interest in her seemed to subside, but only relatively. What was written differed from the more traditional military and religious biographies of the previous two centuries. Especially since the Second World War, there has been an interest in Joan as a woman or, developing later, as a 'cross-dresser'. Although the attraction of her as a saint and as a national hero has persisted, the fact that she achieved what she did by military leadership seems to have been minimized and, in a few of the more recent books, nearly forgotten. Some military historians do not believe that she was a good military leader, while others doubt her role as a leader at all, preferring to view her as the inspirational symbol for continually defeated troops, in other words more a mascot than a general. It is true that some French military officers wrote histories praising Joan's strategy and tactics, but these have become fewer since the end of the First World War, with only three written since 1919 and only two of these written since the end of the Second World War.[20] Moreover, they are not frequently read by Joan of Arc scholars, most of whom justifiably disregard what these officers have to say as they almost always write from secondary sources and in so doing perpetuate errors and myths that originate in earlier military histories of Joan. But when these military histories are so surreptitiously discarded, gone too is what an officer trained in the military arts might reveal to those less well trained in the leadership and skills of war, which Joan was obviously so well versed in. Some kind of middle ground must be found. Joan of Arc, after all, was a soldier. It is this alone that she believed was her mission, and it is what brought both her honors and her condemnations. Wanting to be a French soldier, a leader of men into combat, took her from her simple life in Domrémy to the king in Chinon and Reims, to the battlefields and siege sites of Orléans, Jargeau, Meung, Beaugency, Patay, Saint Denis, St Pierre-le-Moutier, La Charité, Senlis, Crépy-en-Valois, Melun, and Compiègne, and, finally, to the tribunal and then the stake in Rouen. We should not denigrate that legacy; instead, we should study it.

Why Joan of Arc Was Needed

Things had not gone very well for France since the outbreak of the Hundred Years War in 1337. Of the four phases of the war that had already been fought, it can be said that France had only won one, while drawing with England in one, and losing quite dramatically in the other two, including the phase immediately preceding Joan's appearance as a leader of the French army. Numerous studies have been written trying to explain this phenomenon and they have reached different conclusions, usually depending on whether they were authored by an English scholar or a French one. All begin, however, by exclaiming that it should not have happened this way. France had a far larger population than did England.[1] France had a much stronger economy, with a strong agricultural base and the manufacture of many profitable trade goods. France had been led by several good rulers. Believing in the 'divine right' to rule, France's kings had been of one dynasty, the Capetians, from 985 to 1328. (During the same period, England had witnessed more than ten royal dynasties.)[2]

Above all, France had a strong and renowned military. During the thirteenth century under able warrior kings such as Philip II (Augustus) and Philip IV (the Fair), it had won many wars, strengthening the borders against the Spanish kingdoms, Italy, and the Holy Roman Empire, while at the same time restoring almost all of the French lands inherited by the English kings Richard I (Lionhearted) and John through their mother, Eleanor of Aquitaine, and their father, Henry II. (John's nickname, Lackland, came to him because of his loss of so much French territory.) Rebellious lords and heretical sects had also felt the strength of France's military might, ending their days in prisons or, more often, in death. Indeed, Philip IV felt so confident in his military might that he even challenged the Knights of the Temple Mount, the Templars, the largest military monastic order, declaring this crusading relic to be heretical and confiscating its treasures and lands.[3] There were some defeats, it is true, most notably by King Louis IX on crusade in Egypt and North Africa and by noble-led French armies at the battles of Courtrai in 1302 and Arques in 1303, but these were soon forgotten and whatever setbacks had resulted were quickly reclaimed.[4] The definition of a strong military, after all, was not a force that won every battle, clearly an impossibility in the Middle Ages, but one that could quickly recover after a loss.

Yet, a new age seemed to dawn with the outbreak of the Hundred Years War in 1337, an age that forgot France's earlier political, economic, and military strength. When King Edward III launched his first major invasion in 1340, it was ostensibly to recover his crown as king of France, a crown that had been legalistically 'stolen' from him in 1328 when, despite being the closest heir to the dead king, Charles IV, he was declared ineligible to receive it because his royal descent was gained through a woman. The throne instead was given to a cousin, Philip of Valois, who was then crowned as King Philip VI of France.[5]

But there were also other issues at hand. Representatives of the towns and baronies of the southern Low Countries had petitioned Edward to come to their aid as they sought more and more political sovereignty and financial independence from their French governors. Most impressive of the opponents of the French was Jacob van Artevelde, the leader of the county of Flanders. Having led a rebellion manned primarily by urban cloth workers against the count of Flanders, Louis of Nevers, this Ghentenaar cloth-merchant and weaver had cast out the count who, of course, ran off to Paris for solace and aid in putting down the rebellion of his strong towns.[6] Philip VI had not been quick to respond on this occasion – he had previously done so with great speed and success in a similar situation in 1328[7] – and the Flemish towns had grown comfortable in their independence. They did not want to lose it, and with Edward III wanting to wage war against France anyway, why not look to England, their chief supplier of wool, as a means of keeping the French king at bay? They would be joined by other southern Low Countries' powers dependent on English wool, Brabant and Hainault, in an anti-French alliance. Even the Holy Roman Emperor sent some troops and funds to aid the English war effort.[8]

The first major engagement was fought aboard ships in the harbor at Sluys on 24 June 1340. By the end of the day, Edward's navy, ably assisted by Flemings from Sluys and nearby Bruges who watched the fight from the shore and kept any French sailor from escaping to land, won the battle. In doing so, they almost completely annihilated the French navy.[9] It was a devastating loss for the French, so much so that a later English chronicler reports that no one in the French court wished to deliver the news to Philip VI. Finally, a court fool or jester was chosen to inform the king of the result of the battle:

> This fool, placed in the presence of the king, began vehemently to indict the insanity of the English, and he began to multiply his words concerning this matter. However, the king, ignoring the words this moron wished to say to him, asked why he said that the English were so insane. The fool said to him: 'Because they are timid and do not dare to dance in the sea as our generous Normans and French do.' Through these words, the king understood that they had been the victims and that the English were the victors.[10]

Edward III followed this with a siege of the town of Tournai, the largest of the northern towns that had declared their allegiance for the French king. But it was there that Edward's momentum was temporarily halted. Despite destroying many French-allied lands and villages near Tournai, and despite having Philip VI and the French army camped within sight of the besieged town but unwilling to come to battle even though it seemed that the town was on the verge of surrendering, Edward III lost his alliance through bickering and saw his own parliament hold up funds needed for him to carry on the war. He was forced to retreat to England and sign the truce of Espléchin with the French.[11] The Low Countries' baronies, now left without a protector, quickly dissolved into wars against each other; eventually a rival Flemish faction assassinated Jacob van Artevelde, and the county of Flanders returned to its previous comital governance.[12]

What appeared to be a victory for the French quickly proved, however, to be nothing more than a short recess before they suffered even greater defeats. Edward III used the time to remove those elements in his representative government who opposed war with France, and then he planned his return. According to the truce of Espléchin, Edward could not 'legally' wage war against France for five years. However, before that time had elapsed, a civil war broke out in Brittany between two heirs to the vacant ducal throne. Edward used this excuse to re-enter conflict with France, supporting John of Montfort in his claim while France supported the rival candidate, Charles of Blois. Technically this did not violate the terms of the Espléchin treaty, as Brittany was not a part of France proper, and although this war would continue until 1364, by 1342 Edward in the name of Montfort had occupied a large part of the duchy, including the port town of Brest.[13]

Four years later, in 1346, the truce of Espléchin expired, and Edward wasted little time in attacking the French kingdom. Landing in Normandy with a large army, probably as many as 15,000 troops, Edward besieged and quickly captured Caen.[14] He then marched towards the Low Countries, perhaps in an effort to reach Flanders and re-establish his earlier alliance. If he was trying to reach the Low Countries, however, he surprisingly stopped at Crécy, in the county of Ponthieu. The French army, still under the leadership of Philip VI, who was following the English, decided this time to give him a battle, and, on 26 August 1346, the first great land battle of the Hundred Years War was fought. As was to be the pattern repeated throughout the next century, the French soldiers greatly outnumbered their opponents but lost. Philip was able to escape the carnage, departing to Paris under the cover of darkness, but many of his lords and captains were killed.[15] Edward moved victoriously to the town of Calais, and after a year-long siege, again with the French king camping idly by, the townspeople could no longer withstand their forced hunger and the town fell. The English would use Calais as their continental 'beachhead' for the next two centuries.[16]

What the French seemed unable to do, a plague of unprecedented proportions did. The Black Death, as it became known to contemporaries, attacked Europe in 1348–9 and effectively halted the military progress of Edward III and the English. Although no study has yet been undertaken on what effects this plague had on the fighting of the Hundred Years War, on the manpower, leadership, finances, or strategy and tactics, the epidemic's impact seems to have been major. Not only was there a cessation of hostilities for nearly a decade, but when fighting did begin anew, in 1355–6, the armies could be seen to have decreased dramatically in size. There was also a new tactic of warfare which the English began to adopt and which, for the rest of the war, they would practice with regularity and proficiency: the *chevauchée*, a quick cavalry raid through the countryside with the intention of pillaging unfortified villages and towns, destroying crops and houses, stealing livestock, and generally disrupting and terrorizing rural society. The first effect of the Black Death in fact fed the second. With decreased armies on both sides, there would never again in the Hundred Years War be the likes of the battle which was fought at Crécy, with its 15,000–20,000 men per side, or the sieges which were carried out at Tournai and Calais, with upwards of 30,000 besiegers. Indeed, the siege as a means of waging the Hundred Years War, at least for a few decades following the Black Death, was replaced almost entirely by the *chevauchée*.[17]

Of course, the *chevauchée* was not a new tactic. Military raids into the countryside to gather foodstuffs and booty and to spread terror had been conducted throughout the entire Middle Ages. Indeed, during the Hundred Years War, what could be called *chevauchées* were conducted during the sieges of both Tournai and Crécy, as well as at other times during the years preceding the Black Death. But they had never been relied on as military actions by Edward III, who preferred battle and siege as a means of waging war against his enemies, the French and the Scots; nor were they probably his desired tactic after the Black Death. But when he could no longer field an army of the size he felt he needed to provoke a battle or participate in a quick and victorious siege, he began to depend on raiding into the generally unprotected countryside to fight against the French, and perhaps also to bring them to battle. So it happened that in 1356, when Edward's son, Edward the Black Prince, was raiding through the north-central regions of France above Gascony, the then king of France, John II (Philip VI had died in 1350), tried to fight against the smaller forces of the English outside the town of Poitiers. The result was the same as that faced by his father at Crécy: he lost. Only John was unable to flee from the battlefield, and was instead captured and imprisoned in the Tower of London.[18] The French were forced to the negotiating table, where eventually the Treaty of Brétigny was signed. The French promised a ransom for John of 3 million golden crowns and the surrender of the duchies of Aquitaine and Ponthieu and the town of Calais. Edward III, in turn, agreed to renounce his claim to the French throne.[19]

The imprisonment of King John II in London may have been the best thing that could have happened to the French. He is generally considered to have been an ineffective military leader and John II's ransom was long in coming to London – indeed, it was never completely raised. He lingered in his English jail, his expenses paid for out of English coffers. In the meantime, John's son and heir, later to be Charles V, was forced to defend his kingdom's shrinking borders. These were threatened not only by the English, but also the Navarrese, led by his cousin, King Charles of Navarre, who sought to take advantage of what he perceived to be a weakened France, and by roving bands of soldiers left without employment by the Treaty of Brétigny but carrying on their own war by plundering the countryside. In this the dauphin Charles was aided ably by a rising French military superstar, Bertrand du Guesclin. Du Guesclin, a short and ugly Breton, whose French military leadership was unsurpassed in the Hundred Years War until the advent of Joan of Arc, fought in a number of impressive engagements. In some he was dreadfully overmatched and unsuccessful. In fact, he found himself a prisoner after his defeats both at Auray, in 1364, and at Nájera, in Castile, in 1367. At the latter conflict, du Guesclin had taken the side of Henry of Trastamara in his Castilian succession struggles with his half-brother, Pedro the Cruel, who was supported by the Black Prince. However, in most of the engagements that Bertrand du Guesclin fought, he was victorious.[20]

With these victories and others, Charles V – for he had assumed the throne in 1364 on the death of his father in London – saw his military fortunes begin to rise, and slowly he began to regain his kingdom. By 1369 he had taken back Aquitaine; by 1371 he had made peace with Charles of Navarre; that same year he again began to exert authority in Brittany; in 1372 his allies, the Castilians (Henry of Trastamara had eventually defeated and killed Pedro the Cruel and at that time sat on the throne of Castile, always willing to aid the French against the English) defeated the English fleet off the coast of La Rochelle;[21] and by 1377 he had outlived both of his chief enemies when Edward the Black Prince died (in June 1376 of a disease which he had acquired during his campaign in Spain) followed less than a year later by Edward III.[22] This left a child, Richard II, untrained in the warfare of his father or grandfather, as king of England, a situation which Charles V, and after his death in 1380, his son, Charles VI, took full advantage of, pushing the English back until they could barely hold on to Calais and Gascony.[23]

There were several reasons for the French success during the reign of Charles V. Undoubtedly the military leadership shown by him and Bertrand du Guesclin were major factors in regaining what had earlier been lost. This, coupled with the weakened, and in fact ailing, English leadership of the same period, meant that the French soldiers were able frequently to take advantage of the confusion and instability within their enemy's ranks. At the same time, the English must have been feeling fatigued from fighting far away from their homeland and for such a long time for a cause that seemed rather distant and unimportant. The number of English troops available after the Black Death was limited, and those willing to go to France and fight for a diminished and (after the crowning of Richard II), increasingly uninterested military leadership, one that lost far more than it won, was unappealing even to the few soldiers who might have been mustered.[24] Thirdly, the Flemish allies who had always stood by the side of England were having their own military problems. Faced with war first against Brabant during the 1360s and then, from 1379 to 1385, engaged in another attempt to gain independence from the French, the Flemings ultimately saw their alliance with England as doing them little good. The bishop of Norwich's 'crusade' of 1383 in an effort to aid the Flemings against the French was unable even to besiege successfully a town, Ypres, which was not entirely unwilling to surrender. In addition, the Flemings' weak count, Louis of Male, was replaced by his much stronger son-in-law, Duke Philip the Bold of Burgundy, as governor.[25]

Finally, the *chevauchée* form of fighting, which during this phase of the war had been carried out continuously by an increasing number of English captains, both noble and 'mercenary', must also shoulder some of the blame for the declining English military power in France. As a tactic for causing terror among the French while at the same time making its English practitioners wealthy, it was thriving. But none of the territorial gains from this practice could be called permanent, and, while their destruction of the French countryside should not be underestimated, the defense of those areas already occupied by the English was neglected, and in places even abandoned. In the end the *chevauchée* may have harmed the English more than it ever helped.[26]

By 1394 Richard II was forced to counter revolts among the peasants at home and dissatisfaction among his uncles, cousins, and other bellicose English nobles; he decided to push for peace with France. In 1396, a twenty-eight-year truce was arranged in Paris, dependent on the marriage of the still young English monarch to Isabella, one of Charles VI's daughters, and an equal Anglo-French presence on a crusade to the east against the Ottoman Turks.[27] It was a fine peace proposal, but not too realistic considering what occurred during the next five years: since 1392 Charles VI had been suffering the fits of mental illness that would continue until his death;[28] the crusade, which was not well attended to by either the French or English, ended miserably with the defeat and virtual destruction of the Christian army at Nicopolis in 1396;[29] and, in 1399, Richard II was overthrown and killed by his cousin, the Lancastrian warlord, Henry IV.[30] Therefore, the Hundred Years War was destined to continue into a third phase.

Some might claim that this third phase of the conflict was not really a phase at all. In fact, neither France nor England actually fought each other, although each occasionally raided the other's coast, and threats of greater hostilities were always present. But such a claim would erroneously narrow the focus of the Hundred Years War to those two participants only. While France and England may not have exchanged blows during the period between the Treaty of Paris and 1415 when Henry V launched his attack on France, that is not to say that they were not involved in warfare, and that this warfare was not related to the Hundred Years War, which had been waged between the two for most of the previous century. First, in England, Henry IV found that his occupation of the throne after his usurpation of it from Richard II – at least one cause of which was Henry's dissatisfaction at how Richard had pursued the war against France – was anything but simple. Between 1399 and his death in 1413, Henry was continually forced to put down insurrections that threatened his own royal security. In 1400, Owain Glyn Dŵr led a Welsh uprising which captured many fortified places in northern Wales, including the important castle of Harlech, and endured until it petered out on its own around 1410.[31] In Scotland, raids across the English border lands were frequent and supported by the French. An expedition into Scotland in 1400 by the later Henry V could do nothing to halt them and must be seen as one of the few military failures in this powerful general's life.[32] Finally, in 1403, a rebellion of English nobles, led by Henry Percy (Hotspur) was forced to fight a battle at Shrewsbury. On this occasion, in what some historians have called the first contest of the English Wars of the Roses, the future Henry V, who led the royal forces, was victorious.[33]

In France during the same period, the military situation was far more demanding and far less resolved. Charles VI's illness had left an unstable government, with a number of nobles vying for power. Two of these quickly came to the fore and faced each other in what just as quickly became solid opposition. The dukes of Burgundy and Orléans were both cousins to the king, which of course made them cousins to each other. But their family ties did not bring them to an accord, and for almost the rest of the Hundred Years War these two factions, typically known as the Burgundians and Armagnacs, utilized every means of warfare from actual combat to assassination in their fight. It was quite simply a civil war, one that would infect the French and weaken them to such a point that when Henry V did invade the geographical kingdom, he found instead a divided realm, with one side, the Burgundians, willing either to collaborate with his invasion or to ignore it, and the other side, the Armagnacs, unwilling to decide whether it was more keen to fight against the English or the Burgundians.

John the Fearless, the duke of Burgundy and leader of the faction which bore that name, and Louis, duke of Orléans and leader of the party which would later be known as the Armagnacs, agreed on almost nothing except their common desire to rule France in the place of the ill king. They could not even agree on which pope to support: John supported the Roman pontiff, Gregory XII, in consideration of his Flemish subjects, who backed Gregory and who financially bore the greatest amount of the duke's expenses, while Louis supported the pope residing in the southern French town of Avignon, Benedict XIII.[34] But more important was the issue of how the two felt about war with the English. Louis, recognizing the French successes of the past phase of the Hundred Years War, wished to take advantage of Henry IV's problems at home to try to retake those areas of France still in English hands, principally Gascony. John, more a pragmatist than a soldier (despite his military activity at Nicopolis, among other places) desired to make peace with the English. Again, it was the Flemings and their dependence on English wool for their profitable and taxable cloth-making industries that determined John's politics.[35] Still, there had been little more than words between the two parties before 20 November 1407, when Louis of Orléans was assassinated in Paris. John the Fearless was quickly implicated, and the kingdom of France became divided between the two sides, the Armagnac side being led then by Louis's son, Charles of Orléans, and his son-in-law, Bernard, the count of Armagnac.[36]

There seems little doubt among historians that John the Fearless planned this assassination with the idea of taking advantage of the then weakened Armagnacs to extend his own lands and political power, although his initial claim was that it came about 'through the intervention of the devil'.[37] Later, he paid a master in theology at the University of Paris, Jean Petit, to write a *Justification* for the murder, claiming that it was done only to put a stop to Louis of Orléans's 'tyrannicide'.[38] (As will be seen below, this would not be the last time that scholars at the University of Paris would be used to rationalize a political killing.) Such maneuvers convinced King Charles VI that John should not be punished for this crime, and he was able to escape with only a fine. Other French leaders were not so mollified, with some, such as Jean, duke of Berry, Louis II, count of Anjou, and Jean I, duke of Bourbon, joining the Armagnac party.[39] But all of this noble weight against him did not discourage the duke of Burgundy. Indeed, it seems to have strengthened his resolve to reinforce his position by military means. Simply put, he began to wage war against all who opposed him. When not involved in quelling uprisings in his own lands – he spent most of 1408 at war against the Liègeois[40] – he used his large army, well supplied with perhaps the largest, most diverse gunpowder artillery train in Europe, to attack his French enemies. In 1409–10, he besieged and captured Vellexon;[41] in 1411, he besieged and captured Rougemont and Ham;[42] in 1412, he captured Bourges;[43] and in 1414 he took Arras.[44] Other towns surrendered to him without resistance to avoid destruction. So successful was John the Fearless that by 1412 he occupied the entire duchies of Picardy, Champagne, and Berry, threatened Bourbon, and had most of the citizens of Paris sympathetic to his rule. The Treaty of Auxerre, signed in August of that year by most of the high-ranking French nobles and government officials, confirmed these victories.[45]

More important even than these military victories was John the Fearless's truce with the English, made before the murder of Louis of Orléans in 1407. While not particularly well enforced – in fact in 1412 John of Berry actually convinced Henry IV to send a few troops to aid him in trying to recover his lost territory – this set the stage for the later English-Burgundian alliance which was to play such an important part in the next phase of the Hundred Years War.[46]

The French civil war between the Burgundians and the Armagnacs remained unresolved during the life of Joan of Arc. It could even be said that it affected her every bit as much as Henry V's 1415 invasion, for because of it she was faced with having to deal not only with an English enemy, but also a French one. Joan tried to do what she could to bring about a settlement between the two factions. She wrote at least two letters to Philip the Good, John the Fearless's successor as duke of Burgundy, asking for a reconciliation between himself and his cousin, the king. But this king, Charles VII, whom she placed on the throne, was the head of the Armagnac party, and Philip refused to accede to her wishes for unity and peace.[47] In the end, it would be Burgundian troops at Compiègne who would capture Joan and sell her to the English.

In March 1413, the death of Henry IV brought his son, Henry V, to the throne of England. While it could be said that Henry IV had technically complied with the provisions of the 1396 Treaty of Paris signed by his predecessor, Richard II – the only troops that he had sent to France were there at the invitation of the French – Henry V planned no such compliance. On 14 August 1415, Henry's invasion force landed in the mouth of the Seine and began to besiege the nearby town of Harfleur. It was not a large army, probably numbering no more than 8,000–9,000 soldiers, only a quarter of whom were men-at-arms. But the French seem to have been completely unprepared for this attack, and six weeks later on 22 September the town surrendered, having received an extraordinarily large number of gunpowder-propelled projectiles, which, as recorded in a contemporary poem later adapted by Shakespeare, fulfilled a promise made by Henry: 'My gonnes schall play with Harflete/ A game at the tenys, as y wene.'[48]

The French army did not come to the relief of Harfleur, but remained instead at Rouen. Why it did this is not known. Perhaps the French knew how costly the taking of Harfleur had been for Henry; dysentery had caused a large number of his soldiers, primarily the men-at-arms, to die or become disabled. At the same time, they may have thought that, once he had configured Harfleur, the English king would stay put, waiting for reinforcements behind the protective walls of his newly captured town. However, those walls had taken quite a beating and were severely damaged. Besides, the capture of Harfleur was not the only result that Henry wanted from his invasion. So, he determined to march his remaining healthy troops 150 miles north-east to the much safer haven of Calais. On 6 or 7 October, he began his march, hoping, it is argued, not to encounter the French army, but willing, it seems from the result, to engage this army in a battle should they catch him.

After allowing the English army to cross the River Somme near Peronne, undoubtedly a mistake in judgement among the French military leaders, on 25 October 1415, the French finally caught the English outside of the village of Agincourt.[49] As at Crécy (and elsewhere throughout the Hundred Years War), the French forces should have easily defeated their English foes, if for no other reason than that they outnumbered them by almost 5 to 1 (25,000 to just over 5,000), with most of the French soldiers knights and men-at-arms.[50] Yet, they did not. In what was certainly one of the greatest and most immortalized victories of the entire Middle Ages, the English annihilated their opponents. Using his archers on the wings of a central infantry line, a customary English battlefield tactic, but also interspersing groups of them among the men-at-arms in this central line – an entirely non-customary English battlefield tactic forced on Henry by the losses of his men-at-arms to dysentery – the English king took a defensive stand and prepared to meet the charges of the French horse and foot. On came the French. They made charge after charge, but all became disrupted and confused by the archery and muddy field. By the time that the few soldiers who were able to complete their charges met the solid English line, their impetus had been lost, and they were easily dragged off their horses and slaughtered or imprisoned (and later slain). At the end of the day, more than 10,000 French soldiers lay dead; three of these were dukes (Alençon, Brabant, and Bar), and seven were counts (Nevers, Marle, Vaudémont, Blamont, Grandpré, Roucy, and Fauquembergues), with the Constable of France and commanding general, Charles d'Albret, the Admiral of France, Jacques de Châtillon, and more than 90 other lords and 1,560 knights also killed. Charles, duke of Orléans, Jean, duke of Bourbon, Arthur de Richemont, the aged Marshal Boucicaut, and many other French nobles were prisoners. On the English side the casualties were light, with only a few hundred killed, including only two nobles, Edward, duke of York, and Michael de la Pole, count of Suffolk.[51]

Henry V took quick advantage of the French defeat. He also proved himself to be more than a great field general, showing a strategic foresight absent even from his great-grandfather, Edward III. Marching to Calais, he was back in London by 23 November, displaying the high-ranking prisoners. News of the great victory had already reached England before the king returned, and the English greeted him with cheers and accolades everywhere he went. It was now quite easy to recruit men and logistical support. During the next year he built up a large army funded by an impressive war-chest.[52]

There was little military action in 1416. The French did make an attempt to regain Harfleur, blockading the town by land and sea, but on 15 August Henry's brother, John, duke of Bedford, easily defeated the blockading French fleet at the battle of the Seine and relieved the siege.[53] This was to be the first of many skillful military moves that this general would make during the Hundred Years War; later, as commander of the English forces in France, he was to come to know Joan of Arc perhaps better than any of her other enemies.

While it was perhaps not apparent at the time, the French action at Harfleur was quite a weak military response to what had occurred the previous year. It was clear that Agincourt had taken its toll not only on the French army's leadership and numbers, but, perhaps more importantly, on its military confidence as well. It was only a matter of time before more significant places than Harfleur would be lost.

These losses would begin in 1417. Henry V returned on 1 August of that year with a strategic design in mind. He would first take Normandy; using this strong position, he would keep the dukes of Burgundy and Brittany out of the conflict (neither of them had shown any great love for the current French regime anyway); then he would take Paris. This would give him complete control of the north-east and south-west of France (the English, of course, still held Gascony), as well as its capital, with the Burgundians and Bretons holding on to the north-west and east of France, as well as the Low Countries. The rest of France would then either submit to him without conflict or would be simple to defeat without much military effort.[54]

It was a confident plan – some might even say a brazen or foolhardy plan. But it worked, at least it worked before the untimely death of its planner in 1422. With an unprecedented speed of conquest, Henry's large army cut a wide path across Normandy. His first target was the castle of Bonneville; unrelieved, its garrison surrendered to Thomas Montagu, earl of Salisbury, on 9 August. The nearby castle of Auvilliers also fell to him two days later. These sites would protect the main army's rear. Led by Henry himself, it was moving towards Caen, capturing Lisieux and Bernay along the way. Caen was a well-fortified town, with strong walls and a strong castle, dating from the time of William the Conqueror, and a larger garrison than Henry had previously encountered. But without a relief force to aid in its defense, it fell on 20 September. On the heels of this conquest, Henry occupied Bayeux, Tilly, Villers Bocage, and many other nearby towns and villages, all of which surrendered to him without resistance. Moving southwards, Argentan and Alençon also fell, quickly and with little conflict. Falaise, the birthplace of William the Conqueror, was stronger, supported by walls, a castle, and large garrison. Still, the town only held on until 2 January, with the castle surrendering a month later.[55]

Despite the winter, Henry did not halt his invasion. Targeting the Cotentin, before the winter was out he had attacked St Lo, Carentan, Valognes, Cherbourg, Coutances, Avranches, Domfront, Mont-Saint-Michel, and Saint-Saveur-le-Vicomte. Only Cherbourg, Domfront, and Mont-Saint-Michel did not fall before the spring, with Cherbourg and Domfront being captured in summer and Mont-Saint-Michel remaining defiantly out of English possession.[56] As spring arrived, Henry moved toward the capital of Normandy, Rouen. By April, he had captured all of lower Normandy, and in June and July he besieged and reduced the fortified Seine bridge crossing at Pont-de-l'Arche. Rouen would last somewhat longer, enduring a six-month siege, but in the end it, too, fell to the English army.[57]

The English entered Rouen on 19 January 1419. So far there had been little French reaction to their invasion. Opposing garrisons occupying the many castles and towns which Henry had taken were small, and they seemed to have little desire to fight or endure a siege against him. None of them even held out beyond the exhaustion of their food supply. Gone were the days of lingering through a long, hunger-inducing siege like those suffered by the citizens of Tournai or Calais during the previous century. Nor would the garrisons of Arques (later known as Arques-la-Bataille), Lillebourne, Vernon, Mantes, Neufchâtel, Dieppe, Gournay, Eu, Fécamp, Tancarville, or Honfleur, all of which fell to the English before the end of February 1419, or of Gisors, Ivry, La Roche-Guyon, Pontoise, Meulan, Poissy, St Germain, or Château Gaillard, all of which held out a little longer, but were still captured by the end of the year.[58] Why? The obvious reason was the absence in all of these cases of any French relief army. The small numbers of a fortification garrison were never supposed to be able to withstand a concerted attack, especially in an age when gunpowder weapons were significantly lowering the time it took to enter the once nearly impenetrable walls of a castle of fortified town.[59] Their only hope was to be able to endure these attacks until relieved by an army whose numbers could effectively counter those in the ranks of the besiegers. This is why so many of the garrisons agreed to a date when they would surrender if not relieved. (This also guaranteed no loss of life among the soldiers on both sides, as fighting would be suspended until the date set for relief or surrender.) This had been done at Bonneville, Caen, Falaise, and Rouen, all of which had surrendered on the agreed date when no relieving force had arrived. And when no relief came to those more important locations, other garrisons simply surrendered, knowing that they would have no French army coming to their aid either. In view of this, the unique bravery of the defenders of Mont-Saint-Michel must be singled out, for they alone had withstood the English action, and they would continue to do so for the rest of the war.

But the lack of a relief army was not the only reason why these garrisons surrendered with such unprecedented quickness. Since the battle of Agincourt, an obvious attitude of defeat had beset the French. The loss of so many French military leaders, including the Constable and Admiral, as well as the death of so many soldiers, was followed later in 1415 by the death of the dauphin, Louis of Guyenne, who had led them at Agincourt but had escaped death there. Dead, too, by 1419 were Louis's brother and successor as dauphin, Jean of Touraine, Bernard, the count of Armagnac, who had been named as Constable after Agincourt, Jean, duke of Berry, and Louis II, count of Anjou. With the dukes of Orléans and Bourbon still in an English prison, this left only the mentally ill king, Charles VI, and his young son and now dauphin, Charles, as leaders of any military resistance. There were probably other nobles who could have risen to the task, but they did not come forward at this time. In addition, several aristocrats were potential leaders, but in 1419 most were still too young to take over any military leadership. Perhaps military leadership is not always the defining factor in victories or defeats, but for a decade following Agincourt in France, it certainly was. Without it, recruitment ceased, and so too did the gathering of supplies and funds to fight against the English. The kingdom was becoming occupied, not only physically but also in the minds of most French men and women.

Then there were the Burgundians. John the Fearless, who was not with the French army at Agincourt, either through lack of invitation or desire, had not been idle since the battle. He had seen the same opportunities as Henry V in the wake of French, in this case Armagnac, defeat, and had stepped up his own campaigns. By

October 1417 he had conquered Chartres, moving from there to Monthléry, only a few miles to the south-west of Paris, which he took in the same month. Thus while the English were moving across Normandy, the Burgundians were moving on Paris. Still, it seems that the two leaders were not acting in concert. Since Agincourt, John had been in contact with Henry, even meeting with the English king at Calais in 1416, but no formal agreement between them had been made. In fact, it seems that while John the Fearless had made overtures towards the English, he remained suspicious of them and their intentions in France. It is certainly true that he wanted to govern France, but it is less certain that he wanted to share that governing responsibility with the king of England. Henry may have had similar feelings towards the duke of Burgundy. The citizens of Rouen had, after all, submitted to John the Fearless in January 1418 in an effort to protect themselves against the English, a fact that had not kept the English king from attacking and capturing the town. On the other hand, this submission had not meant much to the duke of Burgundy who had done nothing to save Rouen; when the Rouenais requested help from him, John had responded that they should 'rely on their own strength'.[60] He was far more interested in Paris.

Ever since the assassination of Louis of Orléans in their city, the Parisians had been divided on whether to give their allegiance to the Burgundians or to the Armagnacs. Before Agincourt, when the dauphin, Louis, or one of his Armagnac military leaders, Charles of Orléans, Louis of Anjou, or Bernard of Armagnac, had been present in the city, the inhabitants had favored their side. But when the Armagnacs were not present, and especially after Agincourt, the Parisian commitment to the Burgundians had increased. During 1416, several Parisian rebellions had tried to force the city to accept John the Fearless's rule. These had always been harshly quelled by the Armagnacs. But when Burgundian soldiers actually stood outside the city in 1417 and again in 1418, firing their cannon and other gunpowder weapons on to the walls and into Paris, the intensity of the rebellions increased. During one of the uprisings Bernard of Armagnac was murdered. Finally, on 29 May 1418, the citizens of Paris, under attack from without and within, opened their town's gates to John the Fearless's troops.[61] A massacre of Armagnac supporters ensued, with more than 2,000 killed, and Charles VI and his queen, Isabeau of Bavaria (she already held by

and favorable to the Burgundians) welcomed John the Fearless as
the governor and 'protector' of France. Charles and Isabeau's son,
the dauphin and future Charles VII, had fled from the city to
southern lands not in control of his enemies. He would not see Paris
again for another eighteen years.

In 1419 John the Fearless tried to put together a governing
coalition of Burgundians and Armagnacs. In a treaty signed in early
September 1418, he even made sure that the dauphin received the
lands of Dauphiné, Touraine, Berry, and Poitou as an appanage. (It
is there that Joan of Arc would first meet with him.) John allowed
Charles, the now *de facto* Armagnac leader, to name one of three
officials who would handle the state's finances. He also continued to
recognize the dauphin as heir to the French throne. Additionally,
John seems to have been interested in halting any further English
advance and, perhaps, in regaining some of those lands already lost
to them. However, he was never able to carry out this plan, for in
meeting with Charles on the bridge at Montereau under a writ of
'safe passage', he was set upon and murdered by Armagnac
adherents. Unable to forget or forgive the numerous Burgundian
'treasons', including, most notably, the assassination of Louis of
Orléans, the Armagnacs finally had their revenge. But in so doing,
they made sure that there would be little peace in France for the
near future, for the Burgundians, who under John the Fearless had
felt little desire to seek an alliance with the English, now under his
son, Philip the Good, openly sought to join with Henry V.[62]

On 21 May 1420, the Treaty of Troyes was signed between Henry V,
Philip the Good, and Charles VI. This treaty in all its intricacy can be
reduced to one single provision: it made Henry V heir to the throne of
France. Charles VI was still recognized as king, but should he die, and
he was ailing almost all of the time, then Henry V would assume his
throne. Charles's own son, the Dauphin Charles, was effectively
disowned. Henry was also to serve for the time being as regent of the
crown, which placed him effectively in charge of the government.
Finally, Henry V would marry Charles VI's youngest daughter,
Catherine, and their eldest son would become heir to both the French
and the English kingdoms. (The marriage took place less than a month
later, on 2 June 1420, in Troyes Cathedral.)[63] Philip the Good
ostensively received nothing, although he did gain some revenge for
the assassination of his father in the satisfaction of knowing that the
man who was responsible for his father's death had been disinherited.

He also knew that there was little likelihood that Henry would be in his position were it not for the fact that he, the duke of Burgundy, had placed him there. Philip undoubtedly also believed that, should he so desire, he could remove Henry from that position of power at any time.

There were still the Armagnacs to worry about. Of course, they did not accept the Treaty of Troyes and still considered the legitimate heir of the throne to be their leader, the dauphin. However, the Armagnacs were weak. The transformation of power had reduced their numbers even further, and now, because of their assassination of John the Fearless, they would have two enemies to fight. Although they were certainly restless, their plan was to fall back cautiously to more secure lands and try to regroup. It was a position in which they would grow increasingly more comfortable and from which they became less willing to move.

Yet, neither the English nor the Burgundians intended to let them follow this plan, and both allies continued to wage war against their common enemy. Sometimes these actions were done by both together, and sometimes separately, but almost always, at least for the next two years, they were done successfully. Between 1420 and 1422, the English and Burgundian armies captured Ballon, Beaumont-le-Vicomte, Montfort-le-Retrou, Fresnay, Harcourt, Dreux, St Valery-sur-Somme, Gamaches, Crépy, Compiègne, Pontoise, Melun, Epernon, Gallardon, Bonneval, Montereau, Sens, Villeneuve-sur-Yonne, La Charité, and Meaux. Rarely did they encounter any Armagnac opposition, and when they did, such as outside Fresnay, they defeated it with relative ease.[64] At other times, such as at Meaux, there was strong opposition from citizens seemingly unaligned with the Armagnacs, but unwilling to be taken by the English or the Burgundians. Sometimes these towns were even able to hold out against their attackers, unlike Meaux, and remained essentially free from occupation. (Two of these, Domrémy and Vaucouleurs, would later play an important part in the rise of Joan of Arc.) But for every town that opposed the attackers, perhaps ten, trying to stave off the destruction that others had suffered, surrendered to English or Burgundian forces without even having been attacked. Important and sizeable towns, such as Auxerre, Sens, Laon, Soissons, and even Reims, fell to the English and Burgundians in this way. Only at the battle of Baugé fought on 22 March 1421 deep in Armagnac territory by an English army led by Henry's brother, Thomas, duke of Clarence – did a French and Scottish army achieve a victory. (The

Scots, remaining the only allies of the Armagnacs, had sent several thousand soldiers to their aid.) Henry V was then in England, and most historians surmise that he would not have given permission for his brother to raid so deeply into Armagnac territory had he been in France at the time. Clarence paid for the mistake with his life.[65]

Had someone suggested to Henry at the signing of the Treaty of Troyes that he might die before the frail Charles VI, the English king probably would have laughed. However, that is precisely what happened. During the siege of Meaux, Henry V contracted what was probably an intestinal illness, perhaps dysentery, the disease by which he had seen so many of his countrymen perish. He died a few weeks later on 31 August 1422 in Vincennes, on the outskirts of Paris.[66] Charles VI was still alive, although he would follow Henry to the grave later that same year. Also in 1422, Catherine, Charles's daughter and Henry's wife had borne a son, named after his father. That baby was, almost from the moment he was born, Henry VI, king of France and England.[67]

Yet, just because Henry V had met an early death this did not mean that the English conquests were over. Henry VI was far too young to lead an army, but his uncles, John of Bedford and Humphrey of Gloucester, were not. And they had other able generals as well, including Thomas Montagu, earl of Salisbury, and Richard, earl of Warwick, as well as some younger officers who were beginning to show their own military leadership skills, such as John Talbot and John Fastolf. It was their destiny now to lead the English army to victory in memory and following the plan of Henry V. So, even though the Armagnacs began to fight back with more ferocity, during the next seven years the English, together with their Burgundian allies, continued to make significant gains against their Armagnac enemies. They would win the battle of Cravant, fought on 31 July 1423,[68] and the following year, on 7 August 1424, they defeated the French in an even greater battle at Verneuil.[69] In both battles, the English were outnumbered by their French counterparts but still won. Other victories were had at Noyelles, Le Crotoy, Pont-sur-Seine, Montaiguillon, Etampes, Rambouillet, Le Mans, Mayenne, Dol, Meulan and Ivry. (The latter two needed to be retaken after they were lost briefly to the French.) There were also a few defeats, most notably at Montargis, which withstood an English siege in 1427, and at Mont-Saint-Michel, which continued to withstand all attempts to capture it.[70] One bright spot for the Armagnacs was Arthur de Richemont, brother of John V, duke of Brittany. While his brother had so far chosen to remain a neutral bystander in this phase of the Hundred Years War, Richemont was active in fighting successfully on behalf of the dauphin. Named Constable by Charles, Richemont responded by defeating the English at St James-de-Beuvron in 1426 and Pontorson in 1427.[71]

In July 1428 the very experienced and successful Thomas Montagu, earl of Salisbury, decided that it was time to strike a blow into the heart of Armagnac territory. His target was the extremely important Loire river town of Orléans. If he was able to capture Orléans, the English would control the River Loire, and the dauphin, headquartered at Chinon Castle, would be caught in Aquitaine between Salisbury's army and Gascony with little route of escape. He might even be forced to surrender. With a freshly recruited army of some 2,700 men plus more than 2,000 veterans, Salisbury started south from Paris. Every town along his route not previously in English hands fell to him. By August he had even taken Chartres, which had withstood many previous attempts at English capture. The walls of Le Puiset and Janville too were stormed and fell a few days later. Turning along the Loire below Orléans, he captured Meung (8 September) and Beaugency (26 September); to the north of Orléans he captured Jargeau (5 October) and Châteauneuf (6 October). At these sites were bridges which gave Salisbury the ability to surround the larger Orléans. The siege of Orléans began on 12 October.[72] Joan of Arc would arrive to relieve that same siege less than a year later, on 29 April 1429. (What occurred at Orléans between those two dates will be discussed in detail below.)

When Joan of Arc involved herself in the Hundred Years War, she entered a hornets' nest of military and political problems. If anything could have discouraged her, the state of France in 1429 should have. Wracked by a war that had lasted nearly a century by this point, half of it occupied by a foreign military, its society frightened by marauding armies and confused by the political dispute waged between two parties whose arguments had little grass-roots permeation, its economy broken by the constant marching of armies across its agricultural fields, their soldiers largely living off the land, and its industries blocked from the markets and trade routes which had once made them prosperous, with no crowned king, and few others who could or would rise to take over leadership of the government or the armies, the kingdom of France was not even a shadow of its thirteenth-century prototype.[73] Then there was that 'loser's mentality' which seemed to have beset all of the Armagnacs. A less confident person, especially a woman, a member of the gender which was not called on to exert any kind of military leadership, would have stayed in the comfort of their home, especially if that home had as little direct contact with the warring parties as Domrémy seems to have had. But Joan's confidence came from an other-worldly source – or at least she believed that it did.

She had one other extremely important advantage. Certainly a French patriot herself, she was not alone in her patriotism. There were pockets of resistance which had held out and still did hold out against the English. Largely unsupported by the dauphin or his generals, these towns continued to fight against the English, and many were successful. That people in places like Mont-Saint-Michel, Tournai, Vaucouleurs, and Orléans were successful in their own defense, gave hope to the many 'patriots' who felt that the English occupiers of their lands were vulnerable to a concerted, aggressive military effort. Men such as Jean, duc d'Alençon, Robert de Baudricourt, Etienne de Vignolles (dite La Hire), Gilles, maréchal de Rais, Louis de Culan, Ponton de Xaintrailles, Arthur de Richemont, and Jean, the Bastard of Orléans, not to mention many unnamed French soldiers, felt that the English could be defeated, but that they needed inspiration. Dauphin Charles had not provided this inspiration. Nor was he likely to in the near future, especially as he was being counseled to proceed against the English and Burgundians with sluggish, even inactive caution by his favorites, Georges de la Trémoïlle and Archbishop Regnault de Chartres. That this inspiration for military aggressiveness was to be peasant or female was probably not anticipated by any of those willing French warriors. Yet, when Joan appeared, and they felt her confidence and determination, they followed her with a loyalty which few soldiers in history have given their leaders.[74] She responded by leading them to victory.

Yes, the state of France in 1429 should have kept Joan of Arc spinning wool at her home in Domrémy. But it did not. And judging from her results, she may have been just what the French military needed to regain its own confidence and composure and to realize the advantages that it had over its English enemies.

3

A Military Mission?

We really do not know what she looked like. As with Charlemagne, a 'saint' she would invoke at times during her life, there is no accurate contemporary artistic depiction of Joan of Arc. The contemporary picture that is most often referred to as a portrayal of Joan, drawn by Clément de Fauquembergue, *greffier* (or scribe) of the Parlement of Paris, in the margins of his report on the raising of the siege of Orléans, written two days after the Joan's relief of the city, cannot be a true likeness. Neither Fauquembergue nor any other member of the Parlement had ever seen Joan. They were in Paris, and Paris was in the hands of Joan's enemies, the English and the Burgundians. More importantly, Fauquembergue's illustration of Joan portrays her with shoulder-length hair and clothed in a dress, two fashion characteristics to which Joan did not pretend, during the siege of Orléans or at any other time in her brief but extremely significant military career. He does, however, portray Joan's sword and banner, possessions which she had become associated with even at this early date and even within the walls of an occupied city.

There were certainly other contemporary portraits of her. It is recorded at Reims that a Scotsman – nothing more is know of the artist – painted the Maid sometime during her stay in the ecclesiastical capital when Charles VII was crowned.[1] However, this painting has not survived; or, at least, the portrait has not surfaced, and is considered to have been destroyed. Other portraits may also have existed, for it would be odd indeed, considering that there is so much contemporary writing about Joan, if more artistic works had not been produced.[2]

Yet, even though there is an incredible amount of contemporary written material about Joan, it is difficult to arrive at an accurate description of her. Was she tall or was she short? Did she have blond, black, or brown hair? What color were her eyes? How large was her mouth? Did she have the figure of a woman or was she 'boyish' in shape? Was she beautiful or was she ugly? Was she sexually attractive? Hardly any of these questions can be answered with historical certainty. No one, it seems, took notice of Joan's face or head. The only evidence regarding her hair color might be a strand of black hair found in the mid-nineteenth century by Jules Quicherat to have been caught in the wax of her seal attached to the letter which she had written and sent to the inhabitants of Riom on 9 November 1429.[3] The seal and hair have now disappeared, and a black-haired Joan of Arc seems to go against most modern artistic depictions of her. These prefer to have her hair blond. On the other hand, most historians have accepted her hair color to be black because of Quicherat's otherwise accurate historical work on Joan's behalf. But Quicherat also had a romantic vision of the Maid of Orléans, and perhaps this strand of hair, which quite frankly could have been anyone's, caught there at the time of the sealing of the letter or later, is more a part of his search for a trustworthy relic of Joan than evidence of his historical accuracy.

Of course, because of the means of her death, there are no other physical remains of Joan of Arc. Legends of her heart surviving the blaze are numerous and frequently cited as evidence of her sanctity, but even if it did, this organ and her ashes, according to more credible witnesses, were scooped up by her executioner and tossed over a bridge into the Seine. Presumably they then sank to the bottom of the river or out to sea. Naturally, there is the possibility of a bone or flesh fragment surviving that disposal – at least that is the claim for a charred rib bone preserved in a vial at the Joan of Arc display in Chinon Castle – but without more substantial contemporary evidence, Joan seems to be one of the few Catholic saints whose remains are not distributed as relics throughout European churches.

Still, although they were not detailed in their descriptions of her, to her fellow-soldiers Joan was physically quite attractive. 'She was a young girl, beautiful and shapely,' recalled her squire, Jean d'Aulon, at Joan's nullification trial. This was echoed by Jean, duke of Alençon, and many others who had ridden with her and been in her company. And how did they know? They had seen her dress and undress in their presence, as a fellow-soldier concerned little with her privacy while on campaign. Jean d'Aulon continued in his testimony:

> many times when helping to arm her or otherwise he had seen her breasts, and other times when he was dressing her wounds he had

seen her legs quite bare, and he had gone close to her many times – and he said that he was strong, young and vigorous in those days – never, despite any sight or contact he had with the Maid, was his body moved to carnal desire for her, nor did any of her soldiers or squires, as he had heard them say and tell many times.[4]

The duke of Alençon agreed: 'sometimes he saw Joan get ready for the night, and sometimes he saw her breasts, which were beautiful. Nevertheless, he never had any carnal desire for her.'[5]

This, of course, set her apart from other women. Soldiers, no matter when or where they serve, seem inclined to sexual lasciviousness. It seems to be an outgrowth of their macho, misogynist, all-male society and seems to accompany them throughout their military adventures. Of course, this gives employment to the large number of prostitutes who are always found around the camps of the soldiers, but at the same time it often leads soldiers to think of rape either as booty or as a punishment for their opponents' defeat. This did not occur when Joan was around. Aulon's and Alençon's claims to never having had 'any carnal desire for her' were universal among her troops and her officer colleagues alike. The royal esquire, Gobert Thibault, testified that:

> . . . in the field she was always with the soldiers, and he had heard many of Joan's intimates say that they never had any desire for her. That is to say that sometimes they had a carnal urge, but never dared to give way to it; and they believed that it was impossible to desire her. And often when they spoke about the sins of the flesh, and used words that might have aroused carnal thoughts, when they saw her and approached her, they could not speak like this any more, for suddenly their sexual feelings left them.[6]

What is more, her purity so confused the soldiers who fought and lived around her that they even changed their feelings about women as sexual objects. 'For himself and the rest,' declared Count Jean of Dunois, the Bastard of Orléans, at the nullification trial, 'when they were in the Maid's company they had no wish or desire to approach or have intercourse with women. And it seemed to him that this was almost a miracle.'[7]

Thus her beauty may have been more than physical attractiveness, at least to those who fought beside her and loved her. Indeed, there appears to have been no middle ground for anyone who came in contact with the Maid, friend or foe; they either loved her and would do anything for her, or they hated her and would do whatever they could to bring her downfall. As such, even if we possessed the most clear and precise literary descriptions of her, we still could not rely on their validity, for they would be colored by the passion that her contemporaries felt toward Joan.

'She was born in the town of Domrémy which is one with Greux, and the principal church is in Greux.' So Joan answered the simple question, 'Where were you born?' asked during the trial which would lead to her death. This was followed by, 'Her father was called Jacques d'Arc and her mother Isabelle,' in answer to what were 'the names of your father and mother?'[8] (There is little doubt about the veracity of these responses, for, although periodically a book appears which, based on the most spurious of sources and speculation, declares that Joan was a royal bastard, no serious scholar of Joan's life believes that she could have been the illegitimate daughter of Isabeau of Bavaria and Louis, duke of Orléans, and therefore the half-sister of Charles VII.[9])

The purposes of those questions were simple. They may have been the only questions which Pierre Cauchon's wholly biased tribunal asked which did not have ulterior motives. Joan of Arc's answers were also simple. For they told of an upbringing in a small village, one that was less well known than the nearby larger village of Greux, by a father and mother not generally concerned with military matters. Joan's parents undoubtedly knew about the war's progress, about the civil war with the Burgundians and the international conflict with the English, and they may have discussed it around their children. They may also have held a belief in the divine right of the dauphin to succeed his royal father, a belief which they duly passed to Joan, but no one gave testimony to that fact. Theirs seemed to be lives without great concern for what was happening around them, except to feed and shelter themselves and their children – Joan had three brothers, Jacques, Jean, and Pierre, and a sister, Catherine – and to bring them up righteously, humble and true to the Christian religion which they practiced with a devotion neither more or less than their neighbors.

They also seem to have been a bit more wealthy than most 'peasants' of the time, owning twenty hectares of land (about fifty acres), of which some twelve hectares were fields and four were woodland. They owned their own house and furnishings. The house, as judged today, if it is the same domicile which the d'Arc family owned before Joan's exploits,[10] was larger than many in the village, large enough for them to take in travelers. They also had some money left over, which allowed them to travel and purchase religious favors: they paid a parish priest an annual rent for one-and-a-half mowings from the church's lands and for the priest to celebrate two masses each year during the 'week of the Fountains'; additionally, Isabelle may have gone on a pilgrimage to Rome, whereby she earned her surname, Romée, which she proudly carried on all official documentation.[11]

The point of all of this is to show that Joan was not the daughter of warriors. They were not poor, it is true, but neither were they wealthy enough to train their sons for military service, let alone their daughter. Jacques d'Arc and Isabelle Romée were 'laborers', which at that time in Domrémy meant farmers,[12] and witnesses to Joan's youth also saw her participate in farming activities, ploughing fields, harvesting crops, and tending to the communal cattle herd, with some time also spent in 'certain honest work done by women', by which her relative, Durand Laxart, meant primarily spinning flax or wool.[13] So where did she acquire her desire to participate in the military actions of the Hundred Years War?

Joan of Arc was a devoutly religious woman. No one who knows her history will question that. And it was this devotion, starting from a very young age, and not her bellicosity which witnesses remembered at her nullification trial. Béatrice, one of Joan's godmothers, testified:

> Joan was well and sufficiently instructed in the Catholic faith, just as other girls of her age. And from infancy or adolescence until she left from her father's house, she was filled with good morals. She was a chaste girl and well mannered, and attending frequently and devoutly at church and holy places . . . she confessed freely on the correct days, and especially on the most holy feast day of Easter, or the Resurrection of Our Lord Jesus Christ. Thus it did seem to her that there was no one better in the two villages [Domrémy and Greux].

Her godfather, Jean Moreau, agreed:

> Joan, in her youth . . . was well and decently raised in faith and in sound morals, and she was so that almost everyone of the

village of Domrémy loved her. And Joan knew her creed, her *Pater noster* and the *Ave Maria* just as other little girls of her age did.

Perhaps this was 'just as other little girls', at least to adults, but the other children saw her devotion as a bit peculiar, as a childhood friend, Colin, the son of Jean Colin, testified:

> She freely went to church, as he had seen. For almost every Saturday afternoon, Joan, with her sister and other women, went to the hermitage or church of Our Lady in Bermont, carrying candles. She was so devoted to God and the Blessed Virgin, that on account of this devotion, he who was then young, and other boys used to ridicule her.[14]

Of course, this devotion was most manifest in the reception of her visions and voices. But was it widely known in Domrémy that Joan was the recipient of these heavenly gifts? Only Jean Waterin, a childhood friend, testified that it was, although only from his observance and not from her boasting: 'While they played together Joan would draw herself aside and speak with God, so it seemed to him.' As a fellow child, his response to such action was simple, and somewhat cruel, 'He and others made fun of her.'[15] Perhaps this potential ridicule is what kept Joan, as a youth, silent on the topic; or perhaps her 'voices' were simply too special for Joan to talk about. In her later trial, after her accomplishments gave her experiences credibility, she had no problem in recalling what had occurred as a young girl. Shifting from past to present tense with a conviction that her revelations had not ceased, she recalled what had occurred:

> When she was thirteen years old, she had a voice from God to help her govern her youth. And the first time she was very frightened. And came this voice, about the hour of noon, in the summer, in her father's garden . . . And she heard the voice on her right-hand side, towards the church; and rarely did she hear it without a brightness. Indeed, this brightness is from the same side as the voice is heard, and it is generally a great light. And when Joan came into France [in Domrémy, Joan was considered to be in Burgundy], she often heard this voice . . . She said that it seemed to be a dignified voice, and she believed that the voice was

sent to her by God; and, after she had heard this voice three times, she knew that it was the voice of an angel.[16]

This voice initially told her only 'to conduct herself well' and 'to go to church often'. But as she aged, a mission began to be laid out for her:

> It told her, Joan, that it was necessary that she should come into France . . . The voice told her, two or three times a week, that she, Joan, must go away and come to France . . . The voice told her that she should go into France, and she was not able to stay where she was. Also, the voice told her that she should raise the siege placed before the city of Orléans. The aforesaid voice told her that she should go to Robert de Baudricourt in the town of Vaucouleurs, the Captain of that place, that he would give her people to go with her. And she, Joan, responded that she was a poor girl who did not know how to ride or lead in war.[17]

At times, Saint Michael, Saint Catherine, and/or Saint Margaret visited her and gave her advice on how to proceed on her mission. They gave her strength, in what must have appeared to her as a mission that could not possibly be accomplished; they gave her confidence, until she became convinced not only in their authenticity, but in her own abilities:

> The first time [Saint Michael appeared to her] she was young and afraid, and afterwards Saint Michael taught her much and proved himself to her so that she believed firmly that it was him . . . Above all things he told her that she should be a good child and that God would help her. And, among other things he told her that she should come to the help of the King of France . . . And the angel told her about the tribulation that was in the kingdom of France.[18]

She was instructed to keep silent about what was revealed to her – although she believed that her voices would have allowed her to tell her parents had she wished – at least until she was ready to visit Robert de Baudricourt in Vaucouleurs. (The visions, or their veracity, are not in themselves important for this study. What is important, in fact what is key to Joan's history as a military leader, is that *she* believed that they came from God.)

Of course, some ambiguous mention of her mission did slip out. Who can blame her? For it was an exciting message, one that she became convinced would change the history of France. Gérardin d'Épinal, a neighboring farmer who seems to have expressed some sympathy towards the Burgundian side, testified at Joan's nullification trial: 'When she was wanting to go away, she said to me: "Friend, except that you are a Burgundian, I would tell you something."' But, because Joan had never before shown any inclination of her military future, Gérardin 'believed that what she would have said to him was about a friend she wished to marry.'[19] Another witness at the same trial, Michel Lebuin, who seems to have had a special, 'confidential' friendship with Joan, confirmed that it was sometimes difficult for her to keep silent on what was shortly to occur, although the meanings of the words she said to him did not become apparent until later:

> Once Joan told him, on the Eve of Saint John the Baptist, that there was a girl between Coussey and Vaucouleurs who before a year was passed would have the King of France consecrated. And he said that the year that followed the King was consecrated in Reims.[20]

Ultimately, she was also forced to tell what had occurred to her to someone who could help her travel to Vaucouleurs and meet with Robert de Baudricourt. This companion was her mother's cousin's husband, Durand Laxart, a man whom we know very little about, but someone whom she must have trusted and who, in turn, must have trusted her and believed in what she said God and His angels were requiring her to do. Still alive at her nullification trial, Durand recalled the first time Joan told anyone what she planned to do:

> He sought Joan at her father's house and took her to his own home, and she said to him that she wanted to go to France, to the Dauphin, to have him crowned, saying: 'Was it not said that France would be ruined through a woman, and afterwards would be restored by a virgin?'[21]

(The woman who Joan referred to as ruining France is most often interpreted as Charles the dauphin's mother, Queen Isabeau of

Bavaria, who was influential in having Charles VI sign the Treaty of Troyes, which disinherited the dauphin, with Henry V.[22])

Joan of Arc made three trips to Vaucouleurs to meet with Robert de Baudricourt. (Vaucouleurs was the place where one of Joan's 'voices' had told her to go, 'that there she would find a certain captain who would lead her safely to France and into the King's presence.'[23]) This is attested to by a number of witnesses including herself, but chiefly by Durand Laxart, who took her to Vaucouleurs, and by Jean de Novelompont (known more commonly as Jean de Metz), who met her there the first day, remained a constant companion throughout her life and carried on her mission after her death, to the extent that he was ennobled by Charles VII in 1448. According to them, in May 1428, sometime around Ascension, Robert de Baudricourt initially met with Joan and listened to what she had to say. But he refused to lead her to the dauphin, despite her persistent pleadings. Durand Laxart even recalled at the nullification trial that Baudricourt told him to 'take her back to the home of her father, and give her a beating',[24] while Jean de Metz remembered the following interchange with Joan when he first encountered her at the home of Henri le Royer in Vaucouleurs:

He said to her: 'My friend, what are you doing here? Will it not occur that the King shall be expelled from his kingdom, and that we shall all become English?' And the Maid answered him: 'I came here to the royal chamber to speak to Robert de Baudricourt, that he might escort me, or to have me escorted, to the King. But he does not care for me, or for my words.'

Still, her confidence had not declined; the persistence of her mission was even greater than her persistence with the Lord of Baudricourt. Jean continued with what Joan told him:

Nevertheless, before the middle of Lent, it must happen that I will be with the King [Charles, the dauphin], even if I have to wear my legs down to the knees. For there is no one on earth, neither kings, nor dukes, nor daughters of the King of Scotland [there was an idea at the time to marry Charles's eldest son, Louis – later Louis XI – to Margaret of Scotland, which occurred in 1436. Joan seems extremely well informed, if we can rely on Metz's testimony here], or anyone else, who are able to restore the kingdom of France, nor will he have any help except through me, although I would prefer to be next to my poor mother, for this is not my station. But it happens that I must go and I must do this, because the Lord wishes me to do this.[25]

This speech, so filled with enthusiasm and determination, inspired Jean de Metz to promise Joan his assistance to lead her to the dauphin. But apparently that was not enough, for Durand Laxart reported that Joan eventually came to him and requested to return to Domrémy.[26] She would return to Vaucouleurs the following January and again meet with Robert de Baudricourt. Why he granted this second meeting is unknown, although it may have to do with the July 1428 attack of Domrémy by Burgundian troops. What provoked this attack is unknown, although it could possibly have been that rumors of Joan's 'mission' were sweeping throughout the countryside and into the Burgundian court, which was not too far away. Perhaps wishing to quell an insurrection using Joan's visions as a reason to rebel against the duke of Burgundy's alliance with the English, Philip the Good sent troops to Domrémy in an obvious 'show of force'. Little is recorded of their destruction there, except that they burned the church, an obvious sign that they were more powerful than any religious structure or being in the village. Most of the inhabitants of Domrémy had escaped this attack, having taken refuge nearby in Neufchâteau, including Joan and her family.[27] If the attack on Domrémy was because of her, perhaps Baudricourt felt guilty about not defending the village, or perhaps he reasoned that if the duke of Burgundy accepted the possibility of Joan's mission that there might be something in her story. As he had died before the nullification trial, Robert de Baudricourt's reason for granting Joan a second meeting is lost to history.[28]

Also lost to history is what transpired between Robert and Joan at this second meeting, for none of the contemporary sources remarks on it. What results, it seems, is that Joan was not to be accepted by the captain of Vaucouleurs until she first visited first with his superior, Charles II, duke of Lorraine, in his castle at Nancy. Why this visit was made in January 1429 cannot be known for certain, as the duke also did not live to testify at Joan's nullification trial and no other witness was present at the meeting between the two. Durand Laxart, who again accompanied her, reported only that she had 'safe-conduct' to travel to the duke, and that when he met with her, he gave her four francs,[29] while Marguerite la Touroulde, at whose house Joan stayed in Chinon, remembered that the Maid told her that Charles of Lorraine had asked to see her when 'he had a certain infirmity', and that Joan told him that the reason for this was 'that he did evil, and that he would not be cured unless he reformed'. One of the things she required of him was that he 'take back his good wife', Margaret of Bavaria, whom the duke had left for a younger woman, Alison Dumay, with whom he had five children.[30] During her trial, Joan reported a different conversation with the duke. She claimed that while he had enquired what she could do about his ill-health, she had responded 'that she knew nothing about that'. Nor did she say much about her desire to take her message to the dauphin, only that she wished him to give her some men to fight for France:

> She said very little to him about her journey. She did say nonetheless that he should give her his son [actually his son-in-law and the dauphin's brother-in-law, René of Anjou] and men, so that she might lead them to France and that she would pray to God for his health.[31]

Perhaps it was Duke Charles II of Lorraine who instigated Joan's trip to Nancy before she set out for the dauphin. Or, letting Joan think that the duke had summoned her, perhaps Robert de Baudricourt did not wish to accept Joan or to send her to the dauphin without first seeing what a superior noble thought of her. Should the duke have felt that Joan's cause was without merit, Baudricourt could still have returned her to Domrémy without embarrassment. At the same time, once the duke of Lorraine approved of Joan of Arc's mission, he and not Robert de Baudricourt would be blamed should she embarrass them both before the dauphin.

Joan returned to Vaucouleurs in the middle of February 1429. She had been accepted by the duke of Lorraine, and she had also had the opportunity to visit the shrine at St Nicholas on her return.[32] But it was now the beginning of Lent, and Joan had promised to be with the dauphin before the middle of Lent, so she could not spend much more time in Vaucouleurs. Nor does it seem that there was any other reason for Robert de Baudricourt to hold her there, although according to Catherine Royer, Joan's hostess in Vaucouleurs, Baudricourt did order her to be exorcised before he would send her to the dauphin.[33] Despite the picture historians have often painted of the count of Baudricourt as a man completely convinced of Joan's mission, the count seems to have been a very cautious man, not at all sure that he was doing the right thing in sending this peasant girl to 'save France'. Indeed, only after he had visited her on at least three separate occasions, seen her village ravaged by Burgundian soldiers – possibly because of her mystical 'reputation' – had her also visit the duke of Lorraine, arranged for her to be exorcised, and seen a relatively large number of his troops and townspeople believe in her, did Robert de Baudricourt give her his blessing and send her to the dauphin. This shows a leader not at all confident in what he was doing.

But Robert de Baudricourt's lack of confidence did not rub off on the people who seem to have gathered around the Maid, hoping, if not actually believing, that she would fulfill her mission. Jean de Metz and the inhabitants of Vaucouleurs gave her clothing for the journey, men's clothing to make her ride more comfortable, although such attire would later be used against her at her trial.[34] Durand Laxart and Jacques Alain of Vaucouleurs bought her a horse, although Durand reported that Robert de Baudricourt 'afterwards had the money returned to them'.[35] She also received a sword from Robert de Baudricourt, according to Bertrand de Poulengy, less obviously for protection than as a symbol of what she was about to do – fight for the freedom of occupied France.[36]

In February 1429, when Joan left Vaucouleurs to visit him, the dauphin was in the royal castle in Chinon. Only a small number of men accompanied Joan on her trip. But they were devoted to her and would remain with her for most of her military adventures. Four were knights or soldiers of Robert de Baudricourt – Bertrand de Poulengy, Jean de Metz, Colet de Vienne, and Richard Larcher (his soldierly skill suggested by his name) – with two others, Julien and Jean de Honnecourt, servants to Poulengy and Metz respectively.[37]

The distance between Vaucouleurs and Chinon meant that Joan and her companions had to travel for eleven days through enemy territory to reach the dauphin. It was a perilous journey, and not without its adventures. However, Joan's party took the necessary precautions of sometimes traveling at night and resting during the day.[38] Her confidence and her devotion to her mission also aided them, giving them courage in the face of obvious dangers. Even before she left Vaucouleurs, she told Henri Royer that 'she was not afraid of soldiers, for her way was direct; and if there were soldiers on her way, she had God, her Lord, who would make a road for her to go to the lord dauphin, and that for this purpose she was born.'[39] While on the journey she continued to inspire her companions. Bertrand de Poulengy recalled at her nullification trial:

> They were eleven days on the journey, going to the king, then dauphin, and in traveling they had many doubts. But Joan always told them not to fear, because in reaching the town of Chinon, the noble dauphin would give them a warm welcome. She never swore, and he, himself, was greatly inspired by her voices, because it seemed that she had been sent by God. Nor anywhere in her was seen any evil, but she was always such a virtuous girl, just as if she was a saint. And so, entirely without any great difficulties, they traveled to the location of Chinon where the King, then the dauphin, was.[40]

Jean de Metz recalled a similar assurance when he was in the presence of Joan of Arc during the journey:

> And as he was traveling with her, he asked her if she was going to do what she said; and the said Maid always told them that they should not be afraid, because she had done this by commandment. For her brothers in Paradise told her what she had to do, and it was then four or five years ago that her brothers in Paradise and her Lord, that is to say God, told her that she would have to go to the war to recover the kingdom of France . . . And he believed many things that the Maid said, and he was inflamed by what she said, and, as he believed, by a divine love for her.[41]

While the party did not encounter enemy troops on their journey to Chinon, an ambush of sorts seems to have been set up along the way by soldiers loyal to the dauphin. However, there is some confusion about the affair in the testimonies of the two individuals who recalled it at Joan's nullification trial: Seguin Seguin, a professor of Theology at Poitiers, and Husson Lemaitre, a tinker from a town near to Domrémy. Neither of these men was actually present at the ambush, remembering it only as an event told to them by one of the ambushers, and they agree on little about it.

Seguin Seguin claimed that some soldiers – Seguin does not indicate specifically that they were the dauphin's men, although such might be inferred from his testimony – laid in wait 'to capture Joan, and rob her and her company,' while Husson Lemaitre reported that these were soldiers 'who had led her there' and that they 'pretended to be of the enemy.' But both witnesses agree on one thing: the ambush failed because the soldiers laying-in-wait did not attack her and those accompanying her. Lemaitre remembered that she calmed her own company, promising them no harm, and that there was no ambush. While Seguin recalled that the ambushers were unable to move from their positions against the Maid: 'When they were about to do this [to ambush her], they were unable to move from the places where they were, and thus Joan escaped with her company without hindrance.'[42]

Joan did not mention this incident in her own trial, and it may never have happened; undoubtedly it did not happen the way that either of these witnesses tried to reconstruct it. But, if nothing else, at least it is evidence that by the time of the nullification trial, Joan's journey between Vaucouleurs and Chinon had begun to take on a myth of survival against incredible military odds. It also undoubtedly added to the reasons for the dauphin to grant her an audience, especially if these were his soldiers and if they had been sent by Charles to 'test' her, rather than to capture or rob her.

Joan of Arc's only sorrow during the journey was her inability to hear her accustomed daily Mass; because of the danger, she was only able to celebrate this religious ordinance twice on her journey.[43] One stopover spot would become important later. This was at the monastery of Saint-Catherine-de-Fierbois, where she was able to hear Mass, mingle with the monks, and send a letter to the dauphin announcing her imminent arrival in Chinon.[44]

Although that letter no longer survives, Joan testified in her trial that she sent this, and perhaps more letters, to Charles (she used the plural 'letters' in referring to what she sent to Chinon) 'to know if she could enter the city where her . . . king was, because she had traveled 150 leagues to come to him, to his aid, and that she knew many good things for him'. She also promised to 'recognize' the king 'among all others'.[45] But this was not the only announcement of Joan's arrival and her mission. Jean Barbin, a lawyer and advocate to the court of Parlement, testified at Joan's nullification trial that a 'certain Marie d'Avignon' had come to the king several years previously and told him of a vision she had had in which:

> she saw many pieces of armor which were brought to her, which frightened her, that she might be forced to put this armor on. And it was said to her that she should not fear, that it was not she who would have to wear this armor, but a certain maid who would come after her would wear these arms and free the kingdom of France from its enemies. And he firmly believed that Joan was this maid of whom Marie d'Avignon had spoken.[46]

Such prophetic events were easy to recall once Joan had completed her mission and France was out of the hands of the English, but it is clear that before the time of Joan's arrival in Chinon, some in Charles's council, and indeed Charles himself, wondered how they should proceed once she had arrived. Some clearly doubted her 'mission' – she would always have her enemies at the royal court – while others decided that they at least wanted to hear what she could offer them, in the words of Simon Charles, the President of the Chamber of Accounts, 'that as she said that she had been sent by God and had something to say to the king, that the king ought at least to hear her'.[47] Ultimately, the dauphin decided that he would meet with her.

Chinon Castle is still an imposing fortification. Begun in the eleventh century and added on to in each subsequent century before her visit, Joan could see the magnificence of the structure so highly prized by all the kings of France and also those kings of England who had held it as counts of Aquitaine. Indeed, both Henry II and his son, Richard I (the Lionheart), were reported to have died within its walls or in the town below it. The castle is built on a hill, its impressive walls encircling all that lies on top of this hill. Tradition holds that Joan stayed in the town below these walls, awaiting the dauphin's bidding. The road, more a path really, by which she would have made her way up to the castle still remains, narrowly winding between closely built houses. It is a steep climb which ends at a large gatehouse through which she would have passed on her way to meet with the dauphin. His apartments were to the south of the gatehouse, along the wall which overlooked the town. He was to meet her in a sizeable hall at the beginning of these apartments at a large gathering of all his nobles and courtiers.[48] Obviously all were interested in seeing the girl who said God had told her to acquire an army and free

France from its English occupiers. Simon Charles, a member of Charles's court who may not have actually been present at this meeting, although he obviously heard the story from others present, testified as to what happened when Joan entered this hall:

> And when she entered the castle of Chinon to come into the presence of the king, the king, on the advice of the principal councillors of his court, hesitated to speak to her, until the moment when it was reported to him that Robert de Baudricourt had written that he had sent a certain woman to him, that she had been led through the lands of the King's enemies, and that she had, almost miraculously, forded many rivers in order to be led to the king. Because of that the king was moved to hear her, and Joan was given an audience. And when the king learned that she was coming, he withdrew to a place behind the others. However, Joan recognized him totally and showed reverence for him; and she spoke to him for a long time.[49]

Everything that Joan said in this conversation with the king is not recorded, although Raoul de Gaucourt, the Grand Master of the Dauphin's Household and an eyewitness to the event, did report that he heard her say, 'Most beloved Lord Dauphin, I have come and am sent by God to bring help to you and your kingdom.'[50] But this was not her whole message to the dauphin. She also seems to have had a secret communication for Charles alone, one which pleased him immensely. What this was might never be known for certain, although Joan's confessor, Friar Jean Pasquerel, testified that she had told him that the message was that the dauphin was 'the true heir to France, and son of a king, and that God had sent me to you to lead you to Reims, so that there you might receive your coronation and consecration'. Invoking the name of God in making this statement to the dauphin, Joan had so impressed Charles that he said to those gathered there that 'Joan had told him a certain secret which no one knew or could know except God; and that is why he had great confidence in her'.[51] Alain Chartier, the dauphin's secretary at the time, wrote that what she told Charles made him so joyous that it was 'as if the Holy Ghost' had visited him.[52]

For the next three days Joan was housed at Chinon Castle, in the upper chamber of the Tour de Coudray. Next to her lodgings was the Chapel of Saint-Martin, where she passed much of her time, hearing

Mass at least once daily and frequently confessing to ecclesiastics assigned to attend to her spiritual needs. She was relatively free to come and go as she wished, since the Tour de Coudray no longer fulfilled the function of a prison as in earlier days, when it held Templars as prisoners during the reign of Philip the Fair. It is also here where Joan first encountered Jean, duke of Alençon, who would become her staunchest ally and best friend.[53] There were also frequent visits with the dauphin and his councillors during her short stay. Always she proclaimed her mission to whomever would listen; Simon Charles remembered: 'She said that she had two commissions for which she had been sent by the King of Heaven: one to raise the siege of Orléans, the other to lead the King to Reims for his coronation and consecration.'[54] From these two points she did not waver, although Seguin Seguin claimed that when interviewed by him, she added two other military achievements that would also come about, although not necessarily to be achieved by her:

> . . . she said to me and others present four things which were then still to come, and which afterwards occurred. First, she said that the English would be defeated, that the siege before Orléans would be raised, and the town of Orléans would be freed of the English; however, she would first send them a summons. Second, she said that the King would be anointed at Reims. Third, that the city of Paris would return to the King's rule, and that the Duke of Orléans would return from England.[55]

Still, the dauphin was not convinced enough to allow Joan to lead an army to Orléans. He wanted her examined by theological professionals first. This meant sending her to the University of Poitiers, the largest and closest gathering of theologians still loyal to him. She would be interrogated by Gérard Machet, the dauphin's confessor and bishop of Castres; Raphanel, the confessor to the dauphin's wife; Hugues de Combarel, the bishop of Poitiers; Pierre de Versailles, a monk of Saint Denis; Guillaume Le Marié, a canon of Poitiers; the Dominican, Pierre Turelure, the inquisitor of Toulouse; and Pierre Seguin Seguin, a Carmelite from Limousin, one of the counselors of the dauphin, who was trained in canon and civil law.[56] Arriving on 11 March, Joan was questioned in Poitiers for eleven days. Unfortunately, little of what she was asked at this interrogation is known. A transcript was made, but unfortunately it has been lost or destroyed.[57] She passed the examination though. Despite being asked questions which would have confounded the most adept theologian, she answered simply and directly. She refused to be intimidated. When asked in what 'tongue' the voices spoke to her, she answered, according to Seguin Seguin's memory: 'A better tongue than I spoke, . . . which was a Limousin accent'. When asked to provide a sign to have them believe in her, she answered: 'In God's name, I am not come to Poitiers to make signs. But lead me to Orléans; I will show signs to you for which I was sent.' And when she was asked whether she believed in God, Joan replied, 'Yes, better than me.'[58]

In the end, she completely convinced her examiners that her mission had been given to her from God, just as she said it had. Seguin Seguin testified:

> And all of these things were reported to the King's Council, and they were of the opinion that, in view of the urgent need and the peril that there was to the city of Orléans, the King could be aided by her and to send her to Orléans. They enquired – even he and the other commissioners – concerning the life and morals of this Joan, and they found that she was a good Christian, and that she lived as a Catholic, and that she had never been found neglectful.[59]

And later, in Tours, when she had her virginity examined by the dauphin's mother-in-law, the Queen of Sicily, Yolanda of Aragon, and other ladies of the king's court, she passed this test as well. Jean d'Aulon, Joan's later squire, recalled:

> This Maid was put into the hands of the Queen of Sicily, mother of the Queen our sovereign lady, and to certain ladies being with her, by whom the maid was seen, visited and secretly regarded and examined in the secret parts of her body. But after they had seen and looked at all that there was to look at in this case, this lady said and related to the King that she and her ladies found with certainty that she was a true and entire maid, in whom appeared no corruption or violence.[60]

There was nothing left for Charles the dauphin to do but to grant her wishes and send her with an army to the relief of Orléans.[61] Joan designed and had made a special standard which would be with her until her capture at Compiègne. She had been so instructed by her voices. Those who saw it claimed that it was made of white canvas fringed with silk on a field of fleur-de-lys. In the middle was painted 'the world', that is the figure of Christ in His Majesty holding either the world or a fleur-de-lys, flanked by two angels, with the words 'Jesus Maria' written to the side. It was meant as a rallying point and was carried most frequently by the Maid herself, who preferred to wield it rather than a weapon.[62] In addition, the dauphin ordered a set of armor to be made for Joan. Jean d'Aulon reported to her nullification tribunal that it was a 'full harness' and 'fit to her body'.[63]

A new sword she acquired in a more miraculous manner. Probably while at Tours, although she could not later remember whether she was at Tours or Chinon, Joan sent an unidentified man, some say an arms merchant by trade, others a gun-maker, to the monastery of Saint-Catherine-de-Fierbois, a site that had impressed her on her journey from Vaucouleurs to Chinon. Joan instructed him to search in the earth behind the altar for a sword that had been buried there some time before. To the surprise of all the monks present, a sword was located exactly where she had said that it would be. It was a special weapon, rusted but with a fine enough steel blade that when it was cleaned shortly after its discovery, the rust 'fell off'. On the sword, presumably engraved on the blade, were five crosses, which are not explained in any contemporary source.[64] Although Joan would have at least three other swords in her lifetime – one given to her by Robert de Baudricourt, mentioned above; one taken as a prize of war from an Anglo-Burgundian leader, Franquet d'Arras; and two which she held as war-booty and which were given by her as a votive offering at the shrine of Saint-Denis, one of which is presumed to be that acquired from Franquet d'Arras[65] – it is the sword of Saint-Catherine-de-Fierbois that she prized above all others, and that she carried until her first defeat outside the Parisian suburb of Saint-Denis.[66]

Whose sword had it been prior to Joan's acquisition of it? No one knows for sure. Joan herself never attached the weapon to any specific heroic character, and its special engravings exist on no other exemplar. Joan's sword no longer exists, although what happened to it is also a mystery; she testified that it was not in her possession when she was captured at Compiègne, nor was it in the hands of her prosecutors at Rouen. Later legends assign the sword to Charles Martel, claiming that he had used it to defeat the Muslims at the battle of Poitiers in 732,[67] or to even earlier 'noble men of prowess' from the time of Alexander the Great.[68] It may have been a crusader's sword, placed there around 1400 by the great soldier and relic-collector Marshal Boucicaut when he paid for some buildings to be constructed at Saint-Catherine-de-Fierbois.[69] The crosses on the sword could certainly have been found on a crusader's weapon.

How did Joan know it was at Saint-Catherine-de-Fierbois? At her trial, she was asked to recall the circumstances of this sword's discovery to which she repeated the story above. Her judges did this to try to cast doubt on the miraculous nature of this event. They were unsuccessful. Her voices, she told them, had revealed the sword's existence to her.[70] Although it is certainly possible that while at Saint-Catherine-de-Fierbois earlier, Joan had heard of the sword's existence and had conspired to have it raised as a sign of her spiritual veracity, the fact that she did not seek the sword out until after her Poitiers approval, when such a miracle was no longer needed, speaks against this possibility. Nor is there any evidence prior to 1429 that such a legendary weapon could be found at this site, although many chapels did serve as repositories of captured weapons offered in gratitude by soldiers surviving and returning home from a military campaign – Joan's own votive offering at Saint-Denis is proof that such a tradition was still active in France in the fifteenth century. However Joan knew about the sword's presence in the ground behind the altar of the monastic chapel at Saint-Catherine-de-Fierbois, it quickly became reported as one of her many miracles. Almost all of her chronicles ascribe it as such. As the anonymous author of the *Journal du siège d'Orléans* writes:

> The king wished to give her a fine sword. She asked that it might please him to send for one which had five crosses close to the hilt on the blade, and was at Saint-Catherine-de-Fierbois. Then the king marveled greatly and asked if she had ever seen it, to which she answered, no; but she knew that it was there. The king sent there, and that sword was found, along with others that had been given there in times past. And it was brought to the king, who had it honorably decorated and furnished.[71]

All of this equipment completed Joan's transformation into a military leader. Only a few months before she was dressed in peasant woman's clothing, working in the fields and spinning. But now, as Pierre Champion describes, 'she had become a captain, going to command in war, to draw her pay and her equipment, and to serve according to the size of her large heart'.[72]

The recruitment of soldiers was not difficult. Rumors of her travels to Chinon, and the mission for which she traveled were well known,[73] and while it is true that she was a woman, and soldiers should have been reluctant to be led by a woman, by this time, according to Bertrand de Poulengy, who had ridden with her since Vaucouleurs, 'it was as if she were a saint'.[74] Soldiers flocked to her ranks, some 10,000–12,000 in total, a formidable relief force to add to that already serving with the French army at Orléans.[75] As she and her troops departed from Chinon, some time in late May, all were jubilant, feeling a hope that they had rarely felt for the last fifteen years. Before she arrived, as Seguin Seguin remarked, 'the king and his people had no hope, that everyone believed that they should retreat'.[76] Now that Joan of Arc had arrived, the defeatism previously present had given way to a belief in the possibility of victory. The siege of Orléans lay ahead of her; her first mission was ready to be fulfilled.

4

Relieving the Siege of Orléans

If Joan did not own a horse until she received one from Robert de Baudricourt at Vaucouleurs; if she did not have a sword until she received one also from Baudricourt or even later sent for the one which was hidden in the monastery of Saint-Catherine-de-Fierbois; if she had never worn armor, until she first tried on the suit which Charles, the dauphin, ordered to be made for her; and if she had never ridden under any standard, let alone hers, when did she become a soldier or, even better, a military leader? For that is what Joan was destined to be; that is why the dauphin had her tested and approved by so many at Chinon, Poitiers, and Tours. The rather convoluted question can be answered quite simply in two ways. The first is to stand on a historical soapbox and exclaim that a horse, sword, armor, or standard were not necessary to make someone in the late Middle Ages a soldier, let alone a military leader, just as having those items did not automatically improve one's military skill or legitimize one's generalship. Indeed, during the Hundred Years War especially, it was being discovered that many were not made military leaders simply by their noble birth. Far more often, the good generals on all sides – English, French, and Burgundian – rose from obscurity to greatness because they had a natural ability to lead men, formulate strategy and tactics, and, perhaps most importantly, stay alive when others around them were being killed. They also had to have confidence in their abilities, for if they appeared to doubt what they were asking others to do, their leadership was moot; no soldiers would follow them for long. This was more important even than winning (although numerous victories also obviously helped) in leading men into battle or at sieges during the last two centuries of the Middle Ages.

Even during the fourteenth century, the great generals were not always born into their roles – although some obviously were, such as Edward III and Edward, the Black Prince – but often rose through the ranks. Thus it was that a man such as Bertrand du Guesclin, whose minor nobility would never have accorded him the military leadership that he eventually achieved, became the most important general of France. He alone may have been responsible for the positive reversal of French fortunes towards the end of that century.[1] On the English side was Sir Robert Knolles. His origin unknown, Knolles learned the soldiering trade simply by fighting, playing non-leadership parts in earnest battles such as Poitiers and more chivalric displays such as the Combat of the Thirty. Eventually, his ability to lead *chevauchées* successfully through the French countryside made him a popular and very wealthy leader. So popular was he that when peasants threatened London in 1381, the retired and relatively old Knolles was called on to design the defense of the city; so wealthy was he that later, when Richard II ran into money problems he went to Knolles for a loan, the collateral for which were Richard's own crown jewels.[2]

During the fifteenth century, such leaders multiplied. In Joan's own company, men, such as Étienne de Vignolles (dit La Hire), and Ponton de Xantrailles, were every bit the leaders that the more noble-born Jean, the Bastard of Orléans, Jean, the duke of Alençon, and Gilles, the lord of Rais, were. The latter may technically have been in charge of the soldiers who fought in the French armies that Joan was a part of, but the real leaders were those wizened old veterans, men who had proven themselves in warfare and had not been caught or imprisoned, let alone killed. Follow one of the noble leaders into a potential imprisonment, the leader would be ransomed, the more common soldier might be hanged; follow an impoverished, veteran captain into the same situation, and the potential for survival was far greater. One need only look at the signatures of these leaders to know their potential worth on the battlefield. The Bastard of Orléans's, Alençon's, and Rais's signatures are all flowery and full bodied, evidence of an education in the posh surroundings of wealth and title. La Hire's and Xantrailles's, the few times when they can be found, are thin and shaky, evidence of a late-acquired knowledge of how to write, let alone other arts and sciences, learned probably around the campfire. Joan might have been one of these. She was confident in the divinity of her mission, and she had a fire and spirituality, which attracted soldiers to her. As will be seen, when the other leaders questioned her ability, it was often the fact that the soldiers followed her that would cause them to accede to her strategic and tactical wishes.

But that answer may side-step the question entirely. If the horse, weapons, and armor did not make the soldier or leader in the Hundred Years War, why did noble families continue to educate their sons in military skills and leadership? Why pay for them to be so richly attired and educated, when there was the likelihood that a peasant subject with no equipment or training might assume their military responsibilities? The answer is that everyone, including Joan, believed that it was necessary to learn how to fight and lead in a military engagement. And whatever spare time she had between her numerous examinations and ecclesiastical devotions, she spent on the practice of military arts. A short time after the duke of Alençon, who would become Joan's closest friend, first met her, he was astonished to find that she was practicing her riding and fighting on horseback. He was impressed, testifying later:

> And after a meal [at Chinon Castle], the king [and he went] for a walk in the fields, and there Joan ran with the lance [jousted], and seeing Joan conduct herself in the wielding and running with the lance so, [Alençon] gave her a horse.[3]

Marguerite de la Touroulde confirmed this: 'She could ride a horse wielding a lance as well as a more experienced soldier could.'[4] Alençon also testified that the Maid seemed to have been especially adept at sighting the relatively new gunpowder weaponry that the French used in their sieges:

> . . . everyone marveled at this, that she acted so wisely and clearly in waging war, as if she was a captain who had the experience of twenty or thirty years; and especially in the setting up of artillery, for in that she held herself magnificently.[5]

While she did not practice that skill at Chinon or elsewhere, she seems to have had an affinity in learning from and in the engagements which she fought, and she always seemed eager to learn, especially if such learning aided the fulfilment of her mission. Being 'common' may also have allowed her to listen to others, common cannoneers, for example, and to learn from them, something prohibited the more noble French military leaders.

All of this resulted in a European-wide reputation for military skill and leadership which was unsurpassed for her day. No less a contemporary figure than Pope Pius II was incredibly impressed by her military capabilities. He writes:

> The woman was made the leader of war. Arms were brought to her, horses led; the girl mounted with defiance, and burning in her armor, her lance quivering, she compelled her horse to dance, to run, and in no way to turn from its course.[6]

Somehow, somewhere, sometime, perhaps over a long time, in many places, and under many teachers, Joan became a military leader. And it all started at Orléans.

No single military engagement in the Hundred Years War has had more written about it than the siege of Orléans, and primarily the relief of that siege by the French army. The battles of Crécy, Poitiers, Agincourt, Formigny, and Castillon together cannot boast the number of pages devoted to the siege of Orléans. The reason for this is simple. While all of those engagements contained valiant military efforts and sometimes even cinematic scenes of heroism (e.g. the teenage Black Prince's defense of the center of the English line at Crécy, John II's capture at Poitiers, Henry V's battlefield oration before Agincourt, Richemont's march into the battle of Formigny, and the death of the aged Lord John Talbot at Castillon), none of those engagements had the participation of the Maid, Joan of Arc.

Of course, most of the modern authors writing on the siege of Orléans are French, as are most of the chroniclers who wrote about the engagement in the fifteenth century.[7] To modern English commentators, their ancestors' inability to capture the city of Orléans by siege is somewhat of an embarrassment, a sentiment which they share with their late medieval counterparts. Joan's presence, and her role in the relief of the siege, too, is embarrassing. Jean Chartier's comment, written between 1440 and 1450, 'it was a very strange thing to see a woman fight in such an army',[8] works both ways in the Hundred Years War, or in any war, for that matter. If one wins using an unorthodox leader, in this case a woman who claims that she has a divine mission, the victory takes on a miraculous description. However, if one loses to that same unorthodox leader, an excuse for the loss must be found. Naturally, no one who is defeated by a 'mission' can accept it as 'divine', as that calls into question the justification and divinity of their military adventure. So it was with Joan of Arc. No contemporary English or

Burgundian writer credited her victory at Orléans to deity, and few English historians do so today. Such an explanation, if nothing else, would mean that the justice of their cause should be questioned. At the same time, another excuse for defeat must be found.

There is little historical question as to the earl of Salisbury, Thomas Montagu's, boldness or bravery. His military skill had led to significant and impressive acquisitions during Henry V's Normandy campaign, and, after that king's death, he had led several successful military campaigns into the dauphin's territory, including victory at the battle of Verneuil. However, it is his 1428 campaign leading up to and including the siege of Orléans for which this general is best known. This stab into the very center of the dauphin's lands was meant to break that future king's opposition to Anglo-Burgundian rule in the north of France. And, had Orléans been captured and, thereafter, the Loire river basin been controlled, there is little doubt that the dauphin's road to rule would have been delayed for quite a long time, if not completely destroyed.

But was it a task that could have been successfully completed? With only 5,000 men, could Salisbury have expected to be victorious over all of the towns which he needed to control to win the Loire, including the rather large Orléans? By 12 October 1428, when he began the siege of Orléans, Salisbury had occupied no fewer than seven towns, all of which must have cost him soldiers as casualties, not to mention that he needed some troops to remain behind in each of these locations as garrisons. Even if the garrisons were not large, and they do not seem to have been, he appears to have had an army no larger than 4,000 men at the time of the siege of Orléans. M. Boucher de Molandon and Adalbert de Beaucorps' tally is 4,365, including almost 900 pages, while Louis Jarry's total is 3,189; both judgements are based on an English *compte* of Salisbury's army.[9] Even when they were joined by some 1,500 Burgundian soldiers later in the siege,[10] there seem not to have been enough soldiers to surround the city, let alone to capture it by siege. In fact, Salisbury never did completely surround Orléans. Instead, he manned only a few strongholds, boulevards – fortresses made of earth and wood which will be detailed later – some 600 meters from the city walls along the western side of the town (four in total), one more to the north, one on an island in the Loire river to the west of the town, and one more (the boulevard of Saint Loup) along the eastern road from Orléans to Jargeau (this last one located some two kilometers from Orléans's walls).[11] All of these held very few troops. Additionally, almost the entirety of the northern and most of the eastern sides of the city were left vacant of troops. Only the Saint Loup boulevard, located on the bank of the Loire, protected the eastern approaches to the besieged city, and, as will also be seen later, it was easily surpassed by French relief supply convoys, and by Joan and her army.

There was a single bridge across the Loire into Orléans. It was 350 meters long and consisted of nineteen arched spans. It was an old bridge, built sometime in the early twelfth century, but it had served the city well. Along this bridge, at the furthest point away from the city, on the last of the nineteen arches, was a stone castle, the Tourelles. Really just a fortified gate, with two flanking towers and a drawbridge separating it from the Loire bank, the Tourelles was a formidable defensive structure with which any attacking army was forced to contend. On the shore in front of the Tourelles lay an earthwork that further protected the bridge, although what purpose exactly it was to serve and even what shape it was is unknown. English changes to the bridgehead, principally the building of a boulevard, destroyed what had earlier stood there, and no contemporary description of this earthwork remains.[12]

The Tourelles became Salisbury's primary target of attack. He determined that if he occupied this fortress and then the bridge, the city would eventually fall to him, especially as any French relief army would be forced to dislodge him from that same fortress. First, he bombarded the Tourelles and the earthwork in front of it with gunpowder weapons.[13] Then, after the earthwork had fallen to him with relative ease, he brought forward a large number of miners who began to undermine the stone fortification's foundations.

The defenders of Orléans must have decided that they could not resist Salisbury's attack on the bridgehead and that it would be better for them to try and withstand his forces from behind the long and powerful walls of the city. (Although why they held this belief cannot be determined from contemporary documents.) During the time of Salisbury's attack on the Tourelles, Orléanais miners had also been at work, breaking the bridge behind the fort. After a couple of days, to the surprise of the English who had not significantly undermined the walls of the Tourelles, the French defenders retreated to the city, and their final destruction of two arches of the bridge took place.[14]

Despite most English historians claiming this as a victory for the earl of Salisbury,[15] this English military leader cannot have reveled too much in his capture of the Tourelles. After all, with the bridge broken behind the fortress, his occupation of the city was now as far from reality as it had been before. On the other hand, he now had a more comfortable, more fortified location for his future direction of the siege. But this comfort was not to last long. Only a few days after the occupation of the Tourelles, either 17 October, according to Enguerrand de Monstrelet, or 24 October, according to the *Journal du siège d'Orléans* (most modern historians accept the latter), as Thomas Montagu, earl of Salisbury, peered out of one of the upper windows of his captured fortification towards the town, a cannonball fired from one of the Orléanais gunpowder weapons smashed into the window ledge, shattering it, and propelling a piece of the metal window-frame into the face of the English military leader. Carried to the nearby castle of Meung-sur-Loire, the earl received medical attention. But much of his jaw and lower face had been removed by the blow, and, although he lingered for eight days, he could not recover from such a wound.[16]

The death of Salisbury was devastating to English concerns at Orléans. Few leaders in either the English or Burgundian armies could compete with the earl's military capabilities, his brashness, heroism, or skill in leading men to victory even when faced with seemingly insurmountable odds. William de la Pole, earl of Suffolk, took over from Salisbury, and later, at the beginning of December, he was joined by Sir Thomas Scales and John Talbot, earl of Shrewsbury, who then in turn assigned the siege of Orléans to Sir William Glasdale,[17] but one must wonder if Salisbury's death put an end to any serious attempt to capture Orléans. For one thing, earnest attacks on the city stopped – although gunpowder bombardments were exchanged between the city and the English almost daily[18] – with the English troops remaining in their fortresses around Orléans.[19] Second, the English constructed a large boulevard over the earthwork which they had earlier captured outside of the Tourelles. (If Jacques Debal is to be believed, this was actually a reconstruction of the earlier earthwork, also called a boulevard by Debal, built by the French and occupied by Salisbury before his capture of the Tourelles.[20] However, if the earlier structure were a boulevard, based on the later attack of this fortification by Joan, it appears that the English structure was far stronger than its French precursor.) Placed between the bridgehead and an

Augustinian convent, this fortification was meant for one thing only: to be an added defense for the English troops situated in the Tourelles.

A boulevard was a low earthwork defense that was generally placed before a vulnerable gate or wall. In essence, it was a gunpowder artillery fortification, its defense derived from a large number of guns, and, in English boulevards at least, longbowmen (who increased the amount of defensive firepower), a low height (over which it was easier to fire) and earth and timber walls (which more readily absorbed the impact of any attackers' stone and metal cannonballs). Boulevards had been known in France for at least two decades, and their effectiveness had been witnessed in several places. Indeed, so impressed were they by these gunpowder artillery fortifications, that the English too began to adopt them for their own defensive purposes, as witnessed by the use of them to garrison troops around Orléans before their occupation of the Tourelles.[21] But it was the boulevard placed before the Tourelles that was the strongest and most famous at Orléans. This boulevard, called either the boulevard of Tourelles or of the Augustins in contemporary sources, was one of the most imposing fortifications ever built, despite its earth and wood construction. According to Régine Pernoud, it measured 20 meters in length and 26 meters in width, with a ditch surrounding it 8 meters deep.[22] After its completion, Suffolk, and later Talbot, filled it with a large number of men and gunpowder weapons, perhaps the majority of both English soldiers and guns at Orléans.[23]

The boulevard of the Augustins was to become one of the focal points in Joan of Arc's relief of the siege of Orléans. More importantly for the English troops there before Joan's arrival, the construction of this boulevard and the garrisoning of it with men and gunpowder weapons shows that the English meant to alter their strategy away from the more active assault on the city. It is clear that Suffolk and his successors desired to wait patiently for the city's surrender from starvation, bombardment, or despair. They certainly did not anticipate that the dauphin and his French forces would mount an effective attempt to relieve the siege.

That conclusion was not unwarranted. It is true that the Orléanais fought valiantly to keep their city from falling to the English. Unlike several other French cities and towns, even of the size of Auxerre or Troyes, that had surrendered to English besiegers without putting up much of a defense or even suffering much hunger, the inhabitants of Orléans were determined not to fall to the English without a fight. The numbers of arms within the city are not known, although as the earl of Salisbury discovered, the inhabitants of Orléans obviously had some gunpowder weapons. Nor is it known how many Orléanais were capable of using those weapons. What can be determined from the original sources is that those leading the defense of the city had what can best be called a 'defensability', a sense of what to do to prolong their defensive stance without particularly increasing their suffering. Evidence of this can be seen in the decision to abandon the Tourelles, but to use Salisbury's attack of it to mask their own destruction of the bridge behind it. Thus Salisbury held the bridgehead, but not the bridge; and he was no closer to occupying the city. Another example can be seen in the Orléanais reaction to the destruction of their important Loire mills. The *Journal du siège d'Orléans* reports that in the early days of the siege, Salisbury, using his gunpowder weapons, had especially targeted and destroyed these mills, twelve in number situated between the bridge and the eastern-most city tower, the Tour Neuve. However, these mills were quickly replaced by the besieged citizens with eleven horse-operated mills built within the city and outside of the range of the English cannon.[24] Then there are the exploits of Master Jean, a gunner actually mentioned as one who operated a gunpowder weapon known as a 'grosse couleuvrine', who was originally from Lorraine. The *Journal* calls him 'the best master there was from that trade' and Jean seemed to use that expertise to harry the English in the Tourelles. Firing from a fortified position, known as the Belle-Croix and approximately 400 meters across the broken bridge from the Tourelles, 'he wounded and killed many'. But this was not all: 'To mock [the English] he sometimes let himself fall to the earth, feigning either death or wounds, and had himself carried into the town. But he would return quickly to the skirmish, and did such so that the English would know that he was still alive, to their great damage and displeasure.'[25] Finally, the Orléanais sometimes made their own attacks on the English positions without the participation of French soldiers.[26] The response of the Orléanais to Joan's entry into their city also gives evidence of their unwillingness to surrender to the English.

But the inhabitants of Orléans were unlikely to defeat their besiegers without outside assistance. And a similar unwillingness to surrender was not evident among the leaders of the French army sent by the dauphin to relieve the siege. When exactly a French relief force arrived at Orléans is difficult to determine from the sources; nor can it be determined who the leader of this first relief army was. What is known is that by Christmas 1428, Jean, the Bastard of Orléans, was there with a sizeable French force, as was the renowned veteran, La Hire, with his own military contingent. Of the two, the Bastard of Orléans was the chief commander, not only for his royal blood – he was the cousin of the dauphin – but also because he, as the brother, albeit the bastard brother, of the imprisoned Charles, duke of Orléans, was the noble most responsible for the security of the city. That said, at the coming of Joan of Arc to Orléans, it may also have been this Bastard of Orléans who was most willing to abandon the besieged city to the troops of Talbot, Scales, Suffolk, and Glasdale.

Jean, the Bastard of Orléans, later known as Lord Dunois, was born to Duke Louis of Orléans and Mariette d'Enghien, the Lady de Cany, in 1403, four years before his father's murder began the Armagnac-Burgundian civil war that still raged during the 1428–9 siege of Orléans. Born out of wedlock, as his sobriquet indicated – Louis of Orléans' legitimate wife was Valentine Visconti, but his amorous ways were legendary, provoking rumors of his infidelity even with the queen, Isabeau of Bavaria[27] – Jean, the Bastard of Orléans, was nevertheless recognized by his father, which entitled him to similar benefits as his half-brothers. After Charles was captured at the battle of Agincourt in 1415 and his younger brother, Philippe, comte de Vertus and last legitimate son of Louis of Orléans remaining in France, died in 1420, Jean took over the familial leadership as well as the responsibility for raising his half-brother's hefty ransom.[28]

By this time, his own military career had begun. By 1417, only fifteen years old at the time, the Bastard of Orléans had already taken up arms against the enemies of the dauphin, primarily against John the Fearless, the duke of Burgundy. He was captured and lingered under Burgundian imprisonment for two years. However unsuccessful at the beginning, in 1421 the Bastard began to build his military reputation anew, this time with far more success. In that year, he participated in the battle of Baugé and the defense of Blois. In both engagements he acquitted himself well, and, by the end of the year, his twenty-first, he had been dubbed a knight. From then until the end of his life, the Bastard of Orléans participated in nearly every military engagement involving forces of the dauphin, later Charles VII. Indeed, perhaps no one in French military leadership, including the impressive Arthur de Richemont, fought in more military engagements during the fifteenth century, and especially between 1421 and 1428, than did Jean, the Bastard of Orléans. His reputation continued to grow as did his titles and land-holdings. By March 1424, he had been given the county of Mortain, and by December of that same year, he was also awarded the county of Gien. In addition, Jean married well, in 1422, to the daughter of the president of the Parlement, Louvet.

Surprisingly, considering the time in and the side on which he fought, the Bastard of Orléans had known defeat in only a few conflicts. The battle of Baugé must be considered a French victory, despite some English historical attempts to deny its outcome.[29] Additionally, the Bastard participated in the defense of Mont-Saint-Michel in 1425 and the relief of the siege of Montargis in 1427; in the latter, again in the company of La Hire, he won fame by his awe-inspiring attack of the besieging forces, an unconventional offensive that alone effectively raised the siege.[30] Thus it would seem that he would have been the perfect leader for the forces ordered to relieve the siege of Orléans, his own city. Yet, contemporary chronicles paint a portrait of a military leader not prepared at all to repeat his Montargis feats. Rather, he seems to have been reluctant to meet the enemy, frightened by the English-garrisoned fortifications, and eventually, at least until Joan of Arc appeared, willing to retreat from Orléans and allow the city to fall to its adversaries.[31]

The Bastard of Orléans did attempt some military intervention, it is true, but on these few occasions, he seemed hesitant and cautious, exhibiting no leadership qualities. On 30 December, the *Journal du siège d'Orléans* reports, he led a 'great attack' on the English forces which 'pushed back the enemy' but resulted in no change in the status of the siege.[32] And on 15 January, he again attempted a sortie into the English siege positions, leading 'many knights, squires, captains, and citizens of Orléans' against the boulevard of Saint Laurent. But, also according to the author of the *Journal du siège d'Orléans*, 'the English observed it and called their men to arms against the enemy, so that they were armed, such that there followed a large and intense battle. Finally, the French had to retreat . . . because the English sallied out in all of their strength.'[33] (Both of these attacks seem to have been led out of the city against the English; as will be seen, the English troops were so few at Orléans that passage into the city was relatively unimpeded.) La Hire, too, tried other sorties against the besiegers, but they met with similar results.[34] All of these must be counted as setbacks in a military sense, as they brought not even the most modest of positive results. But no setback was quite so severe to the relief of the siege of Orléans than that delivered on 12 February 1429, outside of the village of Rouvray, to the north of Orléans, at what became known as the battle of the Herrings.[35]

Since the outset of the siege by the earl of Salisbury, the English troops had been constantly reinforced and supplied from their territories to the north, especially from Paris. This was important, for nothing plagues any besiegers more than their own lack of supplies; a siege effectively ends if the besiegers run out of supplies before the besieged. In early February, the Bastard of Orléans decided to intercept one of these supply trains, a large one led by an experienced English general, Sir John Fastolf, and outfitted in Paris. The Bastard's purpose was two-fold: not only did he want to keep Fastolf from supplying the Orléans besiegers, but a convoy of this size would do much to alleviate some of the hunger which the citizens of Orléans were beginning to suffer. At the same time, such an attack might remove some of the unhappiness felt by these citizens at the Bastard's inaction. He persuaded the dauphin to send a large army to perform the task. This convoy was filled with fish for approaching Lent, giving it its unusual name.

On the morning of 12 February, the French army, numbering between 3,000 and 4,000, according to the *Journal du siège d'Orléans*,[36] appeared on the horizon between the sleeping English camp and their Orléans destination. Undoubtedly they were hoping to surprise the English, but on this unusually clear morning their approach had in fact been seen, giving the English army ample time to set up their battle lines and protect their supply wagons. (The flat terrain had probably been recognized as a favorable campsite by Fastolf because it would give his scouts ample warning of an approaching army.) Fastolf's army was significantly smaller than its French counterpart, so that, placing his wagons in a make-shift fortification, he took up a defensive formation. Against this, the French leader, Charles of Bourbon, the count of Clermont – the Bastard of Orléans served only as a leader of one of the French battle contingents – began to bombard the English formation/fortification with his gunpowder weapons. This proved to be remarkably successful, as the English had no option but to endure the bombardment or retreat; English casualties grew and wagons were destroyed, spilling their contents on to the field. (It is said by Enguerrand de Monstrelet that the Rouvray villagers profited much from the herrings left on the field following the battle, and that they were the first to call it 'the battle of the Herrings'.[37]) But the French, true to their late medieval military characteristics, decided not to wait for their artillery to take its ultimate toll.[38] A contingent of Scottish infantry serving in the French army, led by the Constable of Scotland, Sir John Stewart of Darnley, marched into the fray, halting the French guns for fear of striking them, but initiating English longbow fire. Not well protected by armor, the Scots were decimated by the English archers shooting from behind their wagon barricade, and they were forced to retreat. In response, or perhaps feeling that the guns and Scots had weakened the English enough to warrant a frontal assault, Clermont ordered a French cavalry attack. French horsemen outnumbered their opponents perhaps as many as ten-to-one and reached the English lines with little effort. But, by this time, their charge had become disordered by constant archery fire and the stakes which English archers had become accustomed to place before their formations. The French impetus was lost, and, as the fight intensified, English soldiers came from behind their wagons and attacked the rear and flanks of the French cavalry. Within a short time, the French army was in retreat, and the English had won the battle. Fastolf was able to continue with the remainder of his convoy and resupply the English besiegers of Orléans. Even more importantly, the English defeat of the French at the battle of the Herrings sent French spirits, especially those of the soldiers in and citizens of Orléans, to an all-time low. The count of Clermont and several other leaders, 'with about 2,000 soldiers', left Orléans for Tours.[39] And, by the time the Bastard of Orléans returned to his city – he had barely escaped with his life from the battle, according to the *Journal du siège d'Orléans*[40] – the thought of abandoning it to the very determined English must have been quite appealing.

But hope was shortly to come to Orléans from quite a different source. On the day that the battle of the Herrings was fought, and lost, by the French, Joan of Arc was meeting with Robert de Baudricourt. It was her final meeting with the count, after which she would leave to meet the dauphin at Chinon. It was not long before word of her mission, in particular her mission to relieve the siege of Orléans, was heard in Orléans. The Bastard, having by then earned the title Lord Dunois, testified at the nullification trial that he had heard 'rumors from the town of Gien . . . that a certain young woman, commonly called the Maid, asserted that she was going to the noble dauphin to raise the siege of Orléans and to lead the dauphin to Reims'.[41] Gien was not far from Orléans and, still faithful to the dauphin, obviously was quite interested in the progress of the siege there. Undoubtedly, should Orléans fall, Gien might be next. It was thus important to the inhabitants of the latter if Joan's mission was to prove divine.

The divinity of Joan's mission was no less important for the Orléanais. Perhaps this is what gave those citizens the energy to continue to resist their besiegers after the disaster at the battle of the Herrings. They must have listened intently to whatever news came from Joan's meeting with the dauphin at Chinon and her trial at Poitiers. Of course, this was not all that they did. The Orléanais also sent a legation under the leadership of the veteran captain, Ponton de Xantrailles, who had joined the besieged at Orléans early in 1429, to Duke Philip of Burgundy, asking him to intercede on their behalf. The duke refused, leaving the citizens of Orléans no recourse except to wait for their inevitable defeat – unless the Maid could assist them.[42] After the battle of the Herrings, it was clear that there would be no other official French response.

For Joan's part, the siege of Orléans stayed foremost in her mind. She spoke of it frequently and showed impatience at her extended interrogation because of it.[43] Once she was accorded ecclesiastical and then royal approval, she sought to relieve the city. Even before she had returned to Chinon, she sent her famous 'Letter to the English', in which she told the besiegers of her mission to relieve the siege and her determination to complete it. Dictated around 22 March at the conclusion of her trial at Poitiers and sent from Blois between 24 and 27 April[44] as she was collecting her weapons and soldiers, the letter is clear in its confidence and in its defiance:

Jesus-Maria,

King of England, and you, duke of Bedford, you call yourself regent of the kingdom of France, you, William de la Pole, Sir John Talbot, and you, Sir Thomas Scales, who call yourself lieutenant of the aforesaid duke of Bedford, render your account to the King of Heaven. Surrender to the Maid, who is sent here from God, the

King of Heaven, the keys to all of the good cities that you have taken and violated in France. She has come here from God to proclaim the blood royal. She is entirely ready to make peace, if you are willing to settle accounts with her, provided that you give up France and pay for having occupied her. And those among you, archers, companions-at-arms, gentlemen, and others who are before the city of Orléans, go back to your own countries, for God's sake. And if you do not do so, wait for the word of the Maid who will come visit you briefly, to your great damage. If you do not do so, I am commander of the armies, and in whatever place I shall meet your French allies, I shall make them leave it, whether they wish to or not; and if they will not obey, I shall have them all killed. I am sent from God, the King of Heaven, to chase you out of all of France, body for body [every last one of you]. And if they wish to obey, I shall have mercy on them. And have no other opinion, for you shall never hold the kingdom of France from God, the King of Heaven, the son of St Mary; but King Charles, the true heir, will hold it; for God, the King of Heaven, wishes it so and has revealed through the Maid, and he will enter Paris with a goodly company. If you do not wish to believe this message from God through the Maid, then wherever we find you we will strike you there, and make a great uproar greater than any made in France for a thousand years, if you do not come to terms. And believe firmly that the King of Heaven will send the Maid more force than you will ever know how to achieve with all of your assaults on her and on her good men-at-arms; and in the exchange of blows we shall see who has better right from the King of Heaven. You, duke of Bedford, the Maid prays you and requests that you cause no more destruction. If you will settle your account, you can join her company, in which the French will achieve the finest feat ever accomplished in Christendom. And give answer, if you wish to make peace in the city of Orléans; and if indeed you do not do so, be mindful soon of your great damages.[45]

Why did Joan dictate and send this letter? It is clear that she believed her mission to relieve the siege of Orléans had come from God, and that she felt it was only fair to give the English the opportunity of withdrawing from the city without the loss of life. She may also have known or been told of the ecclesiastical tradition of 'declaring war' against your adversary as a requirement to ensure that the war fought was a 'just' one (although the fact that the French were attacking the English in order to regain territory that had been earlier lost to them would have made moot this requirement for justice).[46]

Yet, no doubt the English in receiving this epistle simply discarded it; the fact that they did not immediately remove themselves from outside of Orléans indicates that they did not adhere to its contents. Joan of Arc could not have thought that they would. Nor could her purpose in having this letter written have been only to fulfill the requirements of medieval military justification, or to remove the deaths of so many opponents from her conscience. Because this letter was so well known among those on her own side,[47] unlike her earlier letters – Pernoud and Clin refer to three previous letters sent by Joan since she had left Vaucouleurs, none of which were known to anyone but Joan and the recipients of the letters, and all of which were known only through her own testimony[48] – Joan may have written her 'Letter to the English' more for the French than for the English. Evidence for this can be seen in a citizen of Orléans, Jean Lullier's, nullification trial testimony:

> She summoned the English in a letter containing in substance that they must retreat from the siege and go to the kingdom of England, otherwise they would be compelled to retreat by strength or violence . . . from that hour the English were terrified, and no longer had the power of resistance as previously. Only a few men of the town would often fight against a great number of English, and each time they so overwhelmed those besieging them that the English no longer dared to come out of their forts.[49]

Through her 'Letter to the English' Joan of Arc made official what had been rumored throughout France since she had first visited Robert de Baudricourt: the Maid who would come forth to save France, as had been prophesied, had arrived, and her first target was the siege of Orléans. But that was not all. She would not stop her attacks on the English until they had been removed, until 'the true heir', King Charles VII, would 'enter Paris with a goodly company'. This would be the 'uproar' that was 'greater than any made in France for a thousand years'. It would start at Orléans.

Some time after 21 April Joan joined the royal army at Blois in final preparation for her journey to Orléans. She was met there by the Bastard, who, according to Jean d'Aulon, had traveled to Blois especially to meet the Maid and to lead her safely to Orléans.[50] Later, at her nullification trial, the Bastard did not recall his feelings in first meeting with Joan, which may have been an omission meaning little, but may also give an impression that the man in charge of relieving the siege of Orléans was not overly impressed with her.[51] Others, for example, the duke of Alençon, gave long discourses at her nullification trial on their positive first impressions in meeting Joan.[52] The Bastard of Orléans, however, did recall the large numbers of soldiers – Enguerrand de Monstrelet estimates a number of 400–500 soldiers, while Joan's testimony enlarged this number to 10,000–12,000[53] – and the huge convoy of provisions – 'many wagons and carts of grain and a large number of oxen, sheep, cattle, pigs, and other foodstuffs', according to Jean Chartier – that were at Blois,[54] the latter having been collected with much success by the dauphin's mother-in-law, the Queen of Sicily, and paid for by the dauphin.[55] It seems that Joan's prominence had not only led to the recruitment of many soldiers for the relief of the siege, but also to the gathering of an impressive amount of supplies for the relief of the citizens' suffering as well. Additionally, Joan seems to have brought together a sizeable force of ecclesiastics for the journey. These, Jean Pasquerel reports, she had brought together twice a day to sing hymns to St Mary; they were there to hear the soldiers' confessions. She also had a banner made for these priests, on which was painted the 'image of our Lord crucified'.[56] Finally, there was also an impressive number of French military leaders who had come forward to fight. Many of these, including Jean, the duke of Alençon, Gilles de Laval, Baron de Rais, Ambroise de Loré, the later Provost of Paris, Jean de Brosse, the Marshal of Boussac, and Louis de Culan, the Admiral of France, had remained suspiciously absent from combat at or around Orléans to this time, but would stay with Joan throughout most if not all of her military endeavors after the Orléans engagement. Also joining with Joan and the royal army at Blois was La Hire, who had traveled with the Bastard from Orléans.[57]

On 26 April,[58] after all of the soldiers had arrived and all of the foodstuffs and military provisions had been collected, Joan of Arc and the royal army left Blois for Orléans. Jean Pasquerel testified that initially she marched her priests, with their newly made banner and 'singing the *Veni creator Spiritus* and many other anthems', before the rest of the army, but that these remained with them only for two nights, returning to Blois as they neared Orléans.[59]

Joan's desire was to enter Orléans, but on the Blois side of the city there were countless obstacles. Not only were two major Loire towns lying between Blois and Orléans – Beaugency and Meung, both controlled by the English – but on that side (the west side) of Orléans itself was the largest number of English boulevards, all positioned along the routes that Joan and her army would have to use to enter the besieged city. However, the approach to Orléans from the east was guarded only by the English-controlled town of Jargeau and by the boulevard of Saint Loup. So, this was the logical direction to travel. Furthermore, Jargeau posed little problem as there seems to have been a ford or crossing of the Loire between that town and Orléans. Positioned near Checy, the crossing was unknown to or at least unprotected by the English, which allowed Joan's party to cross the river with her relief convoy. That left only the English in the boulevard of Saint Loup to worry about. The journey from Blois to Orléans was uneventful; indeed, the French army may have traveled fairly far south to avoid any conflict. But once they approached the ford at Checy, and then later at the boulevard of Saint Loup on 29 April, problems arose for Joan and her companions. Witnesses testified later, however, that at both locations Joan solved these problems with miracles.

At the crossing to Checy, the Bastard later recalled, the wind was blowing away from Orléans, which prevented the boats that were to carry the relief provisions into the city from traveling. But once Joan became determined to go across the river herself and enter Orléans, 'in a moment, the wind . . . changed and became favorable; accordingly, sails were immediately raised, and she, the boats and ships, entered the city'.[60] Jean Pasquerel's version of this miracle story is slightly different. Joan's confessor, by his own admission not being present at the time, testified that when the party reached the crossing at Checy, they found that 'the river was so low that ships could not travel up it nor come to the shore on the side of the English', but again when Joan arrived, 'immediately the water rose so that ships were able to land on their side, on which boats Joan and some of her soldiers boarded and crossed over to the city of Orléans'.[61]

The boulevard at Saint Loup posed an even greater problem. How would Joan, several soldiers (it is clear from the original sources that most of the army stayed on the south side of the Loire, so that they might have a better approach against the English[62]), and a large supply train cross virtually next to this boulevard without arousing the English besiegers within? Even if their numbers were not large, the Saint Loup soldiers were probably sufficient in strength to keep the small French force, with its slow-moving supply train from entering the city until reinforcements could arrive. Again, the nullification trial witnesses claim, a miracle occurred. Joan and her company passed the boulevard of Saint Loup seemingly without any incident at all. 'They crossed outside the church of Saint Loup, occupied by the English,' recounted the Bastard, and 'from then he had great hope in her, more than before.'[63] Joan then entered the city of Orléans by the Burgundian Gate.

What is to be made of these two miracles? Obviously they continued to impress the memories of those testifying on Joan's sanctity more than a generation after the events themselves. Yet, there are some problems with what was being remembered. With the first miracle, not only is there the problem of two different versions of what happened, but the Bastard's version, despite his being present while Pasquerel was not, plays the most with logic. If the provisions taken by Joan from Blois to Orléans were carried by boat from Blois to Orléans, as many contemporary sources suggest,[64] such a flotilla would have had to pass the English-held Loire towns of Beaugency and Meung-sur-Loire, as well as floating between the English troops and the Orléans walls, before it reached the French army at the Checy crossing. Therefore, it seems doubtful that such a means of transporting these goods would have been used. Moreover, if these were the same boats and they had passed such impediments as those just mentioned, why would they have traveled further up the river to Checy and not simply have stopped outside a closer entrance to Orléans? Of course, these could have been other vessels found by the French to carry the provisions to Orléans, or sent by the Orléanais, as the author of the *Chronique de la Pucelle* claims,[65] but such a number as would have been needed to take the supplies to the city would also undoubtedly have been too many to have been found outside of the English-controlled towns and been previously undetected by them. Or, they could have simply been a few vessels meant to ferry the goods to the other side of the Loire, with the Bastard of Orléans' testimony in error or incomplete on the matter. Pasquerel's testimony is more logical, if he is talking about a ferry unable to travel from one side of the Loire to the other because of its low water, but it must be remembered that Joan's confessor was not present with the troops there and that he omits the chief characteristic used to retell this miracle story for many years after – the wind. His testimony is also somewhat confused in its description of the side of the river that Joan was to travel to as 'the English side', so that at least one nullification trial manuscript transcriber has replaced those words with 'the French side'.[66] Still, it must be agreed, Joan did cross the river safely and made her way past the boulevard of Saint Loup.

What about Joan's failure to disturb the English troops in the Saint Loup boulevard? There is no question about besieger laxity on that side of Orléans. After all, it seems that the Bastard of Orléans himself had passed that way several times in entering and exiting his besieged city. Also, on frequent occasions, supplies, victuals and gunpowder weapons, had been delivered to the Orléanais through the very Burgundian Gate that Joan would use to enter the city on 29 April. So why was the Bastard so impressed by Joan's achievement? Was it simply because of the size of the party in which Joan traveled and the fact that it aroused no attention? This may be the reason for his praise. But was it a miracle, or simply a daring but tactically well-run military operation? For this, one must turn to the *Journal du siège d'Orléans*. In it we can gain a better understanding of exactly what occurred at the boulevard of Saint Loup on 29 April 1429:

On the twenty-ninth of the month [of April], certain news was delivered to Orléans that the King was sending by the [eastern way] victuals, powder, cannon, and other weapons of war under the leadership of the Maid, who came from our Lord to re-provision and comfort the town, and to raise the siege, by which many of those of Orléans were much comforted. And because it was said that the English would take pains to prevent these supplies, it was ordered that everyone should be armed and well prepared throughout the city; which was done . . . On this same day there was a great skirmish because the French wished to give place and time for the victuals to enter, which were brought to them. And to keep the English busy elsewhere, they sallied out in great strength, and went charging and skirmishing before Saint Loup d'Orléans. And they engaged those there so closely that there were many dead, wounded, and captured on both sides, so much so that the French carried into their city one of the English standards. While this skirmish was

being fought, there entered into the city the victuals and the artillery
which the Maid had brought all the way from Checy.[67]

Perhaps this diversionary attack on the boulevard of Saint Loup by
the Orléanais was not Joan's strategem, but she was tactically capable
enough to recognize an advantage when she saw one. While the
citizens of Orléans attacked the boulevard of Saint Loup and kept the
English occupied, Joan of Arc, together with her soldiers and supply
train, entered the besieged city of Orléans without conflict.

The Orléanais were elated and celebrated Joan's arrival, not only
because she had brought badly needed supplies, but also because,
again in the words of the *Journal du siège d'Orléans*, she brought
'divine virtue which was said to be in this simple maid. All regarded
her with much affection, even men, women, and small children.
And there was a very extraordinary rush to touch her, or even to
touch the horse on which she sat.'[68] One of the citizens of Orléans,
Jacques l'Esbahy, later recalled that she asked first to be taken to the
cathedral to 'show her reverence for God her Creator' and
undoubtedly to offer thanks for her safe and successful journey.[69]
But, Louis de Coutes, Joan's page, claimed that she was so exhausted
after her tiresome travels and the tumultuous adventures of the day
that she simply retired to the home appointed for her stay, the house
of Jacques Boucher, the city's treasurer general, and there took the
Eucharist and went to bed.[70]

The Bastard of Orléans remembered it differently. He testified that
Joan was not pleased with the events of the day. At Checy, she
became angry that he was leading her into the city and not into
immediate action against the English troops. He testified:

Then said she to him: 'Did you give counsel that I should come
here, to this side of the river, and that I should go not straight
there where Talbot and the English are?' He answered that he and
others, wiser on this matter, had given this counsel, believing that
they were doing the best and surest. Then Joan said to him, 'In
the name of God, the counsel of our Lord God is surer and wiser
than yours. You thought to deceive me but it is you who are
deceived, for I am bringing you better help than ever came from
any soldier or any city, because it is the help of the King of
Heaven. It does not come through love for me, but from God
himself who, on the petition of Saint Louis and Saint

Charlemagne, has had pity on the town of Orléans, and has refused to suffer the enemy to have both the body of the lord of Orléans and his city.'[71]

(It was after this reprimand, the Bastard remembered, that the miracle of the winds and then the passing of Saint Loup took place.)

The Bastard of Orléans was not used to such an affront to his authority. Nor was he prepared at that time to attack the English, no matter what Joan might have intended or threatened. Joan, on the other hand, did not wish to sit idly by waiting for the action of military leaders who had not shown any previous ability to encounter the English successfully. Louis de Coutes recalled that she was again incensed on the following morning, 30 April, when she discovered that there was to be no attack on that day either: 'on the next day, after they had entered the town of Orléans, Joan came to the Lord, the Bastard of Orléans, and spoke with him. And, in returning, she was very angry because, as she said, it had been decided that on this day there would be no attack.'[72] To Joan this anger was justified. She had a mission to fulfill, one given her by God, and that mission began with the relief of the siege of Orléans. She could not relieve the city living comfortably within its walls. But she was not the general in charge of the French army, and she had to wait for others, individuals who felt that they were 'wiser' on military matters, to attack the English positions before her mission could be completed. She was, naturally, impatient. (There was an attack made that day, according to the *Journal du siège d'Orléans*: La Hire, 'with some citizens', made a charge against the English in their boulevard of Saint Pouër to the north of the city. Nevertheless, despite the fight being long and very hard, with much exchange of gunfire between the two forces, it was little more than an ineffective skirmish. Joan seems also not to have known about it.[73])

While she may have been restrained from active military conflict by the inaction of the Bastard of Orléans, she did not have to like it, and Louis de Coutes testified that following her rebuff by the Bastard,

Joan went to a certain boulevard that the King's armed men held against the boulevard of the English, and there [*she*] spoke with the English in the other boulevard, saying to them that they should retreat in the name of Christ, otherwise she would expel

them. A certain man named the Bastard of Granville spoke many
insults to Joan, asking her if she wished them to surrender to a
woman, and calling the French with her 'unbelieving pimps'.[74]

The *Journal du siège d'Orléans* confirms this nullification trial
testimony, giving it also a time, the evening, and a place, the Belle
Croix stronghold on the end of the Orléanais-controlled side of the
bridge:

> When evening came, [Joan] went to the boulevard of Belle Croix,
> on the bridge, and spoke to Glasdale and other Englishmen who
> were in the Tourelles. And she told them that if they surrendered
> themselves to God, that their lives would be saved. But Glasdale
> and those on his side responded evilly, insulting her and calling
> her 'cow-herd' . . . crying very loudly that they would burn her, if
> they were to capture her. From which she was very angry and
> answered them that they had lied. And this being said, she
> withdrew into the city.[75]

The *Journal du siège d'Orléans* also reports that on that same day, but
preceding this exchange, Joan had sent two heralds to the English:

> demanding that they release the herald who had carried her letter
> from Blois [evidently the herald who had delivered Joan's 'Letter
> to the English' was being held by them]. And if not, she said that
> those heralds who had come to the Bastard of Orléans would not
> be returned, that she would kill with a brutal death all the
> English who were prisoners in Orléans, and also those among the
> lords of English who were being held as ransom for others.

Such an ultimatum seemed to work. The *Journal du siège d'Orléans*
continues: 'The leaders of the English returned all the messengers
and heralds to the Maid,' but they also sent back a message to her,
'that they would torture and burn her, and that she was nothing
but a rustic, and that she should return to herding her cattle'.[76]
It is clear what Joan was doing here: she was provoking a fight. If
the French military leadership was not going to attack the English,
perhaps she could get the English to attack the French. The result
would be the same: she would have the opportunity to raise the
siege of Orléans. Her plan worked, at least indirectly. Although the

English remained behind their protective barricades, the Bastard of Orléans was forced into action. While he continued to refuse to attack the English, on 1 May, the day after Joan's provocations, the Bastard, believing that he needed more men to undertake what Joan desired, left Orléans for Blois to confer with the Count of Clermont and to collect other troops who were waiting there.[77] He would be away until 4 May.

During the days when the Bastard of Orléans was away, as she had been kept from leading the French army against the English, Joan spent her time reconnoitering their positions and endearing herself to the people of the besieged city. On Sunday, 1 May, she rode around Orléans with some of her companions, and met with the citizens, who crowded around her making her passage through the streets nearly impossible.[78] On 2 May, she rode outside the walls of the city and visited all of the English boulevards surrounding it.[79] Staying beyond the range of the besiegers' weapons, she was able to evaluate her opponents' fortified positions and troop strength. Was the raising of the siege feasible? Or, was the inaction of the Bastard of Orléans warranted? The duke of Alençon would later testify that the English fortifications were so strong 'that if he had been in them with a few soldiers, he would have expected to hold out for six or seven days against the entire power of the army, and it seemed to him that they would not have captured him'.[80] Obviously, Joan did not hold the same opinion; she never doubted that this part of her mission, which she knew to have come from God, would be completed. Later that evening she retired to the Church of Sainte-Croix in Orléans and offered prayers for the fulfillment of this task.[81] And on 3 May, the Orléanais held a procession throughout the city in Joan's honor. They presented money and gifts to the Maid and her companions and asked them to deliver their town from its siege.[82]

Leading reinforcements he had found at Blois, the Bastard of Orléans returned to his besieged city on 4 May. Joan was so anxious for his return that Jean d'Aulon remembered her mounting a horse and riding out to meet him. She was, it seems, excited to report her observations on the weaknesses of the enemy's fortifications to the Bastard of Orléans and the other French military leaders. Almost to prove her point, Aulon, who was with the party from Blois, recounted that she, the Bastard, La Hire, and himself, 'in the view and with the knowledge of the enemy entered . . . with their men, into that city without any opposition'.[83] But was Joan finally to get

her desired combat? Apparently not, for the Bastard remained
hesitant to attack the English,[84] unnecessarily hesitant in the Maid's
view, especially after she heard the rumors of an approaching
English army led by John Fastolf that was coming from the north to
reinforce the besiegers of Orléans. The Bastard confirmed these
rumors 'which he knew for certain from a good source', and caused
Joan's anger at her commander's inaction to surface again; Jean
d'Aulon later recalled her words: 'Bastard, Bastard, in the name of
God I command you that as soon as you hear of Fastolf's coming
you will let me know. For, if he gets through without my knowing it,
I swear to you that I will have your head cut off.' To this, the count
'answered that he did not doubt that, and that he would certainly
let her know'.[85]

Dismayed at the French military leaders' unwillingness to believe
that the English at Orléans were vulnerable, as she did, but having
expressed her views forcefully, Joan retired to her lodgings to rest.
However, before long, as attested to by several nullification trial
witnesses, she awoke with a start, claiming that her voices had told
her that she must attack the English, although she was not clear
which boulevard she should target, or even whether she was to
attack the approaching Fastolf. (This is Jean d'Aulon's testimony.
Louis de Coutes and Jean Pasquerel both claimed that her voices
told her that 'the blood of France was being spilled', meaning that a
French attack was already in progress, without her attendance,
although Pasquerel, who was then present, having arrived with the
reinforcements from Blois, insisted that such an attack was because
of 'Joan's appeal' delivered earlier to the Bastard of Orléans.[86])

The French attack on 4 May was against the English boulevard of
Saint Loup. The boulevard having proved more of an irritant than a
threat to any movement in or out of Orléans, the attack on Saint Loup
was to be a show of French determination to raise the siege of the city.
Were it to fail, however, the attack would deflate the French
exuberance, especially in the presence of their virgin savior, Joan of
Arc. French failure would also have increased the English resolve to
conquer Orléans, or at least to hold on until the arrival of Fastolf. Thus
it was, writes the author of the *Journal du siège d'Orléans*, that the
English in the Saint Loup boulevard put up a 'very strong resistance,
because the English, who were very well fortified, defended it very
valiantly for the space of three hours'.[87] Most fought until they were
killed. In the end, however, the French did succeed in conquering the

isolated English stronghold, despite an attempted relief expedition from the boulevard of Saint Pouër; 140 English soldiers were killed, with 40 more taken as prisoners.[88] (The *Chronique de la Pucelle* and Enguerrand de Monstrelet also insist that the French then destroyed the boulevard.[89]) The French capture of Saint Loup was greeted enthusiastically by all on their side. For Joan, whose first military encounter this was, the feeling of victory strengthened her confidence. Jean Pasquerel testified that even though she wept for the slain English soldiers, as they had died without confession, she also promised boldly 'that within five days the siege being waged before Orléans would be raised and no English would remain in front of the city'.[90] She would better her promise by more than a full day.

On 5 May, Ascension Day, Pasquerel insisted that Joan did not participate in active warfare, in view of the holiness of the day. Instead, she chose to write another letter to the English which her confessor remembered read as follows:

> You, Englishmen, who have no right to this kingdom of France, the King of Heaven orders and commands you through me, Joan the Maid, to leave your fortresses and return to your country, or I shall make such an uproar that will be in constant memory. And these things I write to you for the third and last time; I will write no further. Thus signed: *Jhesus-Maria*, Joan the Maid.

She then added:

> I have sent to you my letters honestly, but you have detained my messengers, in French, my heralds, for you have kept my herald named Guyenne. Would you send him to me, and I will send to you some of your men captured in the fortress of Saint Loup, because all of them were not killed.

Joan then delivered the letter to the English in the Tourelles tied to the tip of an arrow, and she shouted at them to 'Read, this is news!' But the English derided her, as they shouted back: 'This is news from the whore of the Armagnacs!' Such mockery, Pasquerel concludes, made Joan 'sigh and weep with abundant tears'.[91] Perhaps Joan was upset that the English had not yet recognized her mission. But she had made her point. She and her army would not be stopped before they had raised the siege of Orléans. The victory over the troops in Saint Loup was but the first step towards that goal.

However, Jean Pasquerel is alone in his assertion that Joan of Arc did not fight on 5 May. Jean d'Aulon, her squire, and Louis de Coutes, her page, both tell a different story. They claim that:

> the Maid and her people, seeing the large victory obtained the preceding day by them over their enemies, marched out of the city in good order to attack a certain other boulevard in front of their city called the boulevard of Saint Jean le Blanc.

As that boulevard was on the opposite shore of the Loire River from the city, she and her troops were forced to cross over to one of the islands in the river – the name of the island is not given by either Aulon or Coutes but was probably the Ile aux Boeufs or the Ile aux Toiles – and there commandeer two boats to use as a bridge to the English-held shore. Once this maneuver had been completed, they discovered that their target, the boulevard of Saint Jean le Blanc, was deserted, the English troops there having retreated into the boulevard of the Augustins or the Tourelles.[92] Bloodless, it was a French victory nonetheless.[93]

At this point in the relief of the siege of Orléans, there were two potential targets. The French could seek to attack the more lightly manned northern and western boulevards, or they could choose to move against the imposing bridgehead fortifications, the Augustins boulevard and then the Tourelles. Should the relief force have moved against the northern and western boulevards, there might have been fewer French casualties, if the attack on Saint Loup was any indication – but only if this forced the English to retreat from their Augustins and Torelles positions. Otherwise, those two fortifications would have to be attacked eventually. In addition, there was the question of the time that attacks on the other English boulevards would require, and this may have been the most influential factor in the decision of which boulevards to target. Undoubtedly, the French wished to raise the English siege before the arrival of Fastolf's reinforcements. Again, there was a dispute among the French military leaders – once more, it seems, principally between the Bastard of Orléans, although he is not named, and Joan of Arc. The President of the Chamber of Accounts, Simon Charles, who by his own witness was with the dauphin in

Chinon and not at Orléans, but heard of the event from Raoul de Gaucourt, testified that:

> On [6 May] the day that the boulevard of the Augustins was captured, it had been concluded through the leaders who had command of the king's army that it did not seem beneficial to make any attack or charge against it. And the Lord Gaucourt was ordered to guard the gates so that no one would leave the town. However, Joan was not content with this. She was of the opinion that the soldiers ought to leave with the people of the town and make a charge against that boulevard and many of the soldiers and men of the town were of the same opinion. Joan said to the Lord de Gaucourt that he was an evil man, saying to him: 'Like it or not, the soldiers will come, and they will obtain what they have obtained elsewhere.' And against the will of the Lord de Gaucourt, the soldiers who were in the town charged out to attack the boulevard of the Augustins, which they captured with strength and violence.[94]

Although this event is confirmed by no other source, including Gaucourt himself, who says nothing of it in his nullification trial testimony, it is quite likely to have happened. Joan's anger at the inaction of the French leaders had erupted almost daily, and, as was witnessed in the attack on the boulevard of Saint Loup, her desire to lift the siege by whatever means possible, even if it meant a high casualty total among the Orléanais and the French soldiers, was echoed by those very individuals who were being called on to make that sacrifice. As mentioned, she believed that her mission had come directly from God, and although she preferred that no Frenchman lose his life in the undertaking of this mission, any who did, she was confident, would go directly to heaven like the martyrs of old. It is clear from Simon Charles's testimony, that those who were to fight for and with her shared this confidence. The Bastard of Orléans and the other French leaders who appeared to want to follow a more cautious tactical approach to the remaining English positions were simply overwhelmed by the Maid and her cause. A dangerous and potentially very costly direct assault on the boulevard of the Augustins, followed undoubtedly by a similar attack on the Tourelles, was to be made, whether they liked it or not.[95]

According to Jean Pasquerel, on the morning of the French attack on the boulevard of the Augustins, Joan prepared herself for the most

difficult undertaking of her young military career. Pasquerel himself
heard her confession and sang mass to her and her soldiers. Then, he
later testified, 'she left for the attack, which lasted from morning to
evening. And on that day, the fortress of the Augustins was captured
by a great attack.' Pasquerel's testimony left out the details of what
was clearly a brutal and rigorous undertaking, although his addition
of 'and Joan, who was accustomed to fast on Fridays, was not able to
fast on that day, because she was very exhausted' gives an impression
that she for one had acquitted herself quite well in this military
engagement.[96] So also did her troops, who pressed on and on,
suffering large numbers of casualties in capturing this boulevard in
the only manner possible, by force in a frontal assault.

From other sources this becomes clear. The author of the *Journal
du siège d'Orléans* reports:

> [The Maid] sallied out of Orléans in the company of the Bastard of
> Orléans, the marshals of Sainte-Sévère and de Rais, the lord of
> Graville, Sir Florent d'Illiers, La Hire, and many other knights and
> squires, and around four thousand soldiers. And they crossed the
> Loire river between Saint Loup and the Tour Neuve . . . And then
> the English sallied out of the Tourelles in great strength, shouting
> loudly, and they made a charge against them which was very
> strong and harsh. But the Maid and La Hire, and all of their army,
> joined together and attacked the English with such great force and
> courage that they caused them to recoil all the way to their
> boulevard and the Tourelles. And then they delivered such an
> assault against the boulevard and bastille there which had earlier
> been fortified by the English in the place where the Church of the
> Augustins had once been, that they took it by force, freeing a large
> number of French who were held there as prisoners, and killing a
> large number of English who were inside and who had defended it
> most harshly, such that there had been many wonderful feats of
> arms, on one side and the other.[97]

Some of those feats of arms are described by Jean d'Aulon in his
nullification trial deposition:

> He [Aulon] was guarding one of the passes with certain others
> who had been picked and ordered to do so, among whom was a
> very brave man-at-arms from Spain named Alfonso de Partada.

They saw a certain man pass in front of their company, a handsome man, large and well armed, who, because he passed in front of them, was asked to remain a little while with the others to put up a defense against the enemy, in case it was needed. But he responded without restraint that he would not do so. And then Alfonso said to him that he also should remain with them and that there were others as brave as he who waited there. He responded to Alfonso that he would not do so. After which there were certain arrogant words said between them, such that they would go together at the same time against the enemy, and that through this they would know who was the more courageous and the better of the two in doing what was before them. And they, running side by side at the fastest speed that they were able, charged against the enemy's boulevard and came all the way to the foot of the palisade.

He [Aulon] said that when they were seen at the palisade of the boulevard, he saw within the palisade a large, strong, and powerful Englishman, well equipped and armed, who resisted them there such that they were unable to enter the palisade. And then he showed the Englishman to one named Master Jean le Cannonier, saying to him that he should fire at that Englishman, because he was causing such grief and doing much damage to those who wished to approach the boulevard. This was done by Master Jean, because as soon as he sited him, he sent his shot against him such that he struck him dead to the ground. And then the two men-at-arms made an entry through which all of their company passed and entered the boulevard. This they attacked very harshly and in great diligence from all sides with such success that in a short time they had overrun and captured it by assault. And the majority of the enemy were killed or captured. And those who were able to escape retreated into the Tourelles at the foot of the bridge. And thus the Maid and those with her obtained victory over her enemy on that day. And the large boulevard was won, and the lords and their men, with the Maid, remained all night beside it.[98]

The victory against the boulevard of the Augustins was an important one, but it had been fatiguing and costly. Pinned between the broken bridge into Orléans, with the feisty inhabitants of the city beyond it, and the French troops of Joan of Arc, there was little chance for the English to break out from the Tourelles. Nor does it seem that the English troops in the other boulevards, or in the nearby towns of Jargeau, Meung-sur-Loire, and Beaugency, had the confidence to try to relieve the Tourelles. Thus the Bastard of Orléans and other French leaders might be excused for their desire to rest and recuperate for a time to consider their recently won victories and perhaps to gain reinforcements for their even more difficult assault on the Tourelles. But Joan would not have it. Jean Pasquerel reported that during the evening after the capture of the boulevard of the Augustins a 'valiant and noble knight', whose name was not remembered by Pasquerel during his testimony, came to speak with her. He told Joan that she had again been excluded from a council of war during which the French leaders had decided that they were still fewer in number than the English, and that it had only been because 'God had given them His great grace' that they had defeated the fortifications already captured. Their answer was to wait until reinforcements arrived: 'Considering that the city was full of foodstuffs, we ought to be able to hold on to the city well until the king's aid arrives; the council does not see it as expedient that soldiers attack tomorrow.' Joan, now seemingly more accustomed to the determined inaction of the French military leadership, responded to the knight simply: 'You were in your council, and I was in mine; and you ought to believe that the counsel of my Lord will be done and will endure, and any other counsel will perish.' She then summoned Pasquerel and asked him to wake early, earlier than he had on this day, and to remain close to her, for 'tomorrow blood will flow from my body above my breast'.[99]

The convenience of Joan's wound the following day and the positive nature of her nullification trial perhaps allowed Pasquerel a little hagiographical embellishment in remembering her prophecy. But what can be certain from his testimony is the confidence which Joan had that she would be supported by her troops in an undertaking for which she felt some urgency, whether because of the threat of the approaching English troops or as a result of the enthusiasm for the completion of her mission's first charge. She was used to the Bastard's and others' desire to slow the pace of the relief effort, which in fact might have been a more safe and more sane strategy. But she also knew that her cause had gained a legitimacy by the victories in which she had participated. The troops would follow her leadership. She sent word to them to prepare for an attack on the Tourelles the following day.[100] So, too, would the citizens of Orléans follow her, and, as evidence of this, the *Journal du siège d'Orléans* recounts, 'those of Orléans were most diligent throughout the night in carrying bread, wine, and other victuals to the men of war carrying on the siege [of the Tourelles]'.[101]

On the morning of 7 May, Joan arose early and prepared for battle as she had every other day during her sojourn in Orléans: she confessed to Jean Pasquerel and heard mass.[102] She then roused her troops for the attack. There is no report that she said anything special to her men about the difficulty of their assault on the Tourelles. She does not appear to have been as eloquent as so many medieval commanders are reported to be.[103] Of course, many of her soldiers would die in the engagement, but she and, it seems, the soldiers themselves believed that such a death would gain them salvation, for they were fulfilling the mission of the Maid, which had been determined for her by God. It also appears that all of the other French military leaders were present as well – their absence is not recorded in any of the original sources – despite what they had concluded in their council the night before.

Perceval de Cagny wrote: 'the place seemed impregnable against assault by soldiers and was filled with all kinds of military equipment . . . it seemed impossible that such a place would not be captured for a month or more.' He also estimates that Glasdale had between 700 and 800 men inside. But 'the Maid said to those who were with her, "By Saint Martin, I will take this today and return to the city over this bridge"'.[104] The following account of the bloodiest military engagement of the Hundred Years War since the battle of Agincourt comes from the *Journal du siège d'Orléans*:

Early in the morning on the day after, which was Saturday, the seventh day of May, the French attacked the Tourelles and the boulevard while the English were attempting to fortify it. And there was a spectacular assault during which there were performed many great feats of arms, both in the attack and in the defense, because the English had a large number of strong soldiers and had strengthened skillfully all of the defensible places. And also they fought well, notwithstanding that the French scaled the different places adeptly and attacked the angles at the highest of the strong and sturdy fortifications so that they seemed by this to be immortal. But the English repulsed them from many places and attacked with artillery both high and low, both with cannon and other weapons, such as axes, lances, pole-arms, lead hammers, and other personal arms, so that they killed and wounded many Frenchmen.[105]

In the midst of the battle, Joan was wounded, precisely, if we are to believe Jean Pasquerel, as she had predicted. Yet, this did not stop her from carrying on the battle. The Bastard of Orléans recalled the event as follows:

On 7 May, early in the morning, when the attack was beginning against the enemy who were within the boulevard of the bridge [the Tourelles], Joan was wounded by an arrow which penetrated her flesh between her neck and her shoulder, for a depth of half a foot. Nevertheless, her wound not restraining her, she did not retreat from the conflict, nor did she take medication for her wound.[106]

While Pasquerel added these details:

In that attack and after lunch, Joan, just as she had predicted, was struck by an arrow above her breast, and when she felt that she was wounded, she was frightened and wept, and she was consoled, as she said. And some of her soldiers, seeing that she was wounded, wished to charm her . . . but she refused it, saying: 'I prefer to die rather than do what I know to be a sin, or to be against will of God.' And well she knew that she would die sometime, however she did not know when, where, or how, nor at what hour, but if a salve could be put on her wound without sin, she would be cured fully. And they placed olive oil with lard on her wound, and after the placing of this, Joan confessed to me with words, tears, and lamentations.[107]

Her wound did not stop Joan. Nor did she stop pushing the attack forward when other leaders, including the Bastard of Orléans, became fatigued and wished to retreat from the fight to rest until the following day. The Bastard continued his testimony:

The attack lasted from early morning until the eighth hour of vespers [eight o'clock in the evening], so that there was almost no hope of victory on this day. On account of this, this lord [the

Bastard of Orléans] chose to break it off and wanted the army to retreat to the city. And then the Maid came to him and requested that he wait for a little while, and at that time she mounted her horse, and retired alone into a vineyard at a distance from the crowd of men. In this vineyard she was in prayer for a space of seven minutes. She returned from that place, immediately took her standard in her hands, and placed it on the side of the ditch. And instantly, once she was there, the English became afraid and trembled. The soldiers of the king regained their courage and began to climb [up the ramparts], making an attack on those against the boulevard, not finding any resistance. And then the boulevard was taken, and the English in it were put to flight.[108]

Joan corroborated this nullification trial testimony when she testified herself that she 'was the first to put her ladder on the boulevard of the Tourelles'.[109] Sometime during the attack the Orléanais also set fire to one of the city barges and drove it under the Tourelles to weaken the resolve of the English defenders if not the structure itself.[110]

Feats of arms, inspired by the Maid's own courage, were remembered long after the siege of Orléans was raised. Jean d'Aulon repeated one such instance which occurred as the French began the retreat initiated by the Bastard of Orléans:

In making their retreat, the soldier who then carried the standard of the Maid and who had held it since the beginning of the attack of the boulevard, being weak and fatigued, gave this standard to one named the Basque, who was a soldier of the lord of Villar. And because he who testified knew that this Basque was a brave man, and knew that only evil would follow a retreat on this occasion, and that this bastille and boulevard would remain in the hands of the enemy, he imagined that if this standard were advanced, because of the great affection that he knew was still held by those soldiers who were there, they might yet capture the boulevard. And he asked the Basque, that if he [Aulon] were to turn and go towards the foot of the boulevard, would he [the Basque] follow, which he promised that he would do. And then the testifier went into the ditch and all the way to the foot of the wall of the boulevard, covering himself with his *target* for fear of the stones and leaving this companion on the other side of the ditch, whom he thought would follow him close behind. But, when the Maid saw her standard in the hands of the Basque, she had thought that it had been lost, as he who was carrying it was now in the ditch, the Maid came and grabbed the standard in such a manner that he was no longer able to hold on to it, crying 'Oh, my standard! my standard!' and she shook this standard in a way that he who was testifying thought that others might think that she was making a sign to them. So he shouted, 'Oh, Basque, is this what you promised me?' And then the Basque pulled at the standard with such strength that he ripped it from the hands of the Maid, and this done, ran to him, carrying the standard. At this time, all of the army gathered by the Maid rallied together and assailed the boulevard so sharply that, a short while afterwards, both the boulevard and the bastille were captured by them, abandoned by the enemy.[111]

Thus, well into the evening of 7 May the English were defeated. Some fled, but many fought until they were slain. One of these was William Glasdale, the commander of the Tourelles. He who had so often mocked Joan was defeated by her. Jean Pasquerel testified to the following exchange between the two of them shortly before his death:

And then she . . . shouted, saying, 'Glasdale, Glasdale, give in, give in to the King of Heaven! You called me a whore. I have great pity for your and your men's souls.' Then Glasdale, armed from head to foot, fell into the Loire river and drowned.[112]

But this and the deaths of so many other Englishmen, enemies though they were, saddened Joan, who seems sincerely to have wanted them to believe in her mission and to retreat from Orléans without attempting to stop her relief of the siege. After all, had she not warned them several times to do this? As they had not retreated, many had been killed. Pasquerel testified that after she saw Glasdale die, 'Joan, moved to pity, began to cry for the souls of Glasdale and others, a great number of whom had drowned. And that day, all of the English who were on the far side of the bridge were captured or killed.'[113]

There was great rejoicing at Joan's victory over the Tourelles. For although the English around Orléans had not been completely defeated – troops were still garrisoned in the boulevards to the west of the city – the fall of the Tourelles was central to the relief of Orléans. In essence, the siege had been raised. The Orléanais placed wood over the destroyed portion of the bridge, and Joan of Arc and her soldiers crossed the bridge into the city. It was the first time that any Frenchman (or French woman for that matter) had done so since the earl of Salisbury's capture of the Tourelles the October before. The *Journal du siège d'Orléans* describes the jubilant scene:

> Everyone was filled with a great joy and praised Our Lord for the great victory which he had given them. And well they should have done so, for it is said that this assault, which lasted from the morning all the way to sunset was so grandly fought and defended. It was one of the most beautiful feats of arms which had been done for a very long time . . . All of the clergy and the people of Orléans sang devoutly *Te Deum laudamus*, and all of the bells of the city were rung, very humbly thanking Our Lord . . . for his glorious divine relief. And there was great joy in all parts, giving wondrous praise to their brave defenders, and especially above all to Joan the Maid, who spent the night, with her lords, captains, and men-at-arms, on the battlefield, to guard the Tourelles which they had bravely conquered, so that they might know whether the English on the side of Saint-Laurent wished to aid or avenge their companions. But they had no wish to do so.[114]

(There is a small disagreement here between the *Journal du siège d'Orléans* and Jean d'Aulon, the latter claiming that, instead of remaining in the field, after the fall of the Tourelles, 'Joan and her soldiers went into the city of Orléans, where . . . she had her wounds tended.'[115])

On 8 May, the English soldiers who remained around Orléans marched out of their boulevards and ordered themselves in preparation to do battle. The French responded with their own battle-ready formation. But no combat was to be fought that day. The Bastard of Orléans, Jean d'Aulon, Louis de Coutes, Jean Pasquerel, and Jean Lullier all later testified as to what happened. These are Lullier's words:

> On the following day, early in the morning, the English left their tents and ordered themselves as an army ready to do battle, so it appeared. Having heard of this, the Maid rose from her bed and

armed herself. But she did not want anyone to attack the English nor anything sought from them. She ordered that they be permitted to leave. And, in fact, they did leave, with no one following after them. And from that hour the town was freed from the enemy.[116]

The *Journal du siège d'Orléans* adds some details and emphases to Lullier's testimony:

The following morning, Sunday 8 May 1429, The English dismantled their boulevards of Saint Pouër and elsewhere, and leaving their siege they ordered themselves for battle. Because of this, the Maid, the marshals of Saint-Sévère and de Rais, the lord of Graville, the baron of Coulonces, Sir Florent d'Illiers, the lord of Corraze, the lord of Xantrailles, La Hire, Alain Giron, Jamet du Tilloy, and many other brave soldiers and citizens sallied out of Orléans in great strength and lined themselves before them in an ordered formation. And in such a position they were very close one to the other for a space of an hour without touching each other. For this the French suffered great anger in obeying the will of the Maid, who had commanded them and forbade them from the beginning that, for the love and honor of this holy Sunday, that they not begin the battle nor attack the English. But if the English should attack them, they should defend themselves strongly and boldly, they should not fear, and they would be the masters. The hour passed, and the English turned and marched off well in good formation and order to Meung-sur-Loire. And they raised and totally left the siege, which they had conducted at Orléans from 12 October 1428 to this day. However, they did not go away nor did they get all of their baggage away safely, because some of the garrison of the city followed them and attacked the rear of their army with many assaults, so that they captured for themselves large numbers of bombards and cannon, bows, crossbows, and other artillery.[117]

Without waiting for Fastolf's troops or any other reinforcements, the English commanders retreated from a city which perhaps they should never have tried to capture by siege. Why they left when they still held a number of boulevards and knew that Fastolf was approaching with reinforcements and supplies is a difficult question to answer without more evidence, especially as Perceval de Cagny insists that the English still had large numbers of men and gunpowder weapons in their remaining boulevards.[118] Perhaps the English leaders felt that it would be better for them to give up these earth-and-wood fortifications which had already proven too weak to hold off the determined frontal assaults of Joan and her soldiers. Jargeau, Meung-sur-Loire, and Beaugency – the three Loire towns that were still occupied by the English – were fortified by stone walls and, at least at Meung and Beaugency, also with stone castles. These would undoubtedly provide stronger defenses against the French. Perhaps the English leaders had also seen too many of their soldiers perish in what had proven to them to be a futile struggle. Continuing a fruitless siege, especially after the fall of the Tourelles, could only have added to this casualty total.[119] Finally, by withdrawing from Orléans then, they could build up strength and, with Fastolf's arrival, perhaps do battle with the French, for their recent battles had all been successful. But all of these reasons for English retreat are just guesses. The only fact that is known for sure is that on 8 May 1429, only ten days after her arrival, Joan of Arc had done what no one but herself thought she could do: she had raised the siege of Orléans.

More celebrations followed the final retreat of the English from the siege fortifications outside of the city. The *Journal du siège d'Orléans* records that for two days processions were made throughout the city with the Maid, the other French leaders, and their soldiers parading up and down all of the streets. Ecclesiastical ceremonies were held in every church throughout this time, with everyone present praising God and thanking Him for their deliverance.[120]

But Orléans was not the only location rejoicing in Joan's victory. News of the successful raising of the siege reached Chinon and the dauphin on 9 May, and the response there was also one of celebration. Charles expressed his own joy in a letter penned to his subjects which he began before hearing of the French victory, but completed after learning of it:

> Dear and well beloved, we believe that you have been well aware of the continuous diligence made by us to give all possible relief to the city of Orléans, for a long time besieged by the English, the ancient enemies of our realm, and the endeavors into which we have placed ourselves on many occasions, having always good hope in Our Lord that finally he would extend His grace and would not permit that

such a notable city and such a loyal people perish or fall into subjection and tyranny of these enemies. [Charles then writes about the capture of the boulevard of Saint Loup, is interrupted with the news of the capture of the boulevard of the Augustins, which he includes, is again interrupted, and then continues] . . . Before the completion of these letters, have arrived to us two gentlemen who were at this work, who certify and confirm all . . . and from there have brought letters from the hands of the sire of Gaucourt . . . Our men had last Saturday taken and demolished the bastion at the end of the bridge, on the morrow at dawn, the English who were in it, decamped and tried to save themselves so hastily that they left their bombards, cannon, artillery, and the best part of their provisions and baggage.[121]

In this letter Charles does not mention Joan's part in the relief of the siege, which has caused some modern historians to wonder if Charles was 'being discreet' about her role in an effort to minimize it.[122] (Later Charles does, however, buy her a suit of fine clothes to thank her for the Orléans victory.[123]) But if this was his purpose, it did not succeed, for throughout the kingdom, in fact, throughout Europe, Joan of Arc was recognized as the savior of Orléans. Alain Chartier, writing to an unnamed prince at the end of July 1429, could not help but extol her virtues in raising the siege. After telling of her initial meeting with the dauphin, he writes:

This Maid, whom divine precept burns to satisfy, immediately asked him to give her an army to succor the Orléanais who were then in danger. He, to whom she showed no fear, at first denied her request, but finally conceded to it. This having been accepted, she took a huge amount of foodstuffs to Orléans. Crossing under the enemy camps, they perceived nothing hostile . . . Leaving the victuals in the city, and attacking these camps, which in a way was a miracle, in a short space of time she captured them, especially that which was erected almost in the middle of the bridge. It was so strong, so well armed with all types of weapons, and so fortified, that, if all people, if all nations fought against it, they could not capture it.

He then compares Joan to Hector, Alexander, Hannibal, and Caesar and ends:

Here is she who seems not to come from anywhere on earth, who seems to be sent from the heaven to sustain with her neck and shoulders a fallen France. She raised the king out of the vast abyss on to the harbor and shore by laboring in storms and tempests, and she lifted up the spirits of the French to a greater hope. By restraining the ferocity of the English, she excited the bravery of the French, she prohibited the ruin of France, and she extinguished the fires of France. O singular virgin, worthy of all glory, worthy of all praise, worthy of divine honors! You are the honor of the reign, you are the light of the lily, you are the beauty, the glory, not only of France, but of all Christendom.[124]

Such sentiments were echoed everywhere within France.[125] But they also found their way into the Holy Roman Empire, the southern Low Countries, and the Italian states.[126]

As can be expected, the English and Burgundians were not so laudatory in their comments about Joan's role in the lifting of the siege of Orléans. They only report the facts of the French victory, while downplaying her leadership, if they report it at all. An example of this is Clément de Fauquembergue, who records the event in his parliamentary register (as well as drawing the now famous marginal portrait of her):

On Tuesday, the tenth day of May, it was reported and publicly said in Paris that on the previous Sunday, the men of the dauphin in great number, after many skirmishes continually undertaken by force of arms, entered the boulevard that William Glasdale and other captains with English men-at-arms held on behalf of the king, along with the tower at the end of the bridge of Orléans [the Tourelles], from the other side of the Loire. And on that day, the other captains and men-at-arms holding the siege and the boulevards along the Loire around the city of Orléans, left from these boulevards and raised their siege in order to go to the aid of Glasdale and his companions and to combat the enemy, who had in their companies a maid all alone holding a banner between the two enemy forces, so it was said.[127]

Or the English and Burgundian reports continue to see her action as something evil; such a view can be seen in this letter of John, the duke of Bedford and Regent of England, written to his nephew, King Henry VI:

> And all things prospered for you until the time that the siege of Orléans was undertaken, God knows by what advice. At which time, after the adventure had fallen to my cousin of Salisbury, whom God assoiled, there fell, by the hand of God, as it seemed, a great offense upon your soldiers who were assembled there in great number, caused to a large party of them . . . by a disciple and follower of the Fiend, called the Pucelle, who used false enchantments and sorcery. This offense and destruction not only lowered by great party the number of your soldiers there, but as well removed the courage of the remnant in a marvelous way, and encouraged your opponents and enemies to assemble themselves afterwards in great number.[128]

But it was at Orléans that this victory was won, and it was Orléans that continued to praise Joan of Arc during her life and to honor her once she was dead. It is true that all of the civic and military leaders were heralded for their role in the fight, but no one was so praised by the Orléanais as Joan. She was singled out among all of the others because everyone knew that she was pivotal in determining that this city would not fall to the English. She fought for command from the lack-luster French military leaders, and she received it. She fought for the allegiance of the French soldiers, and she earned it. She fought for the love of the city's inhabitants, and she gained it. The people would always remember what she had done there early in May 1429. After she was burned, they would grant land and pensions to her family.[129] They would continue to hold festivals and processions in her honor. They would hold an annual 'mystery' recounting her deeds.[130] And for centuries, until it was achieved in 1920, they would push for her sainthood, for what she did for them was a miracle.[131] Perhaps one of the citizens of that city, Jean Lullier, expressed it best in his nullification trial testimony:

> He and likewise all the people of the city believed that, if the Maid had not come from God to aid them, all of the inhabitants and citizens in a short time would have been under the domination and power of the enemy who was carrying on the siege. Nor did

he think that the inhabitants or soldiers who were there would have been able to resist for a long time against the power of the enemy who up to then had prevailed against them.[132]

After she raised the siege of Orléans, Joan no longer simply was 'the Maid', *la Pucelle*. She had become *la Pucelle d'Orléans*, the 'Maid of Orléans'.

5

Cleaning Up the Loire

The speed with which Joan of Arc relieved the siege of Orléans has impressed commentators from 1429 to the present. Even if one is reluctant to accept that she actually predicted the rapidity of this military task, as testified by Jean Pasquerel, who as her confessor seems also to have used his nullification trial testimony as a hagiographical platform,[1] one cannot deny that Joan seemed to have believed that speed was an important tactic. Indeed, during her raising of the siege, on several occasions when other French leaders asked for time to rest and recuperate in between major, costly engagements, in each instance she used her confidence in the divinity of her mission and the loyalty of her soldiers to refuse what were quite reasonable requests. Why? The city of Orléans was not on the verge of falling to the English because of starvation; its walls were not about to be breached – in fact the English had shown little interest in taking Orléans in such a manner after the death of the earl of Salisbury; nor were the spirits of its citizens failing, especially after the arrival of Joan. So why did she feel an urgency to relieve this siege in such a short time?

The question becomes even more complicated when it is noted that Joan's next military adventure, the conquest of Jargeau, was not undertaken until more than a month after she had been victorious at Orléans, despite the fact that Jargeau is less than twenty kilometers east of that relieved city. Yet, after she recaptured Jargeau, which occurred on 12 June, she proceeded to attack and capture Meung-sur-Loire and Beaugency to the west of Orléans, and then to fight the battle of Patay, all before 18 June. Thus the question must be rephrased: why did speed lose its tactical importance to Joan after 8 May 1429, when she had relieved Orléans, only to reappear suddenly on 10 June when she set out to capture those other Loire-based English-held positions?

Most modern historians associate Joan's speedy relief of Orléans with the urgency she felt in the completion of this phase of her mission, and there is some logic in this conclusion. After all, even before arriving at Orléans, Joan was constantly talking about the need to remove the English besiegers from that city swiftly, and when she was not able to hasten the process of her accreditation at Chinon and Poitiers, she became irritated with those whom she believed were to blame for the delay. But there could be other reasons for her desire to get to Orléans as soon as possible: a worry about the health, safety, and spirit of citizens who had suffered a siege of many months; a worry about the defeatist feelings of military leaders who seemed willing to allow the English to take the city without a strong defense of the site, especially after the defeat at the battle of the Herrings; and, finally, a worry about allowing the English to continue to build up their supply of weapons, artillery, and soldiers through reinforcements until their numbers had become so large that the loss of French life would be increased. (She would never have believed that the siege of Orléans *could* not have been relieved, as she believed that God had sent her to perform such a task, no matter how difficult it had become. But she always seemed to be genuinely concerned with lessening the suffering of those individuals with whom she fought and whom she was sent to assist.) Added to this is the fact that the relief of Orléans was only one aspect of her mission. Was there no similar urgency to the second task given her by her voices (the crowning of the king at Reims), a task that could only be accomplished if the English were removed from these Loire towns?

At best, then, the urgency of Joan's mission can only partially explain her tactical speed at Orléans. In fact, there seem to have been two other reasons for Joan's quickness there followed by her slowed pace the next month. The first is of French origin. The French army's numbers had declined badly during their attacks on the English fortifications around Orléans. In choosing to dislodge the English from the boulevard of the Augustins and the Tourelles by direct assaults, the French had lost a number of men, although no contemporary tallies are recorded. A modern estimate, made by Ferdinand de Liocourt, places the total number of soldiers remaining in the Joan's French army at no more than 2,000; if his calculations are to be trusted, this represents an incredibly small number to continue to defend Orléans as well as recapture Jargeau, Meung-sur-Loire, and Beaugency.[2] It was for this reason that in the days following the liberation of Orléans, Joan, the Bastard of Orléans, and other French leaders traveled to Loches Castle, to where the dauphin had moved. They hoped by this to gain extra troops for their continued military effort along the Loire. The Bastard later testified that: '[Joan] urged the king [the dauphin was Charles VII at the time of the Bastard's nullification trial testimony] most incessantly and frequently concerning this matter that he might hasten and not delay further.' In response, according to the always loyal Bastard, the dauphin 'made all possible diligence', quickly recruited more men, and 'sent the duke of Alençon, [the Bastard], and other captains, with Joan, to recover [Meung, Beaugency, and Jargeau]'.[3] The *Chronique de la Pucelle* alters the story by having Joan visit the dauphin at Tours and going there as she 'could not maintain her army because of a lack of victuals and payment' following the victory at Orléans. Still, the dauphin's reaction was the same: 'he commanded the nobles of all of his lands' to provide men and arms for the army which was mustered 'for the cleaning up of the Loire river'.[4] Eventually, Joan's army increased in number – although not by that many, reported Jean, the duke of Alençon, who claimed that Joan only had 1,200 men-at-arms (plus undoubtedly a number of infantry, archers, and cannoneers) when she sought to capture Jargeau[5] – but the gathering of those extra troops took time and could have also accounted for her May to early June delay.

The second added reason for Joan's delay is English in origin. It has to do with the fact that Sir John Fastolf's reinforcement army, which had been rumored to be on its way from Paris to Orléans since 4 May, had not yet reached the Loire. Indeed, at the time of Joan's raising of the siege of Orléans, Fastolf had not yet left Paris, and would not do so until 8 June. Thus one of the ostensible reasons for Joan's speed at Orléans, at least one of the threats that she referred to in her rebuking of the Bastard's inaction there, was never really a factor. But when did Joan learn that the rumor of Fastolf's approach was false? Likewise, when did the English leaders on the Loire know that Fastolf was in no position to reinforce them? Is it possible that John Talbot surrendered Orléans to the French without making them attack all of the English-held boulevards because he knew by then that Fastolf had not yet left Paris? All of these questions can only be answered by conjecture, as no original sources report what was going on with the English in Paris during May 1429. At the same time, Fastolf's own delay in attempting to aid the English troops facing Joan of Arc could add a reason for her own delay in moving against Jargeau, Meung-sur-Loire, and Beaugency.

In addition, once Fastolf did begin his march to the Loire, his pace was incredibly and inexplicably slow.[6] There is no indication that his army was weighed down by an inordinately large gunpowder artillery train or number of supply wagons. Indeed, the only thing that seems to have hindered its progress was his and his soldiers' defeatist attitude. Fastolf's army was marching to face the Maid, and already, it seems, the English were beginning to fear her.

The last time that John Fastolf had faced a French army in this arena, at the battle of the Herrings, he had found success, a success that added to his already strong military reputation. But the celebration of Fastolf's victory in Paris and the rest of English-occupied France had been short-lived, with French recovery after the battle quicker than almost anyone had thought possible. This, coupled with the rumors of a divinely-inspired Maid being sent to relieve Orléans which reached the English-held lands even before her victory there confirmed them,[7] slowed the recruitment of soldiers, especially among their French subjects, and also presented the problem of sending troops that were hard to come by to reinforce a campaign which had brought few positive results and which most English leaders considered to have been ill-advised even at its initiation the year before.[8] Fastolf, too, seems to have been reluctant to take on the duties of leading these reinforcements. He had fought as an English captain in the war in France since 1415, and his military experiences under Henry V and later were almost always successful and very profitable.[9] Never, it seems, had this general shunned or been reluctant to assume a military duty, at least until 1429. However, in his journey south to the Loire in June of that year, and even though his army numbered at least 4,000, Fastolf appears to have been fatigued, demoralized, and defeated, even before he personally had faced Joan of Arc.[10] More importantly, despite his army's size, which when combined with the English forces already in the south seems to have greatly outnumbered its French counterpart, once Fastolf finally arrived on the Loire on 17 June, he was reluctant either to relieve the English troops under French attack at Beaugency or Meung (Jargeau had already been captured by Joan by this time) or to fight against the French in his own battle. Frequently, he made his opinion known that he preferred to fall back and reinforce the English holdings in the north, and, ultimately, he forced the English to withdraw from the Loire. When he was forced to do battle against the French, at Patay, it was only because the French had provoked it, attacking Fastolf during his withdrawal.

Joan, of course, was unaware of Fastolf's feelings about his reinforcing task, even if she was aware of his slowness in marching towards the Loire. Thus her actions between 10 June, when she moved to attack Jargeau, and 18 June, when she assisted in the French victory at the battle of Patay, must be seen in the light of Fastolf's approach. Speed seems again to have become an important tactic in the face of an approaching English army, much as it had done in her relief of the siege of Orléans the month previously.

Early in June 1429, the *Journal du siège d'Orléans* reports, there was a discussion among all the French military leaders in the presence of the dauphin to decide what next to target after Orléans, with many 'diverse opinions, some counseling that they should go into Normandy and others that they should take the other principal places along the Loire river'. Invoking the name of God, Joan had no problem asserting that the next task given her by God was to crown the king at Reims. At this time, the road to Reims was entirely blocked by one English-held town after another, and so it was necessary to start clearing the path, not through Normandy, but through central France. The first places set for clearing would be Jargeau, Meung-sur-Loire, and Beaugency. To this, the dauphin, echoed by the others, answered: 'Child, Go, go, go; I will give you aid. Go.'[11] A short while later she set out towards Jargeau.

On 11 June, Joan arrived across the Loire from Jargeau. The *Journal du siège d'Orléans* reports that the Bastard of Orléans, the Marshal of Saint-Sévère, the lords of Graville, and Corraze, Ponton de Xantrailles, 'and many other knights, squires, and men-at-arms . . . who had come from Bourges, Tours, Angers, Blois, and other good towns of the realm' were with her.[12] Jean Chartier also adds the names of the Lord of Boussac, who was the Marshal of France, Louis de Culan, the Admiral of France, Sir Ambrois de Loré, La Hire, and Gaultier de Brussac.[13] But none of these had been given command over the army there. Nor, in fact, had Joan. That duty had fallen to Jean, the duke of Alençon.[14] The dauphin's decision to place his relative (Alençon was a distant cousin and half brother-in-law of the dauphin) and friend in command at Jargeau may seem like an unusual one, especially as the duke had not been present during the relief of Orléans.[15] But, if Charles knew of some of the disagreements between Joan and the Bastard at Orléans, he may have decided that Alençon would serve as a good man to settle similar arguments that might occur at Jargeau. He was, after all, a close friend to Joan and brother-in-law to the Bastard.

The appointment of Alençon was a positive one for Joan. The 'gentle duke', as she was fond of calling him, may have held the actual power at Jargeau, but by this time he was already devoted to Joan and always allowed her to make all of the military decisions there. This devotion had begun from the very moment that Alençon met the Maid. He recalled in his nullification trial testimony:

When Joan came to the king, he was at the town of Chinon, and [Alençon] at the town of Saint Florent lès Saumur. [Alençon] was out hunting quails . . . when one of his messengers came to him and notified him that a certain maid had come to the king, asserting that she had been sent from God to put the English to flight and to raise the siege placed by the English on Orléans. Because of this, [Alençon] came to the king at Chinon the next day, and he found Joan speaking with the king. And as he approached, Joan asked him who he was, and the king responded that this was the duke of Alençon. Then Joan said to him: 'You have come at the right time. The more royal blood there is together the better.' And the next day, Joan came to the king's Mass, and when she saw the king, she bowed, and the king led Joan into a certain room, and [Alençon] and the Lord de la Trémoïlle, whom the king held back, were with him, with the others commanded that they should retire. Then Joan made many requests to the king, among others that he should give his kingdom to the King of Heaven. After making this gift, God would do to him just as he had his predecessors, and restore to him his original state. And many other things, which he did not remember, were spoken until the afternoon meal.[16]

From that time on, Joan and Alençon were close friends. He was with her at Poitiers, comforting her when she felt that she had been too harshly interrogated.[17] And she stayed at his home at Saint-Laurent between 22 May and 2 June 1429, where he introduced her to his mother, Mary of Brittany, and his wife, Jeanne, the daughter of the imprisoned Duke Charles of Orléans, to whom Joan made a promise of returning the duke 'safe and sound, and in the state he is in now or in a better one' at the end of their campaigning.[18] At Jargeau, she was forced to remind him of this promise, when she warned him of an oncoming attack that would soon cause his death. The duke later testified:

> . . . during the attack on the town of Jargeau, Joan told me at one moment to retire from the place where I was at, for if I did not retire from that place, 'that machine' – and she pointed to a piece of artillery in the town – 'will kill you'. I fell back, and a little later on that very spot where I had been standing someone by the name of my lord du Lude was killed. That made me very much afraid, and I wondered greatly at Joan's sayings after all these events.[19]

Hereafter, the duke of Alençon would be with Joan as much as possible, and he would remain loyal to her long after her death.

Jargeau was not a large city, like Orléans, but in almost every other way it imitated its bigger and more westerly Loire neighbor. It was strongly fortified, with a wall and a ditch encompassing most of the town's buildings and houses – although a suburb had been allowed to grow outside of these walls; five towers and three fortified gates on the walls added to the defense of the town. It also lay on the southern side of the Loire, with a single fortified bridge passing over the river. Finally, it was filled with gunpowder weapons and perhaps as many as 700 enemy troops led by the duke of Suffolk, William de la Pole, and two of his brothers.[20] Thus Alençon and Joan were faced with the same problem that Thomas Montagu, the earl of Salisbury, had faced when first attacking Orléans the year before: how does one quickly capture a fortified town? The French leaders met to discuss their strategy. At Joan's nullification trial, Alençon recalled:

> There was a debate between the captains, because some were of the opinion that they should attack the town, and others asserted to the contrary that the English were very powerful and were there in a large multitude.

During this debate Joan stepped forward and spoke with the confidence that they had all become accustomed to:

Then Joan, seeing that there was this difficulty between them, said that they should not fear any multitude, nor have difficulty in attacking these English, because God was conducting their work. Joan said that unless she was sure that God was leading this work, she would have chosen to herd her sheep rather than expose herself to such dangers.[21]

Taking this as their inspiration, the French troops began to attack the suburbs around Jargeau, but the English were not willing to let them have even these, and they sallied out from behind the protection of the town walls to intercept the French. This tactic seems not to have been anticipated by the French and they began to fall back. But, as Alençon recalled, Joan, 'picking up her standard, went into the attack, entreating her soldiers to be of good heart'. So encouraged, the French rallied and chased the English back into Jargeau. That night, they lodged in the suburbs of their targeted town.[22]

Emboldened by this victory, Joan asked the English to surrender to her. 'Surrender this place to the King of Heaven and to the gentle King Charles, and you can go, otherwise you will be massacred,' are the words she used, according to Perceval de Cagny. It was a speech she had given before at Orléans; the English at Jargeau responded exactly as their Orléans colleagues had – with refusal.[23] (Although the mockery that Joan had to undergo on the earlier occasion seems to have disappeared.) This was followed by an intensive gunpowder bombardment from the French positions across the river and in the suburbs, echoed, to a lesser extent, by the English, who it seems had fewer of these weapons.[24] The French guns began to batter the walls of Jargeau; in particular, writes the anonymous author of the *Journal du siège d'Orléans*, one bombard from Orléans, named *Bergerie* or *Bergière*, brought down one of the larger of the town's towers.[25] Eventually, these gunpowder weapons created enough of a problem for Suffolk and his English soldiers that he tried to negotiate a surrender. They promised to leave Jargeau without further incident should they not be relieved in fifteen days. But these negotiations were attempted not with Alençon or Joan, but with La Hire. More than twenty years later, this still upset Alençon as he testified in the nullification trial that 'he and all who had leadership of any kind over the army were irritated by La Hire. And he commanded La Hire to come to them, and he came.'[26] The English proposal was refused, although Joan recalled at her own trial that she had told the English leaders that they

were welcome to leave then with their horses without suffering further
loss of life; she also announced to the inhabitants of Jargeau that they
too could leave safely at this time, but should they not do so, they also
would suffer in the assault.[27]

With the English having revealed that they were weak and
disheartened, Joan pushed for an assault on the town walls. The
other French leaders agreed, although Alençon admitted that he for
one had some desire to continue the bombardment of the walls for a
while longer before undertaking such a potentially costly attack. But
Joan urged him on:

> Joan said to him: 'Forward, gentle duke, to the assault!' And since
> it seemed to him that it was premature for them to undertake an
> attack so quickly, Joan said to him: 'Do not doubt! The time is
> right when it pleases God. And one ought to act when God
> wishes. Act and God will act.'

She then reminded him of the promise that she had made to his wife
and mother: 'Oh, gentle duke, are you afraid? Do you not know that I
promised your wife to bring you back safe and sound.'[28] Reminded of
his faith in the divinity of her mission, Alençon agreed to the assault
and it went forward. Enguerrand de Monstrelet reports the violence of
the onslaught: 'And the French began in many places to attack very
harshly, which attacks endured for a long time, terrible and very
magnificent.'[29] While the *Journal du siège d'Orléans* adds more details:

> In the morning of Sunday 12 June French soldiers placed
> themselves in the ditch with ladders and other tools necessary to
> make an assault, and they attacked marvelously those who were
> inside, which defended themselves most virtuously for a long time.

One Englishman in particular, 'large and powerful and armed with
many weapons, carrying on his head a bascinet,' defended the walls
strongly, 'splendidly throwing balls of iron and continually knocking
over ladders and the men standing on them'. Only when Jean, the
Master Couleuvrinier who had won fame in defending Orléans,
purposely aimed his gun at this English warrior and killed him were
the French attackers able to make progress against the Jargeau walls.[30]

In the midst of the attack was Joan. Carrying her standard, she
charged forward with the rest of the army, both men-at-arms and

common soldiers, according to Perceval de Cagny. For three or four hours they attacked the walls without breaking over or through them.[31] Joan was constantly in danger, but it was not until the French came close to victory that her life was threatened. Alençon later testified:

> And with the soldiers breaking in . . . Joan was on a ladder, holding her standard in her hands, when the standard was struck, and Joan also was struck on top of her head with a stone which broke on her helmet. She was knocked to the ground, and when she arose, she said to the soldiers: 'Friends, friends, up! up! Our Lord has condemned the English. At this hour they are ours. Have courage!'[32]

This attack and Joan's response to it did two things. First, it caused the French leadership to ignore a call from Suffolk to meet and discuss surrender terms.[33] And, second, the French soldiers, concerned that Joan was wounded, took heart in what she said. They pressed on with even more vigor. Alençon continued: 'and in a short time, the town of Jargeau was taken'.[34]

Those English soldiers who could, fled. But where could they go? The nearest allied troops were in Meung-sur-Loire, along the river past Orléans. Some did succeed in surrendering, but many more were killed. William de la Pole, with one brother, Alexander, killed and another, John, captured, surrendered himself. But in discovering that his would-be captor, Guillaume Regnault, was only a squire from Auvergne, he knighted him. As count of Suffolk, he did not wish to be made a prisoner of anyone other than a knight.[35] Most of his underlings, however, were not so fortunate. English casualties were quite high, with many of the prisoners also being executed, according to Jean Chartier and the *Chronique de la Pucelle*;[36] the death toll may have been as high as 1,100.[37] (The execution of prisoners after the capture of Jargeau naturally poses a problem for those who believe that Joan would never have participated in anything so sinister. Of course, it is possible that this was done without her knowledge, or that some of her soldiers took her threats of an English massacre more seriously than she had intended, as neither of the sources reporting the incident mentions her presence at or knowledge of what had occurred.) French casualties may also have been high due to the means of capturing the town, but these are not given.[38]

That night celebrations were held in both Jargeau and Orléans.[39] In Orléans, to where she and the other French leaders had retired, Joan heard Mass celebrated by one of her favorite preachers, Friar Robert Braignard.[40] But she, Alençon, and the other leaders would not stay long in Orléans. Two more towns on the Loire River were still controlled by the English: Meung-sur-Loire and Beaugency. In addition, John Fastolf's army was still somewhere to the north. (He had actually stopped at Janville at this time, only about twenty kilometers away, but it is uncertain whether Joan of Arc and her colleagues leaders knew this.[41]) That evening in Orléans, says Perceval de Cagny, Joan told the duke of Alençon that she wished to leave for Meung the following day.[42] It would actually take three days for the army to organize and for the gunpowder weapons, so valuable at both Orléans and Jargeau, to be shipped down the Loire. Then, after ensuring that a garrison of soldiers remained in Jargeau, on 15 June, the French army marched the short distance from Orléans to Meung-sur-Loire.[43]

Meung-sur-Loire was surrounded by a strong wall, like the other Loire towns fought over by the French and English in 1429, and, again like those other towns, had a single fortified bridge crossing the river from the north to the town which lay on the Loire's southern bank. Where Meung differed from Jargeau and Orléans, however, was the large castle which existed just outside of the town walls and in which the English leaders, John Talbot and Thomas Scales, were housed. This castle, once owned by the bishops of Orléans and dating from the thirteenth century, was surrounded by its own walls and thus provided an extra fortification that would require siege or assault before the town itself could be secured. That is, should Joan and the other French military leaders have followed their accustomed method of recapturing towns occupied by the English, they would have needed to attack and conquer the fortified bridge, the walled town, and then the castle. But Joan and the others did not follow their customary tactic at Meung-sur-Loire. Instead, they only attacked and occupied the fortified bridge there before moving on to Beaugency. It was a hard fight, but without strong bridge fortifications like the Tourelles – it appears that the English had hastily added some minor fortifications, but as there are no contemporary illustrations of the bridge, nor does it exist any longer, it is difficult to understand how strong these might have been – it quickly fell. The *Journal du siège d'Orléans* reports:

On 15 June 1429, [the French army] went to lay a siege on Beaugency, and on their way, they attacked the bridge of Meung-sur-Loire, which the English had fortified and garrisoned with brave men, who defended it well. But notwithstanding their defense, it was taken by simple assault, without hardly interrupting them.[44]

After this, the French left a large garrison of their own soldiers on the bridge.

What was the purpose of this limited action? Such a change in tactics actually had quite a simple objective, as Jean Chartier explains: 'this was done . . . so that they would enclose them there and to always stand in the way of any English military activities'.[45] By capturing the only easy access across the Loire for the English leaders and their troops, Joan, or whoever the author of this tactic was, had prevented a quick combination of Talbot and Scales' army with that of Fastolf, whenever he should arrive; they would also be unable easily to come to the aid of the English troops in Beaugency. It was a rather intelligent strategy, which has not been given its weight in the study of Joan's campaigns.

Among those who participated in the capture of the bridge at Meung were several nobles and soldiers who had not taken part in Joan's relief of the siege of Orléans or capture of Jargeau. In mustering the army to travel to Meung and Beaugency, the *Journal du siège d'Orléans* reports that:

The duke of Alençon and the Maid . . . had six or seven thousand soldiers, who had come to reinforce the army, more lords, knights, squires, captains, and valiant men-at-arms, and, among the others, the lord of Laval and the lord of Lohéac, his brother, the lord of Chauvigny de Berry, the lord of La Tour d'Auvergne, and the vidame of Chartres.[46]

It seems that Joan's victories at Orléans and at Jargeau had continued to inspire the recruitment of soldiers, both noble and common. But no one was more 'noble' than Arthur de Richemont, the Constable of France, who approached the French army outside Beaugency on 15 or 16 June 1429. At the same time, no problem faced by Joan's army so far perhaps exceeded that created by Richemont's approach. The reason for this is complicated, but does

much to explain some of the background of the dauphin's lack of
military success before the arrival of Joan of Arc, as well as some of
the reasons for her decline as a military leader after the crowning of
the dauphin as King Charles VII.

Arthur de Richemont was born in Succinio Castle, Brittany, on 24
August 1393.[47] As the third son of duke of Brittany, Jean IV, and
Jeanne, the daughter of King Charles 'the Bad' of Navarre, Richemont
was not expected to succeed to the ducal throne – although he would,
for little more than a year at the end of his life, between 1457 and
1458 – but received the military training of every other noble son of
war-torn late medieval western Europe. It was in this training that he
found a particular affinity, and by the time he was seventeen, in
1410, he had taken up arms to involve himself in the
Burgundian–Armagnac civil war. But on whose side would he fight?
Because his father had died when Arthur was quite young, before he
had turned ten, and his mother had gone to England as the new wife
of Henry IV, he had been raised largely in the ducal courts of Philip
the Bold of Burgundy and Jean II of Berry. Additionally, his eldest
brother, then Duke Jean V of Brittany, had awarded him the county of
Richmond in England, which had remained in the holdings of the
dukes of Brittany since the first duke had fought with William the
Conqueror at Hastings (which also meant that for most of his life
Richemont fought against the king whose fealty he was technically
obligated to). This, one might think, would lead him to support the
Burgundian, and later the English, cause in France. But he was also
the close friend of Louis of Guyenne, the dauphin to the throne of
France in 1410. In the end, this friendship determined his allegiance.
He fought against John the Fearless, and, when Henry V invaded
England and fought the battle of Agincourt, Richemont was captured
fighting on the French side. His imprisonment in England for five
years after the battle was not a harsh one, because of his mother's
association with the English king's father, and he was granted
privileges and luxuries, and, in 1423, permission to take as wife
Margaret of Burgundy, the widow of the dead dauphin, Louis. She was
the daughter of John the Fearless and sister of Philip the Good and
Anne of Burgundy – the wife of John of Bedford, regent of England
and commander of all English forces in France.

Yet, more than anything, Richemont wanted to fight, and when
Bedford refused him a command in 1424, he switched to the French
side, urged to do so by Queen Yolanda, the mother-in-law of the

dauphin Charles. In gratitude, Charles appointed him to the office of Constable, the general in charge of all of the dauphin's forces. Richemont set out to reform the army, to recruit new soldiers, to arm them with more and better weapons, including gunpowder weapons, and to defend vigorously the lands of the dauphin, while regaining those that had been lost by him and his father. An assessment of how successful he was depends on which original and secondary sources one reads; Richemont, like every other wealthy military leader of the Hundred Years War, had his own chronicler, Guillaume Gruel – and his detractors had theirs.[48] One thing is certain, it did not take long for the new Constable to come to be at odds with his one-time friend, the chief counselor of the dauphin, Georges de la Trémoïlle. By September 1427, Richemont and La Trémoïlle had quarreled, and, under the influence of this counselor, the dauphin had barred his chief military leader from his court by the time that Joan had arrived in Chinon in 1428. Thus Richemont had not participated in Joan's military activities in Orléans, Jargeau, or Meung-sur-Loire, although he had undoubtedly heard of what occurred there.[49] What was the cause of Richemont's troubles with La Trémoïlle? Gruel indicates that it was the Constable's desire to carry on an aggressive war against the Anglo-Burgundian forces, while the dauphin's counselor was intent on an inactive military strategy, one that preferred diplomacy, patience, and submission to combat. As these would be the complaints that La Trémoïlle would also level at Joan, one suspects that Gruel's biased opinion may be correct. Richemont had appeared with his forces outside of Beaugency because Joan had fought the war against the English in the same manner that he would have.

As he was still discredited and banned from the dauphin's court, Richemont's appearance was not welcomed by some of the more loyal of Charles's adherents. Alençon, for one, later testified:

Being at Beaugency, they heard news that the Lord Constable was approaching with some troops. As such, he, Joan, and others from the army were irritated and wished to retire from the town, because they had been commanded not to receive the Lord Constable into their company. And he said to Joan that if the Constable came there, he would leave.[50]

Whether Joan actually felt this animosity for Richemont, as Alençon claimed, cannot be ascertained. Certainly her devotion to the dauphin would have given her reason enough to be suspicious of Richemont's own loyalty. On the other hand, should she have heard that the Constable's disfavor was caused by his holding similar military opinions to her own – and his appearance at Beaugency seemed to confirm that he approved of her military methods – she might have had some sympathy for her famous would-be companion. This certainly would explain Joan's next actions in connection with Richemont.

However, the accuracy of Alençon's testimony of Joan's initial attitude towards the Constable can never be tested, for historical fate intervened. The fate in this case came in the form of Sir John Fastolf. That English leader, whose reinforcing march had been anticipated for more than a month, finally arrived outside of Beaugency on 17 June while Joan and her army were attacking the town.[51] Jean de Waurin's estimate of the size of Fastolf's army, to which he belonged, is 5,000,[52] although most historians reduce the tally by at least a thousand.[53] At that point it did not matter whether Richemont was *persona non grata* at the French court or not. Joan needed his 1,000–1,200 soldiers. Thus, persuading Alençon also to stay and fight against Fastolf, and even going as far, according to the *Chronique de la Pucelle*, as making promises in writing which guaranteed the Constable's loyalty to those who were offended by his presence,[54] she approached Richemont with the following words, as remembered by Alençon: 'Ah, good Constable, you have not come on my behalf, but because you have come, you are welcome.'[55] Guillaume Gruel, writing from Richemont's side, adds his perspective:

The Maid climbed down from her horse, and the lord [Constable] did also. And the Maid came to embrace the lord around his legs. And he spoke to her, saying, 'Joan, it has been said that you wish to fight with me. I do not know if you are from God or not. If you are from God, I do not fear you, because God knows my good will. If you are from the Devil, I fear you even less.'[56]

Was Joan right to make peace with Richemont? Certainly it did not help her later position with Georges de la Trémoïlle, nor perhaps with Charles, who refused to allow the Constable to attend during his coronation at Reims, despite Richemont's participation in the victories at Beaugency and Patay and also despite the requirement of his attendance as the holder of the constabulary office.[57] (Charles VII would not make peace with Richemont until 1433.) But from a purely military position and in the face of the arrival of an enemy army, Joan had no choice. Even if she did not have any sympathy for Richemont himself or his status at the dauphinal court, she needed his numbers and perhaps his leadership skill to fight against Fastolf. Actually, she needed his numbers either to fight or to intimidate Fastolf so that he would choose not to fight; the latter choice was, of course, the preferable one for Joan, and it was the one chosen by the English reinforcer. Jean de Waurin reports:

> You could have seen all those English riding in very good order at Beauce [the name of the location of Fastolf's army] which is ample and large. Then, when they arrived thus about a league from Meung and very near to Beaugency, the French were alerted of their approach, with around 6,000 soldiers, of which the leaders were Joan the Maid, the duke of Alençon, the Bastard of Orléans, the Marshal of La Fayette, La Hire, Ponton [de Xantrailles], and other captains. They ordered their soldiers into battle formation on top of a small hill, to better see and verify the appearance of the English. Those, plainly perceiving that the French were ordered in battle formation, believing in the fact that they would come against them to fight, made an order especially given by King Henry of England that every man should dismount, and that the archers should have their stakes placed with their points towards the enemy, as they were accustomed to do when they expected to be attacked. Then they sent two heralds to the French, whom they saw had not moved from their places, saying that there were three knights who would fight them, if they had the courage to descend from the hill and come against them. Which response was made for the French by the Maid: 'Go and camp for today, because it is quite late. But tomorrow, at the pleasure of God and Our Lady, we will look more closely at you.' Then the English lords who were not going to fight departed from this place and rode to Meung where they lodged that night.[58]

They would not return.

According to Guillaume Gruel, the reason why Fastolf left Beaugency without fighting was that 'when he saw that the Lord Constable had come there, he changed his mind and accepted the

counsel of those to leave'.[59] Whether Gruel is correct or not, the fact
that Joan was able to accept Richemont's assistance, while also
persuading the rest of her offended leaders to stay, and that this was
followed by Fastolf's departure without combat, surely confirms the
wisdom of her decision to approach the Constable against the
dauphin's wishes. It also affirms her increased status among the
French military leadership. Only one who was perceived as the true
leader of the French forces on the Loire river could have pulled off
such a stunt, and while the dauphin and La Trémoïlle obviously
remained unhappy about Richemont's re-association with the army,
they could not argue about it in the face of Joan's success.

And Joan continued to be successful. For while the above encounter
with Fastolf occurred on 17 June, she and the French army had been
fighting for control of Beaugency. Joan had been at Beaugency since
15 June, and she had not stopped attacking the town since then, not
even during the face-off with Fastolf.[60] There was a wall around
Beaugency and a single fortified bridge across the Loire leading into it,
just as there was at the other Loire towns that Joan had fought over.
Like Meung-sur-Loire, it also had a castle, although unlike its
neighbor, this castle, a five-storey square keep built in the twelfth
century, was located within the town walls, dominating the skyline
and housing a garrison of 500–600 English soldiers, less a few troops
stationed on the bridge, who had occupied the building since its
capture the year before by the earl of Salisbury. The English captains
in charge of this town were Richard Guestin and Matthew Gough.[61]

Fighting began almost as soon as the French army arrived, with,
according to the *Journal du siège d'Orléans*, a 'very strong skirmish'
fought all day between Joan's soldiers and the English troops
occupying the bridge,[62] followed by an intensive gunpowder
weaponry bombardment from French positions across the Loire on
to the town walls and castle. This would last all night and
throughout the next day.[63] The military action taken against
Beaugency was very different to that used against Jargeau. But the
tactical choice should not be questioned, for not only were Joan and
the other French leaders concerned with the arrival of Richemont
and then of Fastolf, but also the strength of the castle, evident even
today, pretty well prohibited any assault.

Eventually, no assault was needed to capture Beaugency. The
continual bombardment of the town's fortifications – although there
is an indication that Joan was running out of gunpowder[64] – the

disparity between English numbers and those of the attacking army, and the inability or unwillingness of Fastolf's relief force to fight a battle against the French forces there, led Guestin and Gough to negotiate for peace. The English would surrender the town in exchange for the promise of safe-conduct for themselves, their horses and harness, and any moveable goods, 'so long as they were not valued at more than one mark of silver'. They also promised not to fight against the French for the following ten days (which Joan must have estimated would take them out of the conflict for Meung-sur-Loire; as it was, it also kept them from participating in the battle of Patay). Surrender terms were accepted, and Beaugency once again became French.[65]

On the night of 17/18 June, the English in Beaugency took their leave, marching north towards Paris. Because of their promise, there really was no reason to go towards Meung-sur-Loire and the remainder of the English troops on the Loire, including Fastolf's ineffective reinforcements who had proved impotent since their arrival two days before. Even when Fastolf did resolve to take action on 18 June, by attempting to recapture the bridge at Meung-sur-Loire from the French, his attacks were poorly timed – French troops from Beaugency had just arrived in preparation to make an attack against the final English-controlled Loire location – and incredibly ineffective. Even though the *Journal du siège d'Orléans* claims that it was a 'very harsh' assault, it was badly organized and completely unsupported by archery or gunpowder weapons.[66] Ultimately, it also proved to the English leadership that their efforts at Meung were destined for failure. They simply could not withstand French attacks like those that had meant the loss of Orléans, Jargeau, and Beaugency. The decision was made to retreat. Whose decision it was is not mentioned in the sources, but the *Journal du siège de l'Orléans* does say, 'they retreated entirely from the town of Meung, and they made their path across the fields in good order, wishing to go to Janville'.[67]

The French leaders could see the retreat of the English army. They had won. In but a very short time they had cleared the Loire of its English occupiers. The celebrations could have begun. No one would have blamed them if they had simply allowed Talbot, Fastolf, Scales, and the others to retreat in peace to Janville, and from there probably to Paris, for none of those English generals had shown much desire to encounter the French. In the previous few years letting the English leave would probably have been the strategy. But this was not the old French army. For one thing, a woman who believed firmly that it was her mission to crown the dauphin king of France held very great influence over the other leaders, and, for another, that woman believed that she could only ensure that crowning if she pushed the English completely back to Paris, and perhaps even to England. She was not about to let a large English army, which had been defeated at every location, simply slip off to the north without attempting one more defeat, a battle in which not only could she whittle down their numbers, but also demoralize them to the extent that her journey to Reims would be made all that easier. It was a risky venture, but then, again, she felt that any of her soldiers who died during the fulfilment of this mission would gain heavenly rewards. Joan pushed for battle against the retreating English. The duke of Alençon later recalled her confident words spoken in a council of French leaders:

> Joan said: 'In the name of God, let us go to fight them! If they were hung in the clouds, we would get them, for God sent them to us that we might punish them!' Asserting that she was certain of victory, she spoke these words in French: 'The gentle king shall have the greatest victory today that he has ever had. And my Counsel says to me that they are ours!'[68]

But it was essential to overtake the retreating army before they reached the fortified town of Janville, as, it seems, Joan wished to fight a battle against them and not another siege. So speed again became an important tactic.[69] Speed might also bring surprise, which would help the French cause, and surprise could be assured, especially if the pursuit of their army with the aim of provoking a battle had not been considered by Talbot, Fastolf, or any of the other English leaders. (And, judging from what occurred at the battle of Patay, none of the English leaders had considered this to be a possibility.)

No doubt the English retreated from Meung-sur-Loire in good order, as the *Journal du siège d'Orléans* insists. But they were a defeated army, most of whom, arriving with Fastolf only a few days before, had never even had the chance to fight the French before their leaders felt the need to turn around, surrender all that had been won the year before, and return to the north. They must have felt like cowards. The others, the minority who had survived the relief of Orléans, the capture of Jargeau and now of Beaugency and

Meung, or perhaps more than one of those engagements, might have been relieved at the prospect of removing themselves from any further conflict with the Maid. Whether she was of God or of the Devil, they probably did not know; but what was becoming obvious to them and – if they could have known the thoughts of those leaders in Paris, Normandy, and England – to the English as a whole, was that she was someone to be feared. Jean de Waurin gives their order of march: the vanguard was commanded by a unnamed English knight carrying a white standard; between the vanguard and the main body wagons carried what little artillery, victuals, and non-combatants still remained with the army; in the main body were Fastolf, Talbot, the other English leaders, and the majority of troops, including soldiers recruited from the lands occupied by the English; and in the rearguard were a group of Englishmen.[70] The whole army was perhaps 5,000 strong.[71]

The French army had a completely different attitude. It had been victorious in all of its most recent encounters with the English. Any of the troops involved in the defeat at the battle of the Herrings might not even remember that they lost there. More importantly, they believed in their living saint, Joan of Arc. The common soldiers had given her their faith and trust, while the noble leaders had given her virtual command over the entire army. Veteran military leaders such as the Constable of France, the duke of Alençon, the Bastard of Orléans, La Hire, Ponton de Xantrailles, and all the rest now listened to her military advice and heeded it, as if she were the most sage veteran in the French leadership corps. Their line of march, as recorded by Guillaume Gruel, was based mainly on the speed of their modes of transport: in the front rode a group of cavalry led by La Hire, Ponton de Xantrailles and 'other men who rode the horse well', with the main body, consisting of both cavalry and infantry, commanded by Richemont, Alençon, the Bastard of Orléans, Gilles de Rais, and others. Joan was in that body also.[72] The French numbered around 6,000, according to the *Journal du siège d'Orléans*.[73]

The English army had marched for close to four hours and around midday reached a site known as Patay; then the rearguard spotted the pursuing French army pressing on them. According to Jean de Waurin, whose account is perhaps the best concerning what actually occurred on the battlefield because of his presence there, riders were sent forward to warn John Fastolf, who seems to have been in command at Patay, of the imminent arrival of their opponents.[74] Rather than run, and perhaps recalling that the English had consistently found success on the battlefield, he chose to order his lines and meet the French army in battle.

Where this exactly was, however, is not known for certain. The battle was only called Patay because, as Monstrelet maintains, that is the village where the Constable and many of the other French captains spent the night after the fight, 'from which village the battle carries the name forever'. In fact, the village of Patay lies more than a league from the site of the battle,[75] which was said to be close to a place named Coinces.[76] Other place names located on the battlefield include Saint-Sigismond, where the English archers were arrayed, and Saint-Péravy, where the French encountered the main body of the English troops. But since these two locations presently are quite far to the south of Coinces, they were not given much credibility by nineteenth- and early twentieth-century historians. Coupled with the lack of archaeological work done in this region, this left many of these historians struggling to determine where exactly the battle of Patay was fought.[77] More modern historians have had somewhat more success locating the battlefield. Based on his study of Roman roads in the area and a chat with the local curé, Alfred H. Burne in 1956 described its location as where the old Lignerolles–Coinces road crosses the Roman road.[78] This was corrected only slightly by Michel de Lombarès in 1966, when, using basically the same technique as Burne, he found that the Lignerolles–Coinces road was a more modern construction and relocated the battlefield slightly more to the south-east where the medieval Grand Chemin de Chartres à Orléans crosses the medieval Grand Chemin de Blois à Paris.[79] Finally, in 1976, Colonel Ferdinand de Liocourt, basing his account on his discovery of a number of medieval English and French horseshoes which had been recovered over a number of years and the fact that a field to the west of Coinces was known traditionally as 'la cimetière aux Anglais' (the cemetery of the English), both widened the battlefield further to the west from Coinces and to the south beyond Saint Péravy and even Saint-Sigismond and shifted the main fighting to Saint-Sigismond, for the first part of the battle, and Lignerolles, for the latter part.[80] Ultimately, what is described by all three of these battlefield detectives is a large, flat plain with relatively few trees and bushes, although quite a few are described in the contemporary sources.

Having discovered the French army's approach, Fastolf set up his order of battle in preparation to receive the attack. Using what had now become a tradition in English tactics, this order of battle was a defensive formation. As at Crécy, Poitiers, Agincourt, Cravant, Verneuil, and the battle of the Herrings, the English were not to make their own initial charges, but were instead to receive those of the generally over-confident French. At those other battles, the French charges invariably became disordered and lost their impetus before they were able to reach the English defensive formation. But at Patay, this would not occur.

According to Jean de Waurin, Fastolf ordered the English vanguard, supplies, artillery, and non-combatants to hide in the woods along the side of where he planned to fight his battle. Lord Talbot then took 500 'élite' mounted archers to a location towards the front of the battlefield, 'between two strong hedges through which he felt that the French would pass'. This position is said to have been near Saint-Sigismond. These troops were to dismount and to try to keep the French from charging the English until after Fastolf had been able to order his main body and rearguard, also all dismounted, for battle some distance to the rear of the archers. Talbot hoped that once this was accomplished, he and his troops could sneak through the woods in front of Patay (the same woods that held the English vanguard and baggage train) and return to the main body without a large loss of life.[81]

On came the French cavalry, having ridden hard from Meung-sur-Loire in pursuit of the English. They had lost the element of surprise, and according to Waurin, they seemed not yet to have seen the English and did not know of the hidden archers. Indeed, it looked as if they would surely be ambushed by those archers. But then something unusual happened which foiled the English secrecy. Waurin writes:

With much excitement came the French after their enemy, whom they could not see nor knew the place where they were, when, during the front-riders' approach, they saw a stag run out of the woods, which made its way towards Patay and crashed into the formation of the English [archers]. These made a very loud cry, not knowing that their enemy was so near to them. Hearing this cry, the French front-riders were certain that there were the English, and also they saw them afterwards very plainly. So they sent some of their companions to notify their captains what they had seen and discovered, and they made known to them that they should ride forward in good order and that it was time to press on. Those [the captains] promptly prepared themselves in all things and rode so that they saw the English very clearly.[82]

Frequently, it is the 'unusual', the unplanned, that turns the tide of a battle. At Patay, it was this stag. The archers, their hiding place uncovered and their planned ambush discovered, fled into the woods and ran directly into the hiding vanguard, supply wagons, and artillery. Fastolf, who had not yet been given enough time to order a defensive formation with the main body and rear-guard of his army,[83] tried to rush to the aid of his archers and those hidden in the woods with reinforcements. But he was too late. Waurin continues:

However, the vanguard thought that all was lost and that [the archers] were in flight. Because of this the captain of the vanguard, thinking that it truly was so, took his white standard, and he and his men took flight and abandoned the hedges.[84]

Fastolf had little recourse but to turn and run in an attempt to save as many as he could from the main body of his army. He would escape. But his noble colleague, John Talbot, would not. Having placed himself with the hidden vanguard, he had become entangled in their disordered flight and was captured.[85]

By this time, the main body of the French army had ridden on to the field. The English forces were by then completely disordered as they all tried to flee. French infantry and cavalry charged on to these disordered troops and a slaughter ensued.[86] At the end of the battle, which had taken less than an hour,[87] English heralds reported a loss of 2,200 soldiers; the French had lost very few. Many more English had been captured, with not only Talbot taken, but Sir Thomas Scales and many other English leaders as well.[88] If that was not enough, those English soldiers who were fortunate enough to escape from the field found that their nearest allied town, Janville, had closed its doors to them; the townspeople there had learned of the French victory and chose to surrender themselves to the victors at Patay rather than suffer what Jargeau and Beaugency had. Most English soldiers did not find refuge until they had reached Étampes or Corbeil, less than fifty kilometers from Paris.[89]

As mentioned, the Constable and several other French leaders stayed that night in Patay, where they celebrated their victory. Joan, the duke of Alençon, the Bastard of Orléans, and others returned to Orléans.[90] But what was Joan's role in the battle of Patay? Certainly she had encouraged the French army to chase after the English and to force them to do battle. But after that, her name seems to disappear from the contemporary records. This may be partly explained by the fact that the best accounts of the battle are written by Waurin and Monstrelet, two individuals who were writing from the English perspective and not the French one. Nor do either of the chronicles that highlight her military career during this period – the *Journal du siège d'Orléans* and the *Chronique de la Pucelle* – report much about the battle. But, more than likely, this is not the sole reason for her absence from the sources. Her role in the battle of Patay may have been limited because she was a member of the main body of the French troops, the force that found only a small amount of 'mopping-up' action there. Only the soldiers in the French vanguard seem to have participated fully in the fighting, and even their role was limited to one of intimidation rather than actual combat because the English force essentially caused its own initial panic and final demise. La Hire and Ponton de Xantrailles were there, but they and the other French cavalry in the vanguard were veteran soldiers whose capability on horseback allowed them to reach the battlefield and, with the help of a frightened stag, win the battle before the rest of the army arrived. However, Joan was there early enough to see what her encouragement had effected. And her response? It was typical for Joan. She mourned for the lost lives and took pity on the wounded regardless of whether they were English or French. Her page, Louis de Coutes, later testified that when she encountered an English prisoner who had been 'hit . . . on the head' at Patay and left for dead by a Frenchman, 'she dismounted and received the Englishman's confession, holding his head and comforting him as much as she could'.[91]

The English army had been chased from the Loire. In but a short time, all of the numerous acquisitions made by the earl of Salisbury in 1428 south of Chartres were returned under French control. As Joan celebrated the victory at Patay with her by-now customary Mass,[92] she was also preparing to undertake the next part of her journey. Even though she had won many great victories, she had still only fulfilled one of her mission's goals – the relief of the siege of Orléans. Her next task was to crown Charles, the dauphin, as Charles VII, the king. The road to Reims lay open.

6

The Road to Reims

The road to Reims lay open, but that did not mean that it was without 'potholes' or other hindrances. Between Orléans and Reims there were many towns and villages held by the English and Burgundians, and they could all have been impediments to a French army intent on crowning its king at the sacred site of such ceremonies, Reims Cathedral, especially as Reims itself was also under Burgundian control. Should each of these towns, as well as the city of Reims, require a military operation like that carried out on Jargeau, Meung-sur-Loire, and Beaugency, the coronation would be greatly delayed.

But there was some hope in the wake of the battle of Patay. The townspeople of Janville had barred the English from returning within their town's walls, essentially surrendering themselves to the French soldiers who were pursuing the fleeing English. And Janville was not alone. Both Jacques Bouvier, the herald of Berry, and the *Chronique de la Pucelle* indicate that other English-controlled towns and villages Mehun, Ferté-Hubert, Montpeyroux, and Saint-Simeon, also surrendered themselves to the French after Patay without violence or bloodshed.[1] It is of course easy to understand why these towns did this. Besides the simple fact that their inhabitants were French themselves, and in most instances had not been under English rule for long enough to formulate solid political or economic bonds, these citizens also could not help but recognize the newly acquired martial skill of the French or the destructiveness that followed an attempted hold-out against them. What had occurred at Jargeau was known widely throughout the land – and not only the ruin of the town's fortifications, church, and some houses, which obviously had resulted in grievous and long-term financial setbacks, but also the execution of the prisoners there. Whether Joan knew about or participated in these executions, and whether or not the victims were only Englishmen, the effect of this incident and what it

France at the beginning of the Hundred Years War.

Letter written by Joan of Arc to the citizens of Riom on 9 November 1429 asking for aid in her attack on La Charité-sur-Loire. This is one of the three extant letters containing her signature. (Riom, Archives communales de Riom, AA.33)

John the Fearless, duke of Burgundy (1371–1419), Burgundian school. (Musée du Louvre, Paris/Giraudon, Paris)

Henry V, king of England. (By courtesy of National Portrait Gallery, London)

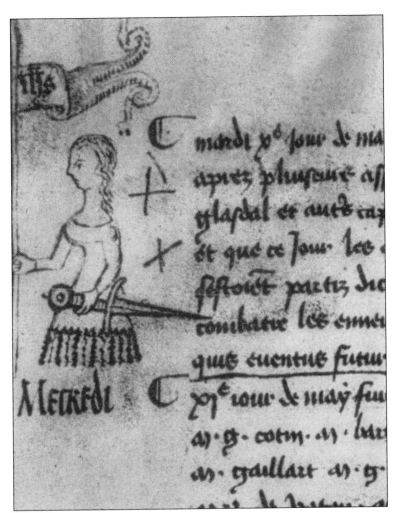

Marginal portrait of Joan of Arc drawn by Clément de Fauquembergue after her relief of the siege of Orléans. Image taken from a parliamentary council register, 10 May 1429. (ET Archive, London)

France in 1429.

House in Domrémy where Joan of Arc was raised and outside of which she received her first visitations. (Image by Timothy J. Frohlick, Courtesy of the Saint Joan of Arc Center, Albuquerque, New Mexico)

Chinon Castle. (Author's photograph)

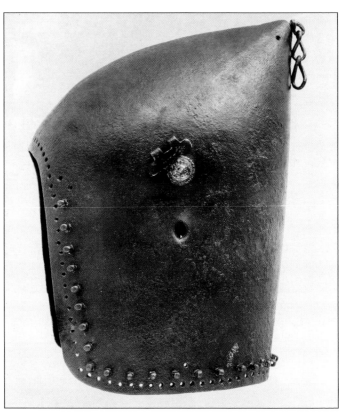

Bascinet from Saint-Pierre-du-Martroi that may have belonged to Joan of Arc. (Metropolitan Museum of Art, New York)

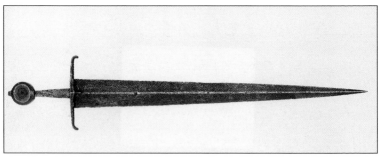

Mid-fifteenth-century sword (western European, possibly French) representative of those used by Joan of Arc and her soldiers. (Courtesy of the Board of the Royal Armouries, IX.3683, Leeds)

Left: Jean, the Bastard of Orléans and later Count Dunois, detail from the *Livre d'heures de Dunois*. (British Library, London, Yates Thompson 3, f. 32v)

Above: Orléans Cathedral, which Joan of Arc visited frequently during and after her relief of the 1429 siege. It has been heavily reconstructed after sustaining damage during the sixteenth-century Wars of Religion and the Second World War. (Jean Feuillie/©CNMHS, Paris)

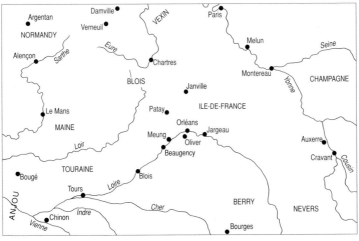

The Loire campaign of June 1429.

The Tour de Cordray, Chinon Castle. Joan of Arc stayed on the first floor. (Author's photograph)

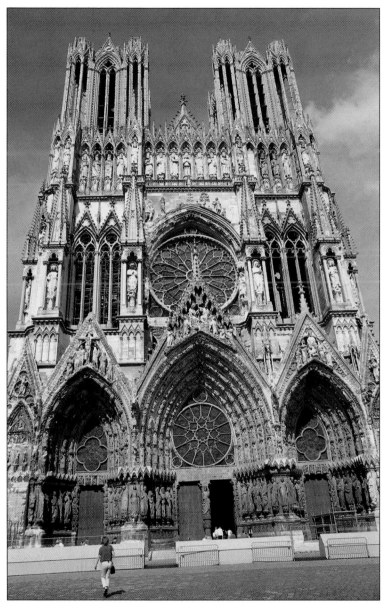

Façade of Reims Cathedral, site of Charles VII's coronation on 17 July 1429.
(Author's photograph)

Joan of Arc being tied to the stake on 30 May 1431, from the *Vigiles de Charles VII*, c. 1470. (Bibliothèque Nationale, Paris, MS fr 5054, f. 71/Giraudon/Bridgeman Art Library, London)

Tour Jeanne D'Arc, the main tower of the twelfth to thirteenth-century castle at Rouen that housed the imprisoned Joan of Arc during her trial. (Author's photograph)

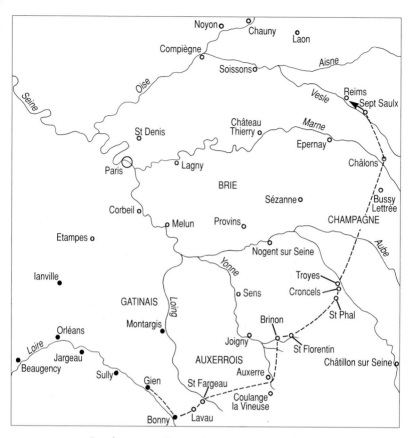

Joan's route to Reims, 26 June–17 July 1429.

Basilica of Saint-Denis outside the walls of medieval Paris and headquarters of the French leadership during Joan of Arc's attack on Paris in September 1429. It was in this basilica that Joan placed her votive offering of captured Burgundian arms and armor. (Author's photograph)

Woodcut from the 1493 printed *Vigiles de Charles VII* portraying the judges
presiding over Joan of Arc's trial.

Medieval gate of Saint-Valery-sur-Somme through which the imprisoned Joan of Arc was marched on her journey to Rouen. (Author's photograph)

Spot in Rouen where Joan of Arc was burned on 30 May 1431.
(Author's photograph)

could mean to other towns undoubtedly frightened some citizens into desiring submission.

But they could not have surrendered if there had been large English or Burgundian garrisons in their towns. Why these garrisons were not in place cannot be explained by the settlements' size, although it is certain that some of the villages and towns in occupied France were simply too small to warrant a gathering of troops. But there were also no garrisons or only small garrisons in far larger towns than those that surrendered after Patay, even towns the size of Auxerre, Châlons, Troyes, and, in fact, Reims itself. The reason for this is, in fact, somewhat complicated, yet it is fundamental to the very nature of fifteenth-century combat. Although this has not been realized by most Hundred Years War historians, especially English ones, the English forces that occupied France in 1429 really had no justifiable reason for their success there. After all, England was a far less populated kingdom than France. Comparative demographic figures show a disparity of more than 300 per cent.[2] This of course meant that the potential number of soldiers from England was much smaller than that from France. Calculations of English soldiers in France provided by Anne Curry based on expeditions sent from England to France between 1415 and 1429 show a total of just 41,327,[3] an incredibly small number of troops to protect all of the occupied regions of France, and to carry on further offensive military actions, even if it was feasible that all of those soldiers remained alive and in military service in France in 1429. This meant, as was seen above, that the English forces besieging Orléans in 1428–9 never had enough numbers even to surround the whole city. To be sure, a small English population and equally small numbers of English soldiers did not seem to hinder the course of the war before 1429. Additionally, the English had been able to capitalize on the civil war that raged throughout France between the Armagnacs and the Burgundians. The English used their allies to help eliminate their personnel problems, assigning them garrison duties in places such as Paris.[4]

All of this had led to a large number of French towns surrendering to the English and Burgundians without being attacked by them. In so doing, they had obviously avoided any of the destruction occurring in the areas that had attempted to withstand an English onslaught: without an effective French army to protect them, the willing subjugation of these towns became a safety measure. Frequently no garrisons were assigned to them, and this gave the occupied towns a relative sovereignty and peacefulness, and enabled the occupiers to spread out their own personnel resources to cover more threatened locations. Leaving these targets exposed to a French offensive was a risk, but it was a risk that the English were forced to take to make up for their low numbers.

Before Joan of Arc's victories along the Loire river, the English risk had been minimal. Few of the 'occupied' towns that were without English garrisons had created a problem for their occupiers. Indeed, contemporary records show that while a small number of towns had dissident groups operating within them who wished to recognize the dauphin and revolt against English control, without dependable promises of French military support, the majority of citizens preferred a less threatened existence to one that carried the threat of a more harsh and violent English or Burgundian presence.[5] But, by 18 June, the situation for many of those towns had changed considerably. By then, not only were there promises of successful French military support for centres of population, especially those to the south and east of Paris, that wished to throw off English control, but at the head of the military was a holy woman, a living saint, whose presence guaranteed divine justification for their decision to go against the English. Joan's reputation as a military 'savior' had traveled widely throughout occupied France. Her mission was well known. She had promised to relieve the siege of Orléans, and she had; and now she promised to lead the king to Reims and his coronation, and no one in France, including the English, doubted that she would.

Consciously or not, Joan perpetuated this image. (Regnault of Chartres, archbishop of Reims and one of her detractors, for one, believed that she was conscious of this perpetuation. After her capture, he would complain to the people of Reims about Joan's pride and independence.[6]) In a letter written on 25 June 1429 (only a week after her victory at Patay) to the citizens of Tournai – and certainly elsewhere, although only the Tournai letter has survived – Joan described her recent victories and what these meant to places like theirs which had continually and at a heavy cost withstood the English forces. She was anything but shy in her enthusiasm:

Jhesus Maria

Gracious loyal Frenchmen of the city of Tournai, the Maid sends you the news that from here in eight days, whether by assault or otherwise, she has chased the English out of every place they held on the River Loire. Many of them are dead or taken prisoners and they are discomfited in battle. And may you well believe that the Earl of Suffolk, La Pole his brother, the Lord Talbot, the lord of Scales, and my lord John Fastolf, and many knights and captains have been taken, and that the brother of the Earl of Suffolk and Glasdale are dead. Hold yourselves fast, loyal Frenchmen, I pray you.

And I pray and demand that you be ready to come to the anointing of the gracious King Charles at Reims, where we shall soon be; come before us when you hear that we are approaching. I commend you to God; may God keep watch over you and give you grace to be able to sustain the good cause of the kingdom of France.[7]

Joan's stature was so high in France at this moment, that even though the road to Reims was not an unhindered one, it would be traveled by her and the king with relative ease, leading to the fulfilment of her second mission, the crowning of a French monarch.

Sometime during the middle of June, Charles, the dauphin of France, moved to Gien. When and why he moved there cannot be determined with exactitude from contemporary sources. Gien is on the eastern side of Orléans, while Chinon and Blois, where Charles had spent much of his time before the arrival of Joan, were to the west of Orléans. Does this mean that the dauphin now felt safe enough to travel to what until recently had been threatened territory as a result of what Joan and the French army had been able to do against the English during the previous two months? That, too, must remain conjecture. But one thing is certain: the location of Gien gave the dauphin a more direct route to Reims. Despite the continued reluctance of some of his counselors, the dauphin himself must have been thinking about the possibility of his coronation.

It might seem unusual that with so many nobles, soldiers, and commoners all joining Joan and her cause, some in Charles's court either openly opposed her methods and achievements or were reluctant to believe that what she had accomplished came from God and would continue. One in particular was especially vocal: Georges de la Trémoïlle,[8] who had been such an adversary to the Constable, Arthur de Richemont, had also begun to oppose Joan. No doubt her acceptance of Richemont into the army had not improved her position at court, but La Trémoïlle's opposition to her seems to have originated even earlier than that incident. Nor had his enmity declined as Joan began to achieve military successes. Indeed, if anything, it seems to have increased.[9]

There were two reasons for La Trémoïlle's reluctance to accept Joan and her methods of retaking the occupied parts of France. The first was a basic personality flaw. While he had been successful in flattering the dauphin enough to secure appointment as the Grand Chamberlain of France and Lieutenant General of Burgundy, as well as serving as Charles's chief counselor, La Trémoïlle seems to have been jealous of anyone else who got close to Charles. He then sought to drive a wedge between the object of his jealousy and the easily influenced dauphin. The second reason for La Trémoïlle's opposition to Joan was his belief that the only way to end the wars between England and France and between Burgundy and France was diplomacy. More importantly, he believed that the only means truly to end the former conflict was to finish the latter one first – to mend the rift between the dauphin and the duke of Burgundy. This philosophy had begun early in his life when La Trémoïlle served as Chamberlain to Duke John the Fearless of Burgundy, and it had not waned when he took up a similar position with the dauphin. Nor had he broken any connections with Burgundy once he joined the dauphin's court. Indeed, although he seems frequently to have come close to what could be called treason when it came to his opposition to successful French military leaders, ultimately, his drive for a diplomatic solution to the Hundred Years War would lead La Trémoïlle to his greatest achievement – the Congress of Arras in 1435, at which he would succeed in inducing Philip the Good to switch allegiances from England to France. But before he effected that pivotal event, he ensured that anyone who sought to 'win' the war by 'warfare' was disliked and was also generally forced out of favor at court.

So, while Joan of Arc and other military leaders both by their words and deeds were urging the dauphin to travel to Reims and his coronation, La Trémoïlle and others were advising him to be patient and wait for further victories, perhaps in Normandy, or for diplomacy to make the trip to Reims more safe. However, Joan continued to push for coronation and promised that she would deliver the dauphin to Reims safely. The Bastard of Orléans testified at her nullification trial:

> After the [Loire] victories, he remembered that the lords of royal blood and captains wished that the king would go to Normandy and not to Reims. But the Maid always was of the opinion that he ought to go to Reims to be consecrated as king, and she added as a reason for her opinion that when the king had been crowned and consecrated, the power of his adversaries would continue to diminish, and that they finally would not be able to hurt him or his kingdom.[10]

Eventually, Joan's opinion prevailed. For although a meeting of the dauphin's council was held on 22 June at which only a few of the successful French military leaders, not including Joan, were present, and at which La Trémoïlle tried to make a different proposal to that which would send the king and his army to Reims, eventually it was decided that the dauphin should be crowned king. Later, La Trémoïlle again tried alternative proposals to those offered by Joan: that the dauphin should first travel to Bourges, or that the army should first besiege the enemy-occupied southern Loire towns of Cosne and La Charité-sur-Loire.[11] But these ideas were also dismissed by Charles, and he prepared to journey to the sacred city of Reims.[12]

During these meetings, Joan had been in Orléans becoming impatient. With her was a growing army, numbering perhaps as many as 12,000.[13] It was a formidable force, one that looked forward to the crowning of the king if not an encounter with the English. All wanted to fight with the Maid, for her triumph seems to have attracted many who were anxious to share in her success, to take part in her mission, and to feel her spirituality.[14] On 24 June, they were allowed to go to Gien. Joan was elated. It seemed that the French army was finally ready to set out on the road to Reims. Perceval de Cagny writes that Joan expressed this to her friend, the duke of Alençon, with the following words: 'Sound the trumpets and mount your horse. It is time to go to the gentle King Charles to put him on the path of his consecration at Reims.'[15] But, once at Gien, the army again had to wait. On 25 June, Joan composed and sent her letter to the inhabitants of Tournai; but otherwise she and the army did little. On 26 June, again no movement towards Reims was made. Finally on 27 June, Joan became frustrated at the inaction of the dauphin, and, while she could not rebuke him as she had the Bastard of Orléans during a similar inactive streak before the relief of the siege of Orléans, she protested against what was happening (or in this case not happening) in the only way she could. She left Gien and camped with the common soldiers in the fields outside of the town. Cagny records her impatience:

> The king was at Gien until Wednesday 29 June. And the Maid was very distressed at the lengthy sojourn which was made at that place because some of the men of his court counseled him not to undertake the road to Reims, saying that he had many cities and other villages closed to him, castles and fortifications well garrisoned with English and Burgundians between Gien and Reims. The Maid said that she knew this well and that she did not take any account of this. And in frustration, she left her lodgings and went to camp in the fields for two days before the departure of the king.

In her absence, it became evident to Charles that the army and its leaders were devoted to Joan. They believed in her and knew that they could deliver the dauphin to Reims without difficulty. Cagny continues:

> And while the king did not have silver to pay his army, all the knights, squires, men of war, and commoners would not refuse to go to serve the king on this journey in the company of the Maid, saying that they would go everywhere she wished to go. And she said: 'By my Martin, I will lead the gentle King Charles and his company safely, and he will be consecrated at Reims.'[16]

Thus, on 29 June, with Joan leading them, and the dauphin and his court also present, the large army began its march north-east to Reims. Its first stop was the town of Auxerre, which was reached on 30 June. Auxerre had been under Burgundian control for almost a decade,[17] and there was even a Burgundian municipal administration, which had been appointed to oversee the governance of the town. But there appear not to have been any soldiers watching over this most southern site of the Burgundian realm. Most importantly, the town and its Burgundian governors were not at all interested in trying to withstand the enormous enemy army led by Joan of Arc. Negotiations for surrender took three days, but in the end the municipal administration capitulated and the townspeople threw open their gates and resupplied the French forces. The dauphin forgave all who were involved with the English and Burgundians, and no blood was shed.[18]

The army marched on, passing the villages of Cravant, Coulanges-la-Vineuse, Saint-Fargeau, Brienon, Saint-Florentin, Evry, and Saint-Phal. All welcomed the soldiers and the Maid, and all made homage to the dauphin.[19] The next large town along the road to Reims was Troyes, but this well-fortified stronghold presented a potential problem to the French forces. Not only had Troyes been within the Anglo-Burgundian orbit for longer than Auxerre, but it had also been the site of the Treaty of Troyes, signed in 1420 by Henry V, Charles VI, and Philip the Good, which had formalized the French situation that Joan and others had opposed for so long. That treaty had disinherited Charles as dauphin, and, only days later, at the church of St Jean in Troyes, Henry V had married Charles's sister, Catherine. The union produced Charles's rival for the French throne, Henry VI.[20] Moreover, unlike the people of Auxerre and elsewhere, the inhabitants of Troyes had actually benefited from and prospered under Anglo-Burgundian rule. There was bound to be some opposition to simple capitulation to the dauphin; perhaps the townspeople might do better to try and hold out against the French until an English or Burgundian army could relieve them.

In anticipation of this possibility, on 4 July, Joan wrote to the citizens of Troyes from Saint Phal, expressing her desire that they recognize her mission and the power of her army, and threatening them if they did not surrender. This letter is much closer to her 'Letter to the English' than it is to her letter to the citizens of Tournai:

Jhesus Maria

Very good and dear friends – lords, townsmen, and residents of the city of Troyes – Joan the Maid commands and informs you on behalf of the King of Heaven our rightful and sovereign Lord, in whose royal service she serves daily, that you should truly obey and recognize the gracious king of France, who will soon be at

the city of Reims and at Paris, come who may against him. And
with the aid of the King Jesus he will be in all good cities in his
holy kingdom. Loyal Frenchmen, come before King Charles. Do
not fail to do so; have no hesitation about your lives and property
if you do so. And if you do not do so, I promise and assure you for
your lives' sake that with God's aid we shall enter all the cities
that should belong to the holy Kingdom; and we will establish a
firm peace there, whoever comes against us. I commend you to
God, may God protect you, if it please Him. Reply soon.[21]

To this, the dauphin added his own guarantees of amnesty, should
the town surrender quickly.

On 5 July, the French army camped outside of Troyes. The gates
of the town were shut tight, the drawbridges erect, so that only the
walls and ditches greeted Joan, the king, and their entourage. The
inhabitants of Troyes, disregarding Joan's letter and the dauphin's
promises, seemed prepared to defend themselves. This, in the words
of C.-R. Pernin, presented the French military leaders with a 'gros
obstacle' (a great obstacle).[22] Part of the reason for this defiance
may have been the fact that, unlike Auxerre and the villages along
the route which had so far surrendered peacefully to the coronation
expedition, Troyes seems to have had a small garrison of 500–600
English and Burgundian troops. This may have led to some
unwillingness on the part of the Troyennes to capitulate, at least
without seeing whether there was a possibility of English or
Burgundian relief. This can be the only explanation of why, shortly
after the arrival of the French army, these soldiers would sortie out
of the town in a show of force, only to be sent scrambling back
inside its walls after a small skirmish showed them that their
opponents possessed a very large force, something which seems not
to have been entirely evident to them initially.[23]

This would be the last military encounter between the two
opposing forces. For the next four days, ambassadors, heralds, and
messengers went back and forth between the townspeople and the
army. Joan and the dauphin continued to plead with the inhabitants
of Troyes for submission, while the townspeople continued to hold
out for either a relief army or better terms of surrender.[24] There was
also some obvious concern among the Troyennes over the presence
of Joan with the French force. They had undoubtedly heard of her
exploits, but they had been continually told by their Anglo-

Burgundian leaders that she was led by a source other than God.
How else could she have accomplished what she had against
superior English foes? In response, on one of these ambassadorial
exchanges, these citizens sent Friar Richard to confront her. He was
a Franciscan brother who had been accorded some form of
theological popularity as a result of his sermons predicting the end
of the world (in 1430), and was well respected by the Troyennes for
his spirituality – although this same respect had not been given him
by other communities, since he had been driven out of Paris in April
1429, a fate that would be repeated later at Troyes. He was sent to
examine Joan and to ascertain her theological credibility. At her
trial, Joan recalled her encounter with him:

> Those from the town of Troyes, she believed, sent him to her,
> saying that they doubted that she was something which had
> come from God. And when this brother approached her, he made
> the sign of the cross and sprinkled holy water. And then she said
> to him: 'Come boldly. I will not fly away.'[25]

Joan was clearly unimpressed by this man whose own orthodoxy
was to be questioned. Friar Richard's reaction to her is not known.

As the days wore on, the situation at Troyes began to demand a
solution. Such a large army as that with the dauphin needed to be
fed, and victuals were beginning to run short.[26] Finally, on 8 July,
the dauphin chose to convene a council of war. Again, surprisingly,
Joan was excluded from this meeting, but this seems to be evidence
of the opposition beginning to grow against her among some of the
king's counselors. The question was whether to continue to camp
around Troyes or to bypass it and proceed on to Reims. Speaking for
the latter possibility was Archbishop Regnault of Chartres.
According to the *Journal du siège d'Orléans* and Jean Chartier, the
two sources which report on this council in greatest detail, the
archbishop felt that they had spent too much time already
attempting to gain the capitulation of this town, and that because of
their lack of supplies, it was essential that they move on to Reims
where they would be greeted with kindness and sustenance. In
opposition to him rose Robert le Maçon, the lord of Trèves, described
by Chartier as an 'ancient counselor'. He eloquently addressed the
gathering, saying that they should summon Joan of Arc and ask for
her advice, that she had 'always pushed to go for the king's

coronation at Reims', and that she, through her military victories, had made it possible for them to travel this far. Le Maçon's words were convincing, and Joan was summoned to give her opinion. The Bastard of Orléans later recalled her appearance before the council:

> Joan came and entered the council, saying these or similar words: 'Noble dauphin, order your people to come and besiege the town of Troyes, and stay no longer in council. For, in the name of God, before three days are out, I will lead you into the city of Troyes, by love or strength or courage, and the false Burgundians will be amazed.'[27]

Joan's promise persuaded the council to increase the military effort at Troyes, and she was put in charge of the siege. She began quickly. First, she set up all of the French gunpowder artillery against the walls and prepared for its use.[28] Then she ordered her soldiers to make bundles of sticks in order to fill in the moat around the town.[29] All of this was done in sight of the Troyennes, and these actions denoted that soon there was to be a serious offensive action against the town. This would mean death and destruction; it would also mean that, according to the traditional laws of war, the dauphin, without impunity, could deal as harshly with the town's inhabitants as he chose after what would be their inevitable surrender, for they had forced the increase in violence. They held out only until morning, for according to Simon Charles, 'Joan cried "to the attack", signifying that [her soldiers] were to put the sticks into the moat. And seeing this, the citizens of Troyes, fearing any attack, sent to negotiate a surrender with the king. And the king made a surrender pact with the citizens, and he entered the town of Troyes with great ceremony, Joan carrying her standard next to him.'[30] After a victory procession through the streets, the dauphin dealt mercifully and without punishment with the Troyennes, who quickly resupplied his army. Again, no blood had been shed.

On 12 July, the French army again set off towards Reims. Further villages, Arcy-sur-Aube and Lettrée, submitted to Joan and the dauphin. Perceval de Cagny claimed that villages had done this there and elsewhere, 'because the Maid always sent her standard to those she wished to submit and said to those in each fortification she passed: "Surrender yourselves to the King of Heaven and to gentle King Charles."'[31] The townspeople of Châlons-sur-Marne, the next large town on the route, also opened their gates and welcomed the soon-to-be Charles VII. Charles had sent a herald forward to them, offering amnesty in return for capitulation, and their bishop greeted him warmly when the army arrived.[32] At Châlons, Joan was back home, or at least as near to it as she had been since she had left Vaucouleurs the previous February. Several from her home town traveled to visit her there. One of these, a farmer, Gérardin d'Épinal said that he went there specifically to meet with the girl who had once told him that she had a secret which she could not divulge to him because he was a 'Burgundian'. Now, he recalled, she greeted him and his four traveling companions warmly and spoke with them. He remembered that she told him at that time that 'she feared nothing except treason'.[33] Was this a prophecy of what would happen to her in the future?

On Saturday 16 July, Joan, the dauphin, his court, and his army arrived at Reims. The next day, the dauphin was crowned as King Charles VII of France. One member of Charles's court, Simon Charles, testified that as they approached the city, the dauphin began to worry that it, deep in Burgundian territory, might choose to hold out against him. Again, Joan comforted him:

> Joan said to the king: 'Do not doubt, as the burgesses of the town of Reims will come to meet with you.' But the king feared the resistence of those of Reims because they did not have artillery . . . nor machines to place in siege, if they were to rebel. And Joan told the king that he ought to proceed boldly and not doubt, because, if he proceeded strongly, he would obtain his entire kingdom.

Again, Joan was correct, the courtier concluded, for even 'before they approached Reims, the burgesses had surrendered to him'.[34]

There seemed in fact to have been no opposition whatsoever in Reims to the crowning of the king. As Joan and Charles entered the town, they were greeted with cheers. Knowing of this possibility and also of their inability to prevent it, the English had tried to strip the cathedral of its liturgical vestments and vessels. They had not been able to do so completely and had left behind the most important and sacred vial of oil – which had been secreted away by monks loyal to the dauphin – traditionally used for the consecration of French kings since Clovis. Four knights had been appointed as guardians of this vial: the marshal de Boussac, the Admiral of France, the lord of

Graville, and Gilles de Rais. All had been present in numerous of
Joan's victories. With the guardians marched a lengthy procession
of canons, bishops, and ecclesiastics. Ten of these represented the
twelve peers of France, five laymen and five ecclesiastics. Others,
including the duke of Alençon and the Bastard of Orléans, carried
the royal insignia: the crown, the golden spurs, the scepter, and the
'hand of justice'. Regnault of Chartres, the archbishop of Reims,
performed the ceremony, with Georges de la Trémoïlle standing
nearby. Where was Joan? She was by the king's side, dressed in her
armor and carrying her standard. (Later, at her trial when she was
asked why she had carried her standard during the coronation, she
answered: 'It had suffered for this; there was good reason that it had
this honor.'[35]) Once the ceremony was concluded and the king was
crowned, Joan did homage to him. The *Journal du siège d'Orléans*
records:

> When the Maid saw that the king had been consecrated and
> crowned, she knelt before him, in front of all of the lords standing
> around them, and she embraced his legs, saying as she cried
> warm tears: 'Gentle king, the pleasure of God has been executed.
> He Who wished that I relieve the siege of Orléans, and Who
> brought you into this city of Reims to receive your holy
> consecration, demonstrated that you are the true king and the
> one to whom the kingdom should belong.' And there was a great
> pity from all who saw this.[36]

Joan of Arc had fulfilled the second task of her mission: she had
crowned the dauphin king of France. She had stood next to him
during the crowning, and she had wept with joy when it was
completed. She had reached the pinnacle of power, prestige, and
sanctity. Nothing, it seemed, could bring her down.

7

The Decline of a Military Leader

Enguerrand de Monstrelet reports that after his coronation, the new King Charles VII retired to the archiepiscopal palace for a celebratory feast. Accompanying him was Archbishop Regnault of Chartres, who was the host of the gathering, Jean, the duke of Alençon, Charles, the count of Clermont, both of whom are said to have 'served the king his meal', and 'many other high nobles'.[1] Joan's presence is not recorded. Her absence may simply have been an omission in Monstrelet's text – his chronicle never shows any affinity for the Maid. Or, she might have been absent because of her non-noble status – she was to be ennobled later, but was not at this time, which may be the reason for her absence not only at this feast, but at the numerous council meetings that had been held by the king since he decided to march to Reims almost a month earlier. Finally, she might have been absent from the archbishop's celebration because, although still greatly esteemed after Charles's crowning, her prominence was beginning to wane; after all, one of the men who was soon to become one of the most persistent opponents to Joan was hosting the meal. Yet, whether she was included in this function or not, Joan certainly celebrated the completion of this second part of her mission somewhere.

In Paris, the English were understandably concerned about recent events. Not only had they suffered significant military setbacks on the Loire river, relatively far to the south of Paris, but with the movement of the French army to Reims, their enemies had come increasingly closer to that very important city. For, even though Rouen was the administrative capital of English-occupied France, Paris, which was actually governed by both the English and the Burgundians,[2] was still the largest city and, more importantly, should Paris fall to the French, the symbolism of such a fall could lead to a complete reversal of all that had been accomplished by the English since Henry V's great victory in 1415. Norman towns, never completely secure in their English occupation, might erupt in rebellion. And the Burgundians, whose duke was a cousin of Charles VII, might break their alliance with England and either seek an agreement with the new French king, or decide to adopt a more singular, independent place in western European politics. In either case, they, too, had the potential to become enemies of the English; there certainly was little chance that Burgundians would remain friendly to foreigners whom they felt had no right to the French throne or any French territory.

Therefore, more positive action needed to be taken to improve the English position. First, the defenses of Paris were strengthened. The Bourgeois of Paris indicates that in the aftermath of the French successes boulevards were constructed in front of the gates, houses built next to the walls were knocked down, gunpowder weapons were mounted and stones were gathered – an inventory notes that 1,176 cannonballs were delivered to the gates of Paris at this time[3] – and placed near the city walls. The ditches and moats around the city were cleared of their debris and deepened 'to make a barrier between the town and them [the French]'.[4]

Second, a peace treaty was signed with Brittany. Making the unprecedented offer of the county of Poitou, English diplomats enticed the independent Duke Jean V to ally with them. While no military aid was promised, the duke did assure the English ambassadors who negotiated the treaty that he would remain out of the conflict. Additionally, his brother, the French Constable, Arthur de Richemont, whose omission at the coronation, his chronicler Guillaume Gruel insists, was intensely objected to by Joan, was offered the same constabulary position in the English army and also the lordship of Touraine, Saintogne, Aunis, and La Rochelle. Richemont refused, but, at least for the moment, he stayed away from the new king and even, unfortunately for her, from Joan.[5]

Third, the English remained defiant in their opposition to Charles's assumption of the title of king of France and in their willingness to defend what lands already had and to attempt to capture or recapture French lands. In a letter written by John, the duke of Bedford and regent to King Henry VI, to Charles VII on 7 August 1429, this defiance is evident, as is the duke's hatred of the means by which the recent French successes had been brought about – Joan of Arc:

We, John of Lancaster, regent of France and duke of Bedford, make known to you, Charles of Valois, who name yourself the dauphin of Viennois, and now, without reason, call yourself king, because you made a new, offensive undertaking against the crown and lordship of the very noble and excellent prince, and my sovereign lord, Henry, by the grace of God, true, natural, and lawful king of France and England, by giving a hearing to simple people who had come to give up their peace and security. That which is not, nor should be, through the means which you have held and hold, which seduce and abuse the ignorant people and which build more a superstitious and reproved people, that is a disordered and defamed woman, dressed in men's clothing and base in conduct, and also a mendicant friar, heretical and seditious, as we are informed [evidently Bedford had heard that Friar Richard had played more of a role in recent events than was true], both, according to the Holy Scriptures, abominable to God, who, by force and power of arms, have occupied in the lands of Champagne and other places certain cities, towns, and castles belonging to my lord the King, and have constrained his subjects in them and induced them to be disloyal and perjurious, and made them destroy and violate the peace finalized between the realms of France and England, solemnly sworn to by the kings of France and England, which was then signed by the great lords, peers, prelates, barons, and the three states of each realm . . . We, who, desiring with all our heart to shorten the war, summon and require that, if you are such a prince who is honorable, and has pity and compassion for poor Christian people, who for such a long time for your cause have been inhumanely treated and defiled and oppressed, and who briefly were away from their afflictions and sorrows, without continuing the war more, choose in the land of Brie, where you and we are, or in the Ile de France which is well known to us and to you, some place in the fields, convenient and reasonable, one day soon and suitable, and close to the places where we and you are for the present to suffer and demand, at which day and place, if you will appear in person with the above-mentioned defamed woman and heretic, and all the perjurers, and such other power which you wish and are able to have, we, at the pleasure of Our Lord, will appear on behalf of the lord the king in our person. And there, if you have anything to offer or place before us, regarding the making of peace, we, hearing and doing what a good Catholic prince ought and will do, always will be inclined and willing in all good ways to make peace, not idle, corrupt, secret, violated, nor perjured, as was done at Montereau-Fault-Yonne, where was, by your culpability and consent, perpetrated the terrible, detestable, and cruel murder committed, against the law and honor of chivalry, in the person of which our very beloved and very honored father, the Duke John of Burgundy, God has taken.

Only half the letter is translated here. The rest becomes repetitious as Bedford goes on to accuse the French of more evils and abuses, all of which would prohibit the English from making the peace which he claims to desire.[6] It was quite certain that there would be no diplomatic solution to the war between these two enemies.

Finally, Bedford himself, not only regent to the English king, but also leader of all English forces in France, decided that he should take command of the army that would oppose Joan.[7] Actually this last decision should not be a surprising one, for not only had Bedford been a successful military leader under his brother, Henry V, but he had also run out of other generals. With Salisbury dead, Scales, Talbot, and Suffolk captured and not yet ransomed, and Fastolf, whose flight from Patay was regarded by some as cowardice, in disgrace, there were very few others with any military experience whom Bedford could call upon to lead his armies. Ultimately, Bedford would be successful, or better put, not unsuccessful, against the Maid, as so many others had been during this reversal of fortune for the English during the Hundred Years War.

The reaction of Philip the Good, the duke of Burgundy, to what had occurred along the Loire and on the road to Reims is not recorded in any contemporary source. But it cannot have been positive. The Loire defeats may not have concerned him, except where his few soldiers there were involved, but those towns which had surrendered to the French army on its march to Reims, principally Auxerre, Troyes, Châlons, and Reims itself, were Burgundian and not English holdings. Their submission to Charles and Joan without resistance was an embarrassment to him. It showed him to be militarily weak. Moreover, such submission was contagious. No sooner had Charles VII been crowned than two more of Philip's large and important towns, Laon and Soissons, located deep within Burgundian territory, also declared themselves for the new French king, even though no French army even threatened them. These would soon be followed by the towns of Château-Thierry, Provins, Coulommiers, Crécy-en-Brie, Senlis, Lagny, and Compiègne.[8] This was a situation which Philip obviously could not allow to continue.

Philip the Good also had to deal with the question of peace with France. Georges de la Trémoïlle had been diligently seeking peace with the duke of Burgundy since 30 June 1429, although it is unclear whether the dauphin or his court were aware of or authorized these negotiations. Even during the march to Reims, the negotiations had continued, with Philip at his home in Paris receiving progress reports on both the negotiations and Charles's movement towards his coronation.[9] Then there was the letter written to him on 17 July, the day of that coronation, by Joan of Arc. Echoing earlier missives which she had sent to him, this letter again sought peace between Burgundy and France:

Jhesus Maria

High and dread prince, duke of Burgundy, the Maid calls upon you by the King of Heaven, my rightful and sovereign Lord, to make a firm and lasting peace with the king of France. You two must pardon one another fully with a sincere heart, as loyal Christians should; and if it pleases you to make war, go and wage it on the Saracens. Prince of Burgundy, I pray you, supplicate, and humbly request rather than require you, make war no more on the holy kingdom of France. Withdraw at once and swiftly those of your men who are in certain places and fortresses of the aforesaid holy kingdom. As for the gentle king of France, he is ready to make peace with you, saving his honor, if it has to do with you alone. And I must make known to you from the King of Heaven, my rightful and sovereign Lord, for your good and for your honor and upon your life, that you will win no more battles against loyal Frenchmen and that all those who wage war against the aforesaid holy kingdom of France are warring against King Jesus, King of Heaven and of all earth, my rightful and sovereign Lord. And I pray you and call upon you with hands joined not to seek any battle nor war against us, neither you nor your men nor subjects, and believe firmly that no number of men that you bring against us will win, and that there will be great pity for the battle and the bloodshed there of those who come against us.[10]

Of course, her promise that should no peace be made by Philip, he would not be successful in any further military engagements, was not as friendly as most diplomats would have preferred. It is important that Joan still held out hope for a union between the two sections of the French kingdom.

If only to buy himself some time, Philip did make peace with the French. While still at Reims, Charles VII received the following offer: that the Burgundians would observe a truce for fifteen days; that Paris would be delivered to the French at the end of that time; and that negotiations would continue until a more definitive peace could be concluded.[11] This was everything that Joan, and presumably the king, wanted. Joan expressed this in a letter written from Provins to the citizens of Reims on 5 August:

> My dear and good friends, the good and loyal Frenchmen of the city of Reims, Joan the Maid sends you her news, and begs and requires you to have no doubt about the good fight she is waging for the blood royal. I promise and certify that I shall never abandon you as long as I shall live. And it is true that the king has made a truce with the duke of Burgundy for a period of fifteen days, by which the duke will surrender the city of Paris to him peacefully at the end of those fifteen days. Nevertheless, you should not wonder at seeing me not enter that city so swiftly. No matter how many truces are made, I am never content and do not know if I will keep them. But if I do, it will be only to preserve the King's honor. No matter how much they mock the blood royal, I shall hold the King's army and keep it together lest, at the end of those fifteen days, they do not make peace. On that account, my dear and perfect friends, I beg you not to grieve yourselves about this as long as I shall live, but I do require that you keep good watch and guard the king's good city. Let me know if there are any traitors who would do you grief. Briefly, I shall do all I can to combat them; let me know your news. I commend you to God; may He protect you.[12]

Joan still wished to fight, and she was suspicious of the duke of Burgundy's promises, but her promise to keep the truce, as well as her repetition of its planks, gives evidence of the hope that she held for what Philip had promised. However, by the end of the fifteen days, Philip had recanted his promises. Negotiations for a more definitive peace had broken down, and Paris remained closed to the French. (The Greffier de la Rochelle claims that Philip only offered this to the French 'to amuse the king' and keep him away from Paris until that city could prepare for such an attack.[13]) Such a dishonest if not treasonous display made Paris Joan's next target.

But what about the limits of Joan's mission? Was she not supposed only to relieve the siege of Orléans and crown the king at Reims? As that had been accomplished, perhaps she should have returned to Domrémy with her parents, Jacques and Isabelle, who were at Reims for the coronation. The limits of Joan's mission pose a question not easily answered: did it include the capture of Paris? Some critics have complained that in going to that city, Joan had overstepped her divine calling and, because of that, she met defeat. Even beyond the fact that such a conclusion speculates not only on historical direction but also on divine will, there is ample evidence that the Maid intended to capture Paris from her very earliest examinations at Chinon and Poitiers. Both the duke of Alençon and Seguin Seguin testified at her nullification trial that they had heard her say very early on that her mission contained the capture of Paris as well as the relief of Orléans and Charles's coronation (also the return of the duke of Orléans from his imprisonment in England).[14] Still, when she testified at her own trial in Rouen that her voices did not direct her to go against this very well fortified city, but that she went there 'at the request of noblemen who wished to make a skirmish or a show of force against Paris',[15] one can only wonder if it was not the failure of Philip the Good to keep his side of the truce that drove her to what would be her first military defeat.

The other aspect of Joan's attacks on Paris and elsewhere during the remainder of 1429 is her declining favor with the king and members of his court, chiefly Regnault of Chartres and Georges de la Trémoïlle. While certainly beginning to show signs of a waning position even before the coronation, as her military leadership responsibilities at Troyes and her position at the side of the king during his consecration and crowning show, Joan was still a highly respected, much relied upon individual, at least for the king and some of his courtiers and counselors. One could be cynical and claim that this was only because she was still well loved by her soldiers, and that any disfavor shown her before the coronation might have meant military upheaval. But such a denial of Charles's sincerity, replacing it with what would have necessitated one of the

most well acted and devious plots in history, seeks a solution that is
neither simple not logical. With the exception of some of its basic
elements – for example, La Trémoïlle's rising jealousy and Joan's
acceptance of Richemont when she had specifically been ordered
not to do so – the greatest part of Joan's decline must effectively
date from after the coronation and must be tied directly to her
inability to gain military success at Paris.

When exactly Joan made her mind up to go against Paris is
difficult to know. However, her movement towards that city began
sometime in early August 1429. Philip's truce lapsed during the
first week of August, exactly when cannot be known because it is
not known when the fifteen days began. Joan's letter to the citizens
of Reims written on 5 August mentions the truce and perhaps
indicates that it was still in effect on that date. After leaving Reims
on 21 July, Joan's army, generally in the company of the king, made
a slow, but continual movement towards Paris. On 21 July, she was
with the king at the abbey of Saint-Marcoul-de-Corbény.[16] From
there she traveled to Soissons, arriving on 23 July, when the king
accepted the town's surrender.[17] Four days later, on 27 July, she was
at Château-Thierry, where Perceval de Cagny writes, 'the army
waited all day in battle formation, hoping that the duke of Bedford
would come to do battle. In the evening the place surrendered and
the king lodged there until Monday 1 August.'[18] Although there
was a rumor that he might appear, apparently the English regent
was not yet ready to face the French. During his stay in Château-
Thierry, King Charles VII also honored Joan by granting her request
that the inhabitants of her home-town, Domrémy, and its close
neighbor, Greux, be exempt from taxation in perpetuity, an honor
which only the French Revolution reversed.[19] On 1 August, she
camped at Montmirail,[20] and the next day her entourage traveled to
Provins. For its size, Provins was a very heavily fortified town and
could have been expected to hold out for quite some time. Yet,
Perceval de Cagny remarks, 'they were received the best that the
town was able to'.[21] Also, at Provins, Rene of Anjou, the duke of
Bar, joined the French army. He was a welcome addition, one which
Joan had asked for when she visited his father-in-law, Charles, the
duke of Lorraine, before she left Vaucouleurs.[22] On 6 August, the
French army marched to Coulommiers, on 10 August to La Ferté-
Milon, on 11 August to Crépy-en-Valois, on 12 August to Lagny,
and on 13 August to Dammartin. At none of these places was there

any military action, even though at Dammartin the English army was nearby and, according to the *Journal du siège d'Orléans*, 'ordered in a good formation and placed in an advantageous position';[23] each town subjected itself peacefully to the new French king.[24]

But on 15 August, as the French army camped in fields outside of Senlis at a place known as Montépilloy, the duke of Bedford decided to make his move against it. Perceval de Cagny, the chronicler of the duke of Alençon and an eyewitness to what occurred at Montépilloy, gives the best account of the engagement. The following, with additions from some of his contemporaries, is his story.[25]

There were 6,000–7,000 French soldiers gathered at Montépilloy, including, according to Enguerrand de Monstrelet, a large number of allied Scotsmen,[26] who camped about two leagues from Senlis. The English army was closer to the town, about half a league away, with a slightly larger army, 8,000–9,000 combatants, including, again according to Monstrelet, 600–800 Burgundians.[27] The fields in between the two armies were flat and without forestation, but with a small stream, the Nonette, and a small village (not so appropriately named as it turned out), Notre-Dame des Victoires, located behind the English forces.[28] The English army had arrived late in the evening of 14 August and began to set up camp. While this was going on, groups of French soldiers, the French being by far the most confident of the two sides – Monstrelet's phrase is 'very strong and anxious for combat' – snuck out towards the English camp and skirmished with some of its guards and outlying campers. This did very little, although Cagny claims that some soldiers were captured and others wounded on both sides, with the English losing '10 or 12 men', including one captain, and no French deaths.

By nightfall, all of this had ended, and both sides 'retreated to their lodgings'. The next morning, 15 August, both armies prepared for battle. The French heard Mass, and then moved forward towards the English lines in battle formation.[29] During the night, the English army had established its accustomed defensive formation, a field fortification really, by surrounding the camp with stakes, ditches, and wagons.[30] It was a formation similar to the one which had brought victory to Sir John Fastolf at the battle of the Herrings. How close were the two battle lines? Jacques Bouvier, the herald of Berry, writes that they were not farther from one another 'than the shot of a couleuvrine [a small, mostly hand-held gunpowder weapon]'.[31] There the two forces sat for the whole of the very hot and dusty day

– Jean Chartier writes that the dust was so thick that it obscured the vision of all soldiers on both sides[32] – but there was little fighting, except for some skirmishing by soldiers from both armies. The English wanted to provoke a charge by the French on to their fortified lines, but refused to move from the protection which those same lines gave them. And the French refused to charge into what had proven in the past to be suicide; nor could they provoke the English to come out from behind their stakes, ditches, and wagons. Not even when Joan, knowing how the English would prize her capture, took her standard and placed herself in the front of the vanguard, marching it 'all the way to the fortification of the English', did the English army move out from their camp. Eventually, she retreated to her own lines, 'because the English did not wish to sally out in large numbers'.[33] The Maid, accompanied by Alençon and others, tried to taunt the English into breaking out of their camp, saying 'that if they wished to come out of their place to do battle, [they] would withdraw and allow them to order their battle formation'.[34] But this, too, failed to budge the English. Eventually, with night falling, the French returned to their camp. The next morning, at 6 a.m., the English army left the battlefield, marching first to Senlis and then to Paris.

Perhaps the two armies knew each other too well. While there is no doubt that the French definitely wanted to engage the English in battle at Montépilloy, they were wise enough not to try to charge into the English fortified lines, as Sir John Stewart had, with disastrous consequences, at the battle of the Herrings. Instead, they stayed in their own formation, trying to weaken the English resolve until they had abandoned their field fortification. It did not work, and, ultimately, the English, who were unable to provoke the French into an attack of their own, retreated from the battlefield. While, technically, victory at Montépilloy must be given to the French, it was a hollow victory. Although the submission of Anglo-Burgundian towns continued, with Senlis, Beauvais, Creil, Pont-Sainte-Maxence, and several others surrendering to the French by the end of August,[35] and problems in Normandy drove Bedford from Paris to Rouen in order to quell a growing rebellion there,[36] a 'true' victory at Montépilloy might have meant the submission of Paris, and this would have kept Joan's military record free from defeat.

Four hours after the English had retreated from Montépilloy, Charles VII also left the battlefield, returning first to Crépy-en-Valois and then traveling to Compiègne. Officially, he was there to receive the town's surrender. But, because of the luxury afforded to him by Compiègne's royal residence, Charles decided to stay on for several days. (He actually remained in the town until 28 August.) Before long, Joan, who was still with the king, became impatient. Undoubtedly, the French counted the engagement at Montépilloy as a victory, and they probably knew that Bedford had moved to Rouen. Joan must have believed that if Paris was to be attacked, this was the time to do it. She had never been in favor of delay as a military strategy, and especially as Philip the Good had not kept his promise to surrender Paris to them, it was time for the French army to push towards the city and attack it. Once again, she found herself dissatisfied with the military leaders placed over her and petitioned the king to allow her to march an army to Paris. Perceval de Cagny writes:

> When the king found himself at Compiègne, the Maid was very saddened by the sojourn which he wished to make. And it seemed by this that he was content with what the grace of God had given him without attempting any other undertaking. She appealed to the duke of Alençon and said to him: 'My fair duke, equip your men and those of the other captains. By my Martin, I want to go to see Paris from closer than I have ever seen it.[37]

The dean of the Collegiate Church in Metz reports that La Trémoïlle spoke against such a venture, but that the king allowed Joan to go anyway.[38] So, on 23 August, Joan left Compiègne, together with her co-leaders in the Loire campaign, Alençon, the duke of Bourbon, the counts of Vendôme and of Laval, the lord d'Albreth, the two marshals of France, the lords de Rais and Boussac, La Hire, Ponton de Xantrailles, and an unknown number of soldiers.[39] While seemingly not a large army, it was increased in numbers by those soldiers who had been sent to receive the surrender of Senlis and who then joined Joan as she passed by that city on her way to Paris.[40]

It took three days to march to the suburbs of Paris, which Joan and her troops did without facing any resistance, and on the night of 26 August, she lodged in Saint-Denis, in sight of the massive Parisian walls.[41] (She would later locate her camp at La Chapelle, a small village between Saint-Denis and Paris.) Joan's purpose in choosing Saint-Denis as the location of her attack on Paris is obvious. This suburb housed the basilica of Saint-Denis in which the bones of so many earlier French kings lay. It was a symbol of her mission, to return all of France, including Paris, to the French, for whom Charles VII had only the month before been crowned as their king. That the English and Burgundians had not chosen to defend this suburb and its basilica, but to retire behind the walls of Paris, shows that they did not hold the site in the same esteem.

Seemingly unknown to Joan and her colleagues was the ambassadorial journey that was then being made to Philip the Good by Archbishop Regnault of Chartres and other French legates. At the very time that she was marching south to Paris, the archbishop was making offers to the duke of Burgundy that would certainly have angered the Maid. In reparation for the murder of the duke's father, John the Fearless, for which Charles VII suddenly seems to have taken responsibility, and in order to keep the Burgundians out of the war which he intended to fight against the English, the king was willing to allow Philip to set his own requirements. A few days later, when a Burgundian legation traveled to Compiègne to state what those requirements were, Charles willingly surrendered Compiègne, Senlis, Creil, and Pont-Sainte-Maxence, all four having surrendered themselves only recently to the king. In return, Philip promised a four-month truce during which both sides promised not to attack or receive in surrender the towns of the other. Philip also promised to remain neutral in the Anglo-French conflict during that same period. A truce was signed on 28 August.[42] (Yet, at the same time that he was negotiating this truce with France, this duplicitous Burgundian duke was making plans with the English to increase the number of Burgundian soldiers who would oppose the French once his truce with them had ended; in return Philip was to receive the counties of Champagne and Brie and the office of lieutenant of France, making him second only to Bedford in authority over the English holdings there.[43])

Why did Charles VII's attitude towards his Burgundian cousin change between his coronation and the end of August? Not a month earlier, it was Philip the Good who had seemed willing to offer almost anything to the French to make peace with them. Then Philip had retreated from his most major concession of that truce, the surrender of Paris, thus necessitating the attacks which Joan was about to make on that city. Now, it seems, it was Charles who was willing to offer almost anything to enter into a peace with

Philip. Why? The answer can only lie in the fact that Charles, having received his desired coronation, was more than willing to listen to the advice of his more diplomacy-oriented counselors. While Joan of Arc and others had been calling for a more intensive push to regain all of France, Georges de la Trémoïlle, Regnault of Chartres, and perhaps others, were advising the king to slow down his military efforts and make peace with the duke of Burgundy before marching his army against the English. In addition, Joan was continuing to make a pest of herself. If Monstrelet is correct, at Montépilloy she had called for an attack on the fortified English line against everyone else's better judgement[44] and no matter how many soldiers it might have cost to defeat it. But the tactics of the other French leaders at that battle had prevailed, and the English had fled the field, giving the French victory, or so it was believed. Then, there was the problem of her impatience at Compiègne. Her desire to march quickly against Paris had split the army and its leadership, no doubt creating an embarrassing situation for a king who was trying to make peace no matter what the cost with the man who was the titular leader of that city. Charles may have been willing to indulge her eagerness and impatience when the goal was something he desired, such as his coronation, but when it was something he was the least bit unsure of, as the capture of Paris seems to have been, he was unwilling to support her much at all. Thus it was that Joan and her army were going into an engagement in which they not only fought the English, but also the apathy of their monarch. This fact may in part explain why in the end she was not able to fulfil this 'task' of her mission.

Unquestionably, Joan's attacks on the walled towns of Jargeau, Meung-sur-Loire, and Beaugency were impressive affairs, and their success greatly increased her military leadership skills. Mistakes made at Jargeau were not repeated at Meung or Beaugency, for example. But it is questionable whether those attacks could have taught Joan how to wage a successful assault against Paris. For one thing, the Parisian city walls were enormous, no doubt the largest and strongest in France, if not in all of Europe west of Constantinople. The ones that Joan faced had been rebuilt fairly recently. In the late fourteenth century, King Charles V, enjoying a time of peace in the Hundred Years War, had spent a fortune on the strengthening of these fortifications. In 1429, the Parisian walls were around 8 meters in height, topped with wall-walks and arrow-

slits. Every 110–120 meters along the walls stood strong
rectangular towers that rose high above them. Six gates pierced the
walls into the city. These, the Saint-Antoine, Temple, Saint-Martin,
Saint-Denis, Montmartre, and Saint-Honoré, were all protected by
massive gate-houses – the Saint-Honoré gate, which would receive
Joan's most determined assault, is known from archaeological
excavations to have measured 18.5 meters by 8.34 meters – with
angular towers, arrowslits, gunports, murder-holes, portcullises, and
drawbridges built into them, their chambers capable of garrisoning
a large number of soldiers. Still, gates were generally considered the
weak points in any urban fortifications, because they had to be
made to allow traders, merchants, travelers, and others access.
Therefore, boulevards, like those which had been the focal point of
Joan's attacks at Orléans, had been constructed in front of most of
these gates. All along the walls and throughout the towers and
gatehouses were mounted a large number of gunpowder weapons.
Often only small in caliber, these would still assist in the defense of
the city by disrupting artillery fire from or charges made by the
attackers. Also around the Paris city walls was a moat, 3 meters
deep and 32 meters in width in some places (again confirmed by
archaeology) and, depending on the level of the Seine, filled with
water.[45] The entire fortification was a formidable defensive structure,
built as much to intimidate any enemy into *not* attacking as it was
to defend against any onslaught. Jean Chartier maintains that Joan
'was not well informed about the large amount of water in the
moat' nor about the fortifications surrounding the city, but she
would not be intimidated by them.[46]

In addition, Paris was awfully large, especially in comparison
with the more southern locales that Joan had conquered. While she
never did surround Jargeau, Meung-sur-Loire, or Beaugency, once
she had captured, or threatened to capture, just one part of the
walls of those towns, she could practically guarantee that the town
would fall. And each time it did. Of course, at Paris there was also
no way that the city walls could be completely surrounded, so an
attack against only one section had to be attempted. But should that
section of wall fall, would the rest of Paris surrender as well? In the
case of John the Fearless's successful assault on Paris in 1418, only
one part of the fortifications had fallen and then the city followed
afterwards, but John had a large number of Armagnac supporters
within Paris whom he could count on for assistance.[47] For Joan,

there was no indication of similar Parisian assistance; in fact, rumors of Joan's 'atrocities' had been spread throughout the city.[48]

Finally, while Joan had never faced an army larger than 700–800 – at Jargeau, with much smaller numbers at Meung and Beaugency – Paris's defending garrisons were much larger. Although exactly how many defenders there were in Paris is not recorded, most of these men would have responded to any attack that she made on the walls. It was going to be a hard and lengthy military adventure.

None of this deterred the Maid. When she undertook this attack, as she had those on the Loire, she believed that God would assist her, and this belief led her to assume that he had a means for the great city to fall. But God would not help those who would not help themselves, so on 26 August, shortly after she had arrived outside Paris, she began to try to discover where the walls were the weakest. This was done, according to Perceval de Cagny, who again witnessed the engagement, by sending out skirmishers 'each day, two or three times a day'. They rode or marched up to the base of the gates or walls, 'one time in one place, and then another'. No day passed without Joan sending out these skirmishers, and in this way, she 'very willingly studied the situation of the town of Paris, and with this, which place seemed to her to be the best for making an assault'.[49] Jean Chartier adds that during these early days, Joan also bombarded the walls continually with her cannon and couleuvrines.[50] This was done less in the hope of breaching the targeted walls or killing the soldiers defending them, than with the intention of weakening the resolve of those defenders.

Yet, carrying out more than these skirmishes was impossible without the permission of the king. At least that seems to have been the order given her when she petitioned Charles to allow her to take an army to Paris. Charles VII's arrival was anticipated daily, but he had still not appeared by the end of August. On 1 September, the duke of Alençon rode north to discover where he was and when he would arrive in Saint-Denis so that the attack could proceed. He found Charles in Senlis, having moved there, Cagny writes, 'with great regret', once he had discovered that the French troops led by Joan were camped in La Chapelle.[51] Alençon was told that the king would leave the following day for Saint-Denis, and he returned with that welcome news to Joan and the others. But the king did not come south. On 5 September, Alençon again rode north. The king still had not moved from Senlis. This time, Alençon was able to persuade him to travel to Saint-Denis; in fact, it seems that the duke refused to leave without the king in tow. On 7 September, Charles VII arrived in Saint-Denis, and he and the military leaders there determined that on the following day the attack on Paris, which seemingly had been planned for almost a week, would begin.[52]

Early on 8 September, Joan led her forces – knights, men-at-arms, and archers – to her predesignated place of attack, the Saint-Honoré gate. They began by bombarding the walls with their gunpowder weapons and by throwing large bundles of sticks, wood, carts, and barrels into the moat. She, Gilles de Rais, Raoul de Gaucourt and others prepared to lead the main assault against the gate, with Cagny writing that she 'took her standard in her hand and was among the first to enter the moat near to the Pigmarket'. He continues:

> The attack was hard and long, and it was a marvel to hear the sound and noise of the cannon and couleuvrines which those inside fired at those outside, and all manner of missiles in such a great multitude as to be innumerable. And although the Maid and a great number of knights, squires, and other soldiers had descended into the moat at the edge or around there, very few were wounded. And there were many on foot and on horse which were struck and knocked to the ground by blows from cannon stones, but by the grace of God and the presence of the Maid, not any man was killed or was wounded who was not able to return to his side and his tent without aid.[53]

(Clément de Fauquembergue, on the other hand, insists that many French soldiers were wounded and killed by gunfire at Saint-Denis.[54] Fauquembergue is most certainly correct.) As the day wore on, the French began to tire. Then Joan was wounded:

> And after sunset, the Maid was struck by a crossbow bolt in the thigh. And since she was so struck, she forced herself to cry more strongly that each man should approach the walls and that they should take that place. But because it was night and she was wounded and the men-at-arms were fatigued from the long assault which they had made, the lord of Gaucourt and others came and took the Maid, and, against her will, they took her out

of the moat. And thus the assault ended. And she had very great regret to have thus departed, saying 'by my Martin, the place should have been taken'. They put her on her horse and took her to her tent in La Chapelle.[55]

From inside the city there was another kind of reaction to the end of the day's fighting, and hence the Bourgeois of Paris's decidedly different and more hostile response:

On the eve of the Nativity of Our Lady in September, the Armagnacs came to attack the walls of Paris, which they hoped to take by assault. But what they won by conquest was only sadness, shame, and mischief, because many of them were wounded for the rest of their lives, who, before the assault, were quite healthy. But a fool does not fear so long as he is successful. I say that to those who were filled with such a large amount of bad luck and such evil belief. I say that to a creature who was with them in the form of a woman, who they called the Maid. Who was it? God knows.

On the day of the Nativity of Our Lady, they came together, all of one accord, to attack Paris on that day. And they assembled at least twelve thousand or more, and came around the hour of High Mass, between eleven and twelve, their Maid with them, and a large number of wagons, carts, and horses, all filled with great bundles of sticks in three lines, to fill the moat of Paris. And they began to make their attack between the Saint-Honoré gate and the Saint-Denis gate, and they made a very savage attack, and during the attack they said said many vile insults to the Parisians: 'You must surrender to us quickly, for Jesus's sake, for if you do not surrender yourselves before it becomes night, we will invade you by force, willing or not, and you will be put to death without mercy.' 'See here,' said one [of the Parisians], 'bawd! wench!' And he shot a bolt from his crossbow right at her, and it pierced her leg straight through, and she fled. Another completely pierced the foot of the man carrying her standard. When he felt himself wounded, he raised his visor and looked to draw the bolt from his foot, and another shot hit him between the eyes, and he was mortally wounded. Then the Maid and the duke of Alençon swore that they would rather have lost forty of their better men at arms in their company.

The attack was very violent, on the one side and then the other, and lasted until four hours after noon, without knowing which one would be the better. A little after four o'clock, the Parisians became confident in themselves, so that they fired their cannon and other artillery so many times that the army charging at them recoiled and stopped their attack, and they left. As they were leaving, it became even more disastrous, for the Parisians had a large cannon which fired from the Saint-Denis gate as far as all the way to Saint-Lazare [about a kilometer]. This they fired into their backs, which was very terrible. Thus was it put to an end.[56]

Despite the failed and fatiguing efforts of the previous day, the French army rose early on 9 September, prepared to assault the walls of Paris again. Even Joan, wounded as she was, woke with the intention of carrying on the struggle. Cagny reports that she 'sent for the fair duke of Alençon, by whom she would be led, and asked him to sound the trumpets and mount the horses to return to Paris. And she said, by her Martin, that she never wanted to leave there until she had taken that town.'[57] She was further encouraged by the arrival of the count of Montmorency and fifty to sixty 'gentlemen' (presumably cavalry), who had defected from the city, wishing to fight with her and the French army against their former allies.[58] But as these leaders prepared their soldiers for a new assault on the walls, they were stopped by the appearance of René of Anjou, the duke of Bar, and Charles, the count of Clermont, who had come from Charles VII to summon Joan to a royal interview in Saint-Denis. The Maid was understandably irritated by this interruption, but she was even more angry when she discovered that the king had ordered the destruction of a bridge which Alençon had built across the Seine to allow for another section of the Parisian walls to be attacked. There is no indication that that attack was to have taken place on that day, despite the supposition by many modern historians that it would[59] – the bridge was actually destroyed on 12 September, claims Perceval de Cagny, which disrupted the French retreat plans. Her anger increased even more when she found that the king had also decided to postpone any further military action against the city until he could first hold a council meeting to discuss whether it was wise to continue with Joan's operation there.[60] In the end, it was decided by the council, over the vehement objections of Joan, Alençon, and others, not to carry out further attacks on Paris. No details of the discussion are found in contemporary sources, although Jacques Bouvier does remark that 'the Lord of La Trémoïlle had caused the soldiers to return to Saint-Denis'.[61] (The official reason given for the retreat, as found in the *Chronique* of Jean Lefèvre de Saint-Rémy, was that 'the king saw that the town of Paris was too strongly fortified' to risk further attacks.[62]) Thus it seems that the French faction in favor of peace and a diplomatic solution to the war had prevailed. After so often trying in vain to thwart Joan of Arc's military mission, La Trémoïlle finally achieved his goal at Paris.

On Saturday 12 September, the French army retreated from Paris. However, it did not return to the north, to Senlis or Compiègne, but to the Loire, from where its journey had started more than two months earlier.[63] The towns and villages along the roads to Reims and Paris which had willingly and without resistance surrendered themselves to Joan and the king were given small garrisons commanded by captains not associated with her conquests on the Loire or elsewhere.[64] Many of these were returned by violent means into the hands of their former occupiers, some with dire consequences for their citizens who so recently had enthusiastically joined Joan's cause. This was, for most of them, treason of the highest degree, and they suffered greatly for putting their trust in the new French king. Even more significantly for Joan, on 21 September, once the king had returned safely to his royal lodgings at Gien, he dissolved the army that had enabled his coronation to take place.[65] Finally, to make matters worse for the Maid, Charles discharged her best friend and military confidant, the duke of Alençon, and sent him back to his wife and family. Later, Alençon would request that Joan join him in some military operations against the English in Normandy, which he was conducting in conjunction with another old friend of hers, Arthur de Richemont, but that request was denied. Perceval de Cagny, who went with the duke, writes:

> Lord Regnault de Chartres, the lord of La Trémoïlle, and the lord of Gaucourt, who governed the body of the king and the waging of the war, did not wish to consent to this, nor make, nor suffer that the Maid and the duke of Alençon be together. [The duke] was never to see her again.[66]

While Joan was convalescing with her wound, she had also been stripped of her friends and her power. Cagny sums up the situation succinctly: 'And thus were the will of the Maid and the army of the king broken.'[67]

Before she left Saint-Denis, Joan had placed a white suit of armor in the basilica of Saint-Denis as a votive offering in gratitude to God for the victories that He had given her so far. She had taken this from a Burgundian knight whom she defeated at Paris. Later, she testified that it was placed in the church 'in devotion, as was the custom among men of arms when they are wounded. And because she was wounded before the town of Paris, she offered it to Saint-Denis, because that is the war-cry of France.'[68] (Jean Chartier claims that after the French retreated from Paris, the English troops pillaged Saint-Denis and found the arms that Joan had left in the basilica 'which were taken away by order of the bishop of Thérouanne, chancellor of those obeying the king of England, without making any recompense to the said church, which was a sacrilege'. Still, it persists in French histories of Joan of Arc that this suit of armor remained in the basilica until at least the late seventeenth century, if not until today.[69]) This was practically the final war-cry that Joan would be allowed to make; indeed, it was the last she would be able to make on behalf of her mission.

What happened at Paris? Was Joan to blame for the loss there? Did she give in to overconfidence or even pride in her military abilities? Using words found in the *Journal du siège d'Orléans*: did 'she wish to attack such a strong town and so well stocked with men and artillery, simply because it was the city of Paris',[70] when she should have been content with the two tasks of her mission which she had already completed, the relief of Orléans and the crowning of the king? Perhaps she should have returned to Domrémy and a life with her family and friends, or have remained at court, content with the limited military action in which the king wished her to take part. Of course, this presupposes that Paris could not have been conquered. Joan certainly felt that it was vulnerable. After reconnoitering the Parisian fortifications, it seems that she and the other military leaders there had made a plan – a plan that they were confident would succeed. But then came the first of many frustrations in executing this plan. The king had failed to come to the battlefield when he said he would. Initially halted by his apathy, Alençon was eventually to gain his attendance, although 'with regret', but once there, Charles continued to be uninterested in Joan's military affairs, allowing himself to be swayed by equally uninterested advisors. This frustration affected Joan's attitudes and behavior. The duke of Alençon's testimony, that 'he had seen her at Saint-Denis . . . with her sword drawn, chase a girl [no doubt a prostitute] who was with the soldiers so that she broke her sword',[71] which was given by him at her nullification trial to emphasize her spirituality and devotion to God, just as easily could be seen as an example of her attempts to understand why God had not intervened with Charles VII to change his mind about her warfare at Paris. It appears that she wanted to purify her troops and their surroundings until God forced the king to accede to her will.

When the planned attacks on Paris were allowed to go forth, they were predictably violent and lengthy, but French morale did not wane, even when Joan of Arc was wounded. Instead, if Perceval de Cagny can be believed, on 9 September, Joan's troops were ready to begin their fighting again for a second day. They knew that it would take more than a single day to capture such a large and important city. So, too, did the military leadership which, having built a bridge across the Seine, expected to be able to launch attacks against other sections of the walls. The strategy was diverse and well planned, but they knew it would take some time to work.[72] These plans were not allowed to reach fruition. The king's apathetic impatience and propensity for what in the end proved to be bad counsel meant the halting of all attempts to take the city. Who knows whether Paris might have fallen if time had been allowed for Joan's long-term military strategy to be put into effect. It was, as the *Journal du siège d'Orléans* says, 'a strong town and so well-stocked with men and artillery'. But Joan's confidence and determination, coupled with her disregard for the lives of her soldiers, whom she thought would become martyrs if they sacrificed their lives for her mission, had brought many victories against 'invincible' foes before. Paris might have been the next one.

8

The End of a Military Leader

Joan of Arc was clearly not to blame for the defeat at Paris. But this was not the prevailing opinion in Charles VII's court. Joan had failed, and her failure cast doubt on the divinity of her mission. It also cast doubt on the tactical method that she had used to gain her Loire victories and that she had also employed against the Saint-Honoré gate at Paris. It had cost France many men to attack the Parisian walls, and it had gained them nothing. Over the objections of numerous military leaders, the king had listened to the overly cautious advice of Georges de la Trémoïlle, Regnault de Chartres, and others, and, at least for a few months following the Paris débâcle, it seemed to him and others that he had been correct in listening to that advice. While Joan had been victorious, others had been able to replace La Trémoïlle in Charles's favor, but after she had lost at Paris, and had been badly wounded in the process, the former king's favorite returned to his chief counselor position with even greater power and influence. For example, no one received more pay from the king for his military and diplomatic service on the road to Reims and around Paris; indeed, his pay far exceeded that of any of the major military leaders – for example, La Trémoïlle received 5,890 *livres tournois* in comparison to Joan's 479.[1] During the march northwards to the coronation and Paris, he had continually cautioned the king to move slowly so that he would not bring Philip the Good, the duke of Burgundy, more actively into the fray. Undoubtedly, although not always recorded as such in contemporary sources, La Trémoïlle was the author of the numerous peace negotiations held between Charles and Philip during this time. As La Trémoïlle became more desperate to stop the Maid, the peace proposals to the Burgundians became more generous, until Charles's advantages in the north were practically erased; much to the disappointment and suffering of those who had accepted him as their new king and had submitted their towns to his rule. It would be in attempting to preserve and defend the allegiance of one Compiègne, of those towns that had surrendered to the French king, that Joan would finally meet her military end.

Once they had returned to the Loire, La Trémoïlle continued to caution Charles VII against attempting military adventures that might hamper his hopes of a reunited Franco-Burgundian realm. Even after Philip proved time and time again not to adhere to many of the peace accords and truces made with the French, or when he did adhere to them, to also be dealing with the English on the side, La Trémoïlle continued to try to manage the French war effort to the benefit of his diplomacy. Thus, once Joan recovered from her wounds, La Trémoïlle was able to persuade the king to send her to a less significant theater of operations, along the southern (or upper) Loire, where she would not be able to offend the Burgundians. That her targeted opponent was a mercenary captain, Perrinet Gressart, who had once imprisoned the counselor, causing him to pay a heavy ransom from his personal funds for his freedom, no doubt also played a role in the decision to send the Maid there.

In October 1429, after having healed her wounded leg, but certainly not her spirits, Joan departed for Saint-Pierre-le-Moutier. Her army, of which she was only a minor commander, was woefully undersupplied. Nor was she enthusiastic about the task assigned to her. She was not to fight the English, nor even the Burgundians. She was instead headed to an area controlled by the leader of a free company, Perrinet Gressart. It is true that Gressart was effectively in the service of the Burgundians and the English and had received funds from them to control what he did in central France.[2] But he was a soldier for hire. He had fought previously for the Burgundians and the English and even, on occasion, for the French. Had the English and the Burgundians lost Paris and been pushed back into Normandy and Burgundy, they would probably have forgotten about Gressart, and he would also probably have been looking for a new employer. Surely, he could have been 'enticed' to abandon his Loire territories, or at least to rule them as a French governor instead of an Anglo-Burgundian one. He was, in fact, little more than an irritant in this phase of the Hundred Years War, and Joan was greatly underutilized as the means of removing him. Not only was her war *materiél* low, but so too were her spirits.

Gressart was one of the last members of what in the Hundred Years War was becoming a dying breed.[3] Leaders of the free

companies, mercenary captains, were quite numerous during the
fourteenth century. Men such as John Hawkwood and Robert
Knolles led armies of mercenaries who fought for whomever would
pay them, while supplementing their income with whatever booty
they could gain; even the great Bertrand du Guesclin, revered by
Joan of Arc for his French patriotism and fighting ability, fought in
Spain against the Black Prince as the leader of a free company in
the employ of the eventually victorious Henry of Trastamara.[4]
Such employment was profitable, if they survived. They led skilled
warriors who fought for them loyally and with frequent victories.
But they remained leaders only until they began to be defeated,
and then their troops sought new leadership.[5] However, during the
fifteenth century mercenary captains were rare in France. Possibly
this was because of the lack of funds available to the principal
warring parties: England, France, and Burgundy. Possibly it was
the lack of booty available in a country that had suffered almost a
century of constant warfare. Possibly it was because the more
profitable military employment had shifted to Italy and the Holy
Roman Empire. Whatever the reason, Perrinet Gressart was one of
the last, and it was decided late in 1429 that he should be engaged
by Joan and a small French army.

Gressart's holdings were impressive if not widespread. A
Picardian by birth, he had been encouraged in his leadership by his
experiences fighting with Duke John the Fearless in the early phases
of the Armagnac-Burgundian civil war. Although probably not
awarded such officially, he declared himself a noble in 1417 and
created a coat-of-arms – a fess with three cinquefoils – under which
he fought the rest of his days. Like most mercenary captains, he was
paid to perform military service, in this case by the Burgundians
early on, but became rich on what he stole or pillaged from the
areas he raided. (Only rarely did these captains do anything more
dangerous than raiding during warfare.) By 1426, he was wealthy
enough to purchase a small fortress, La Motte-Josserand, which he
used as a base, and he began to call himself the 'lord of La Motte-
Josserand'. From that fortified location and under the cover of the
campaign of Earl Thomas Montagu of Salisbury, Gressart had
stretched out his holdings into the surrounding countryside. He
soon captured towns such as Saint-Pierre-le-Moutier, Cosne, Bonny,
Dompierre, and La Charité-sur-Loire. Into this last town, with its
large monastery and strong castle surrounded by formidable town

walls, Gressart moved his forces and set up his headquarters. It was an ideal place, for not only was it strongly fortified, but it also protected a vital section of the Loire, one that catered to merchants – whom Gressart could tax heavily – as well as to armies. It was also central to his land holdings.

Gressart had first come to the notice of the French as more than a minor player in 1427 when it appears that first Arthur de Richemont and then Georges de la Trémoïlle tried to stop the raids he was conducting into the neighboring counties of Berry and Nevers. On one occasion and despite having a writ of 'safe-conduct' to protect him, La Trémoïlle had been captured by Gressart as he travelled to La Charité to negotiate with the mercenary captain. To gain his freedom, La Trémoïlle was forced to pay a ransom of 14,000 écus, an incredibly large amount, to give gifts and praise to Gressart's wife, and to grant a pardon to his captor. It must have been extremely embarrassing, as well as economically punishing, to the egotistical French courtier. In fact, it seems that he never forgot the indignity or the insult.[6] The official reason for Joan's campaign against Gressart's territory was, as given by Jean d'Aulon at Joan's nullification trial, 'that it was very necessary to recover the town of La Charité, which was held by the enemy, but that it was important first to capture the town of Saint-Pierre-le-Moutier, which was also held by the enemy'.[7] But there can be little doubt that revenge for La Trémoïlle's imprisonment, ransom, and embarrassment was also a factor. (The ironic hypocrisy of La Trémoïlle using for this task an individual, the Maid, whose past methods he had shown such disdain for, probably does not need to be noted.)

Many of the details of Joan's campaign on the upper Loire cannot be known, for the sources on her life are fewer for this period; some of the more complete ones for the earlier events, like the *Journal du siège d'Orléans* and the *Chronique de la Pucelle*, have given out all together by this point, with the authors of others, such as Perceval de Cagny's chronicle, removed from her presence and seemingly unable to know or discover enough about what occurred at Saint-Pierre-le- Moutier and La Charité to write much down. In addition, with the exception of Jean d'Aulon, Joan's squire, and Reginald Thierry, who was along as an army surgeon, none of the witnesses at her nullification trial testified about the campaign – and these two only spoke about her victory at Saint-Pierre-le-Moutier, not about her defeat at La Charité, which is perhaps more of a comment on what the judges at that trial were concerned with (her victories) than what was known by the witnesses.

She set out from Bourges late in October, but the exact date is unknown. With her was an army, its size unknown, although Aulon's phrase 'a certain number of men', 'does not', in the words of J.-L. Jaladon de la Barre, 'imply the idea of a very important army'.[8] Joan was not in charge of the expedition: that responsibility fell to Charles d'Albret, the lieutenant-general for the county of Berry and half-brother to Georges de la Trémoïlle. However, it is certain that she wielded great authority. Also along as a military leader was Louis of Bourbon, the count of Montpensier. Although Albret had participated in some of Joan's previous military ventures, principally along the road to Reims and in the north, Montpensier was new to the Maid. Later, the marshal de Boussac, an old ally of Joan's, would also join the campaign.[9]

The first target of the journey was one of Gressart's southernmost towns, Saint-Pierre-le-Moutier. The reason for choosing this as the first site of campaign against Gressart is not known, although it may simply have been because of its geography: lying quite far south and away from the River Loire might have made it difficult for Gressart to reach it with reinforcements. It might also have increased the element of surprise, which could prove advantageous to the French. Still, when the next target was La Charité-sur-Loire, Gressart's base, keeping away from the mercenary captain does not seem to have been a strategy. Presumably, had La Charité also fallen, the other of Gressart's holdings, Dompierre, Cosne, and Bonny would have been Joan's next destinations, either for attack or to accept their capitulation. But that, too, is speculation.

Because it is not known when Joan and her French army left Bourges, it is also not known when she began her siege of Saint-Pierre-le-Moutier. It was before 1 November, as news of the siege being undertaken there had reached Charles VII by that time.[10] Saint-Pierre-le-Moutier was not a large town, more the size of a village really, but it was surrounded by a wall, with a deep moat, six flanking towers, and three fortifed gates, all of which had been augmented and repaired in 1421.[11] In the center stood (in fact, still stands) a beautiful Romanesque church dedicated to St Peter; also within the walls stood a Benedictine monastery dedicated to the same saint. In addition, Saint-Pierre-le-Moutier seems to have been sparsely populated, with most of its inhabitants having fled from the town to avoid the bloodshed and financial burdens imposed by Gressart. Nor does it appear that the self-styled 'lord of La Motte-Josserand' had left much of a garrison to watch over the location, although Aulon later testified that there were a 'large number of soldiers in the town'.[12]

Such a target should have been easy to attack, but the fact that it was walled, with few weaknesses in the walls, and that the French were undermanned and underarmed, especially in the gunpowder weapons which Joan had become so accustomed to using in her attacks on this type of site, meant that Saint-Pierre-le-Moutier proved to be more formidable than it should have been to such a force. By 4 November, it had still not fallen. Finally, according to Aulon, Joan took matters into her own hands and called for an attack that would capture the town:

And after the Maid and her soldiers had besieged [Saint-Pierre-le-Moutier] for some time, an order was given to attack the town. And thus an attack was made, and those who were there before the town tried to take it, but, because of the large number of soldiers in the town, and their great strength, and also the marvellous resistance which those inside gave, the French were compelled and forced to retreat. And at that time, he, who had been wounded by an arrow in his heel, such that he could not stand or walk without crutches, saw that the Maid and a very small number of her men and others had been left behind. And sure that harm would come to her, he mounted a horse and rode towards her, demanding to know why she had not retreated with the others. She, after taking her helmet from her head, responded to him that she was not alone, that she had in her company fifty thousand soldiers, and that she was not going to leave until she had taken the town. At that time, whatever she may have said, she did not have more than four or five men, as he knew for certain, and so do many others who also saw her. For which reason, he had said frankly that she should leave from there and retire to the rear with the rest. And then she said to him to get bundles of sticks and hurdles to make a bridge across the moat of the town so that it might be easier to make an approach. And when she said this she shouted in a loud voice: 'Everyone, to the faggots and hurdles to make a bridge!' which was soon after done and put into place. That such a thing was done was very astonishing, because afterwards the village was taken by assault, without finding there very much resistance.[13]

Saint-Pierre-le-Moutier was conquered, although not without a struggle. The French troops streamed into the town, and many wished to treat its capture violently. But Joan would not allow it. Reginald Thierry explained to the nullification tribunal:

When the town of Saint-Pierre-le-Moutier was captured by assault, where she was, the soldiers wished to do violence to the church and to steal the holy relics and other goods stored there. But Joan strongly prohibited this and defended the place, nor did she ever allow anything to be stolen.[14]

This could have been the soldiers' attitude as a result of the frustration of having to fight a tiresome battle to conquer the town, or perhaps this was what soldiers were accustomed to do after having taken a location that had not willingly surrendered to them. (One need only recall the aftermath of the conquest of Jargeau.) On the other hand, these may not have been soldiers who had fought with the Maid before; what they might have been accustomed to, she forbade. Her mission did not allow for abuses of the French population.

For a brief moment Joan had regained her confidence and military authority. Those with her, whether the four or five which Jean d'Aulon saw, or the 50,000 Joan claimed, all witnessed the kind of military action that had brought about the relief of Orléans, the recapture of Jargeau, Meung-sur-Loire, and Beaugency, the victory at the battle of Patay, the submission of many central and northern villages and towns, and the crowning of the king of France. But it would be the last time that anyone would witness such an event. Saint-Pierre-le-Moutier was the last of Joan's major victories.

The action at Saint-Pierre-le-Moutier had taken its toll on the French army. Its supplies were utterly depleted. Whatever disposable weapons, such as arrows, gunpowder, and cannonballs, which the forces had brought with them from Bourges the month previously, never very numerous, were now gone. And no one in Charles's court seems to have remembered to send Joan's army more. Bows without arrows, crossbows without bolts, and cannon without gunpowder or cannonballs were useless, especially against a strongly fortified and well-stocked town filled with soldiers who were not likely to surrender unless forced and who were led by a captain whose capture meant certain execution. Such was Joan's next

target, La Charité-sur-Loire. In desperation both Albret and Joan
sent letters to nearby towns asking for whatever assistance could be
granted them. Joan's letter to the town of Riom (dated 9 November
1429) still survives:

Dear and good friends, you know well how the city of Saint-
Pierre-le-Moutier was taken by assault, and with the help of God,
I have the intention of emptying the other places which are
hostile to the king. But, because of the great quantities of
gunpowder, arrows, and other equipment of war that were
expended before the said town, and because the lords who are in
this town and I are so poorly provided to besiege La Charité,
where we are going presently, I beseech you, that as you love the
good and honor of the king and also those others here, that you
would instantly send help for this siege, of gunpowder, saltpeter,
sulphur, arrows, heavy crossbows, and other equipment of war.
And do this so that, for lack of the said powder and other
equipment of war, the situation will not be prolonged, and that
you will not be said to be neglectful or rejecting. Dear and good
friends, may Our Lord watch over you. Written at Moulins on the
ninth day of November.

Jehanne[15]

Charles d'Albret's letters said essentially the same.[16]

The reasons for Joan's and her army's lack of success at La
Charité can be seen in these letters. The despair at having to fight
an offensive war when the army was completely unprepared can be
felt in the tenor of her words, if not seen absolutely in the letter
itself. Joan, it appears, had difficulty in condemning nearby
townspeople for not providing for her army, when the king and his
court seemed completely apathetic to the expedition. (The French
army was sent a large number of gunpowder weapons from Orléans
which they used in the siege, and they also received money from the
citizens of both Orléans and Bourges. What this was spent on,
however, is not reported.)[17]

And La Charité was going to be a more difficult conquest than
Saint-Pierre-le-Moutier, especially during the height of winter. The
weather was 'very harsh', writes Jacques Bouvier, as the French
army marched along the River Loire towards the Perrinet Gressart's

capital, something which certainly did not help raise the spirits of this undersupplied force.[18] Nor did matters improve once the army arrived, even after the appearance of the marshal of Boussac and reinforcements (especially as it seems that he brought no new supplies). La Charité could only be approached across its single bridge, and once that was crossed, the besiegers were forced to contend with a strong town wall built by Charles V and then a large castle complex, with several keeps, towers, and a huge inner courtyard which allowed for a large and well-stocked garrison to live quite comfortably; indeed, the soldiers inside were probably far more comfortable than their besiegers outside.[19]

The siege lasted for almost a month. Every day the French fired their 'bombards, cannon, and other artillery' from 'three or four places' across the river. But, although it appears that it was a single-sided bombardment, they made no headway. Eventually, they left without taking the town. So fatigued were they by the experience as a whole, the French did not even take away much of their artillery. With a long return march to the north over wet and frozen roads ahead, there probably seemed no point.[20] Joan's role in the siege is not known; the sources hardly even mention that she was present. For Perceval de Cagny, it is clear that the blame lay elsewhere: 'because the king had not paid to send victuals or money to maintain the army there, they decided to lift the siege and departed in great displeasure'.[21] Asked about the defeat at her trial, 'why had she not entered the town of La Charité, after she had a commandment from God to do so', Joan was indignant in her answer: 'Who said to you that I had a commandment from God to do so?' Later she testified 'that she wished to go into France, but that the men of arms told her that it was better to go first against the town of La Charité.'[22]

On Christmas Day 1429, Joan returned to Jargeau.[23] Waiting for her was news that she and her descendants had been ennobled, through both the male and female lines.[24] It was a consolation prize for what she wanted most: to be able to drive the English from France.

The early months of 1430 cannot have been pleasant ones for the Maid. Little is known about what she did during this time or even where she went. Her presence at court is not often recorded, nor is she said to have visited old friends, like Alençon or Richemont.[25] She wrote letters, it is known, as three written during these winter and early spring months still exist in one form or another. All show the growing desperation she felt at being stuck so far from the action. Two were written to the citizens of Reims. The first, dated 16 March, talks about the citizens' fear of being besieged. She mentions enemies from within and without the city who were conspiring to turn it over to the duke of Burgundy. Do not fear the Burgundians, she writes:

> Know well that you should not be at all distressed if I can confront them. If they come near, shut your gates, for I will be very direct with you: if they come there, I will make them fasten their spurs so fast that they will not know how to put them on and get out of there, and very quickly at that.[26]

The second, written twelve days later, on 28 March, seeks to clarify what she had written in the previous letter, especially concerning those inside the city who wished to surrender to Philip the Good. Again it promises assistance against those who conspire with the Burgundians:

> Very good and dear friends, may it please you to know that I have received your letters which mention the report to the king that in the good city of Reims there are many wicked people. If you want to know the real truth, this report said to him that there are many who are a part of a plot to betray the city and install the Burgundians. And since the king has learned that from you, it will not happen, and he is very pleased with you. Believe that you are high in his grace and that if you have to fight he will assist you in the event of any siege. He knows well that you have suffered much because of the hardships these treasonous Burgundian adversaries have imposed on you. So surrender yourselves to the will of God; rest assured that relief will be sent as soon as possible. I pray and require you, my dear friends, to guard your good city well for the king; keep good watch.[27]

However, the idea that she or Charles VII would go to Reims or anywhere in the north may only have been an idle threat. Charles had shown no signs of uprooting himself from his comfort on the Loire, even if it meant a repeat of his triumphs the year before. Nor does it seem that he would allow Joan to leave. Perhaps the Maid thought that she should try her luck fighting elsewhere for God. This may be why she had a letter written for her to the heretical Hussites who were fighting against their Catholic lords in Bohemia, dated 23 March 1430:

Jesus-Maria

For some time now, rumor and public information have reported to me, Joan the Maid, that from true Christians you have become heretics and that, like the Saracens, you have destroyed true religion and worship; embracing a shameful and criminal superstition and wishing to protect and propagate it, there is no shameful deed or belief you do not dare. You ruin the sacraments of the Church, you rend the articles of Faith, you destroy churches, you smash and burn the statues which have been erected as memorable monuments, you massacre Christians simply because they have kept the true Faith.

What is the frenzy? What rage or madness drives you? This Faith, which Almighty God, which is the Son, which the Holy Spirit have revealed, established, given sway and glorified a thousandfold through miracles is the faith which you persecute, which you wish to overturn and obliterate. You are blind, not because you lack foresight. Do you think that you will not be punished for this? Or do you not realize that God will block your criminal efforts? Do you think He will allow you to remain in darkness and error? The more you give yourselves over to criminal sacrilege, the more He will ready great punishment and torment for you.

As for myself, I tell you frankly that if I were not kept busy with these English wars I would have come to see you a long time ago. But if I do not hear that you have corrected yourselves, I may well leave these English and set off against you, so that, by the sword if I cannot otherwise, I may remove your madness and foul superstition, taking either your heresy or your lives. But if you choose instead to return to the Catholic faith and to the original source of light, send me your ambassadors and I shall tell them what you must do. If you do not wish to do so and persist in resisting the spur, recall how much criminal harm you have done and wait for me, who will deal with you comparably with the aid of divine and human force.[28]

Some wonder if this is Joan's letter or someone else's, who, writing in her name, sought to gain the legitimacy that she would bring to such a threatening epistle. Jean Pasquerel, her confessor, signed the letter, and it is possibly his work, for it seems unlikely that she would promise the citizens of Reims, both a week before and a few days later, that she would come running to them if they were attacked, were she thinking about the possibility of a crusade against the Hussites.[29] On the other hand, should Charles VII not have been willing to let her go to fight the Anglo-Burgundians in the north, she might have pondered the possibility of leaving from France and fulfilling *a* mission, if not *her* mission, elsewhere.

As seen in her letters to the inhabitants of Reims, Joan was not happy about the Burgundian attacks on French territory that she had won just a few months before. Nor could she have been pleased with the increased closeness of the English and Burgundians, news of which had spread everywhere throughout France by this time. But, then again, neither probably was the king or his counselors, especially Georges de la Trémoïlle and Regnault de Chartres, who had brokered the disadvantageous peace with Duke Philip the Good based on the promises of neutrality, if not alliance, which he had frequently given them.[30] What was Charles VII's response to the crisis? He went into council meetings to listen to the very people who had put him into this situation. (Eventually, he would have to accept the fact that he had been duped. In a letter, dated 6 May 1430, the king admitted his mistake in dealing so ignorantly with the duke of Burgundy. It was co-signed by Archbishop Regnault of Chartres.[31])

Then came the news in March 1430 that Philip was planning to lay siege to Compiègne. The people of the town which Charles VII had so quickly and willingly returned to the duke of Burgundy the September before had decided that they would not surrender to him. Like Tournai, Vaucouleurs, and Mont-Saint-Michel, Compiègne decided to remain French and that meant it was forced to resist military attempts to capture it.[32] The citizens of Compiègne began to stockpile supplies and weapons.

Such bravery in a people whom Joan had met just a short time before, but who like her were willing to do whatever they could to stay within the French realm, seems to have encouraged her that there was still hope, still a mission, even if she had to deal with political figures whose apathy was killing far more Frenchmen than any of her military exploits had. She decided not to wait for permission to travel north to aid the people of Compiègne. Sometime at the end of March, with a renewed confidence and determination to rid her land of the evil forces which occupied it, Joan simply left. Perceval de Cagny remarks:

> When the king was in the town of Sully-sur-Loire, the Maid, who had seen and heard all the fact and the manner that the king and his council planned for the recovery of his kingdom, and being very irritated concerning that, found a means of departing from them. And without the knowledge of the king, and not taking leave from him, she seemed to be gone on some business, but, without returning, she went to the town of Lagny-sur-Marne [on the road to Compiègne], because those of that place were making good war against the English in Paris and elsewhere.[33]

Of course, she was committing treason, and this may have been one of the reasons why Charles showed no desire to try to ransom her after her capture. But, who can blame Joan? She had reached the point when she was willing to betray the king whose throne she had helped obtain, to whom she had been so loyal, simply because she knew that she had to try to fulfil her mission, even if the king, who had played such an important part in that same mission earlier, was then too apathetic or too badly counselled to let her continue to fight on his behalf.

By 29 March, she was in Lagny, dated there by the miracle of her restoring the life of a baby long enough for it to be baptised, thereby earning it the right to be buried in holy ground.[34] At Easter, she was in Melun. There she reported that she had received a revelation that she would soon be captured.[35] She was at Senlis on 24 April.[36]

When she had begun her journey, Joan only had a few soldiers in her company, but throughout her journey she had acquired more men who wished to ride with 'the Maid'. Even though this force never became large, at each of these stops, she tried to engage the English in battle. But only at Lagny was she able to accomplish more than a few small skirmishes.

While there, Joan heard of a detachment of Anglo-Burgundian soldiers, numbering between 300 and 400, who had ridden out of Paris towards the north and were passing not far outside of Lagny.[37] They were commanded by a Burgundian, Franquet d'Arras, who,

Georges Chastellain writes, 'had not thought about nor wished for the honor of fighting a battle, except that the name of the Maid was so great and so famous'.[38] Such pride would prove to be his undoing. Joan's force was the larger, at more than 400, and it seems to have been mostly, if not entirely cavalry. Arras's troops were a mixture of men-at-arms and archers. There may also have been some surprise involved; either that or Arras was simply a poor leader, for according to Chastellain and Monstrelet, both Burgundian writers, he was never able to deploy his archers effectively, and, according to Jean Chartier, he formed his men with their backs to a hedge, affording them no room to fight or retreat.[39] The Maid charged down on these soldiers, 'courageously and vigorously', are the words Monstrelet uses.[40] The Anglo-Burgundians withstood two attacks, but they could not withstand a third. Almost all were killed or captured. Joan herself took Arras prisoner; she kept the sword which he presented her at his surrender until she herself was caught.[41] For a while, she kept Arras, too, wishing to trade him for a French prisoner, Jacquet Guillaume, but when she discovered that Guillaume had been executed, she surrendered Arras to the townspeople of Senlis, who, with Joan's consent, executed him for murder, theft, and treason.[42] Her consenting to Arras's execution would be used as evidence against her at her own trial a year later.[43]

Where else she travelled during her journey to Compiègne is not recorded but by 14 May, Joan had reached her goal. She may have arrived earlier, but this is the first date that her presence in the town is recorded, for on this date the town gave a reception in her honor. Also in attendance were Louis of Bourbon, the count of Vendôme, and Archbishop Regnault de Chartres, the latter – since his 6 May declaration of having been duped by the Burgundians – ostensibly repentant of his earlier disapproval of Joan's military methods, although only for the moment.[44] By this time, Philip the Good had begun his move on Compiègne in earnest.[45] Using funds provided by the English,[46] whose interest in seeing the return of Compiègne to Burgundian control is obvious, Philip amassed a large army and an impressive artillery train. To this date, there was no power with a stronger or more numerous gunpowder weaponry arsenal than the Burgundians.[47] And almost all of it was directed entirely at Compiègne and Joan. Contemporary chroniclers report the existence of at least five large bombards, two veuglaires, one large and one small, innumerable couleuvrines, and two 'engins' among the besieging Burgundian army;[48] other sources record the transportation of at least 17,000 lb of gunpowder with the artillery train.[49] Extant artillery comptes for the Burgundian forces have shown that these tallies are in fact too low.[50]

But this show of technological power did not intimidate either Joan or Guillaume de Flavy, the governor of Compiègne and leader of its defense effort. The fortifications of the town were very strong. The town walls were tall and thick; indeed, several still stand today as extremely impressive examples of medieval defensive power. More than 2,600 meters long, they surrounded a town of 53 hectares. A large number of towers had been built along these walls, with no fewer than forty-four of these towers running parallel to the Oise river. This river served as a 'moat' on one side of Compiègne, while its water also filled a wide and deep ditch surrounding the rest of the walls. A rampart, made from the dirt taken out of the ditch, added to the town's defenses as a counterscarp outside the moat. Should these defenses be breached, there was also a large royal castle, modelled after the Louvre in Paris, located within the walls. This castle functioned as a residence for Charles VII when he had stayed in the town after his coronation. The only weak defensive points seem to have been the numerous gates into the town through the walls – these were protected by large gatehouses – and the single bridge over the Oise, running 450 feet long and built on ten or eleven arches. This bridge was lined with houses and ended on the town's shore in a large fortified gate and on the shore opposite the town in a boulevard.[51] Additionally, the defenders of Compiègne had their own gunpowder weaponry arsenal, and they had prepared their defenses to use it by destroying any superfluous fortifications which hindered gunfire.[52] These guns would prove very effective, particularly, as reported by an anonymous eyewitness, 'the great number of small engines, called couleuvrines, which were made of bronze and which fired lead balls'. He even boasted that these balls were able to penetrate the armor of a man-at-arms.[53]

Joan was familiar with the use of gunpowder weapons, although most often to destroy walls, not to protect them. But staying behind protective walls was not her military style. Up to this point she had always been the aggressor, the attacker. At Compiègne, she was one of the town's defensive forces, and defense had never been a part of her tactical regimen. Thus on frequent occasions she sortied out against the attacking

Burgundian troops, or as Jean Chartier puts it, 'every day she fought large skirmishes against the English and Burgundians'.[54]

The first one of these sorties which proved to be a more major engagement took place at Choisy-au-Bac, a village surrounding a bridge crossing the Aisne river north-west of Compiègne a day or two after Joan had been welcomed there. Choisy was an important site; should the French be able to keep the Burgundians from capturing it, the likelihood of the latter surrounding Compiègne with troops and gunpowder weapons was slight. Therefore, Guillaume de Flavy had put the defense of the bridge under the command of his brother, Louis. Joan became involved when she discovered that the fighting there was harsh: she was never one to turn down a challenge. It was a see-saw affair, with heavy casualties taken on both sides, but eventually the continual bombardment of Burgundian gunpowder weapons against the make-shift French fortifications at Choisy proved to be too fierce, and, on 16 May, Joan, Louis de Flavy, and the other soldiers were forced to withdraw to Compiègne.[55]

Two days later, Joan, Archbishop Regnault de Chartres, and Louis of Bourbon decided to ride with their troops up the Aisne river, cross at the Soissons bridge, and try to maneuver behind and attack the rear of the Burgundian army. Such an attack probably would not have been able to prevent the siege of Compiègne, but it would have caused enough harassment and general mischief to make Philip the Good aware of Joan's presence and perhaps also to frighten these soldiers who had yet to face the Maid in battle. Yet, it was not allowed to succeed. Soissons was a French town, having surrendered the previous year to Charles VII, and its governor, Guichard Bournel, was a French appointee, having been assigned to that position as the king retreated to the Loire in the previous year. But neither the townspeople nor the governor there had the same desire as the Compiègnoise and Guillaume de Flavy to try to withstand Burgundian attempts at recapture. The herald of Berry, Jacques Bouvier, describes the incident:

And when they arrived at the town of Soissons, a Picardian squire named Guichard Bournel, who the count of Clermont, son of the duke of Bourbon, had made captain of the place, refused entry into the town to all those lords and men-at-arms, and he bought off the people of the town so that they thought that those lords and men-at-arms had come to be garrisoned with them, and the people were of the opinion that they did not want to entertain them in the town. The soldiers camped all night in the fields, and in the end, the captain did entertain the archbishop, the Maid, the count of Vendôme, and a small group of them.[56]

The following day, the French returned to Compiègne, frustrated in their efforts to fight the Burgundians by some who lacked their patriotism. A little while later, Bournel sold Soissons to the duke of Burgundy for 4,000 gold *saluts*.[57]

A day or so after her frustration at Soissons, Joan rode south to Crépy-en-Valois and returned with 300–400 more soldiers who had come to fight for the freedom of Compiègne. On her return, during the night of 22/3 May, she discovered that the town had been surrounded by Burgundian and English troops. According to Perceval de Cagny, Joan was forced to sneak into Compiègne without arousing the Anglo-Burgundians. This she accomplished successfully:

> Although her men said that she had few soldiers to pass through the army of the Burgundians and the English, she said: 'By my Martin, we are enough. I wish to see my good friends in Compiègne.' She arrived there about sunrise and without confusion nor disturbance from either herself or her men, they entered the town.[58]

The siege in its full intensity had begun. The knowledge that the Maid was inside the town made the Anglo-Burgundians wish to capture it even more. At the same time, those inside were strengthened by her presence, and they fought more vigorously because of her inspiration.[59] Joan herself did not rest, nor did she change her tactics. On 23 May, without even taking time to sleep after her daring entry into the town, she decided to act forcefully against the besiegers. Cagny again provides one of the best reports as to how Joan of Arc's last day as an active French soldier began:

> And around nine o'clock in the morning, the Maid heard that a large and forceful skirmish was being fought on the meadows outside of town [at Margny]. She armed herself and had her men arm themselves. They mounted their horses, and went out to join in the mêlée.[60]

Georges Chastellain describes the confidence in her appearance and her demeanor:

> She mounted her horse, armed as would a man, and adorned in a doublet of rich cloth-of-gold over her armor. She rode a grey steed, very handsome and very proud, and displayed herself in the armor and manners that a captain who led a large army would. And in that state, with her standard raised high and blowing in the wind, and accompanied by many noble men, around four hours before midday, she charged out of the town.[61]

She must have presented a great inspiration to those inside the town . . . and a great target to those besieging it.

There are three different versions of how she was captured. For Perceval de Cagny, giving what might be called the French version, Joan's tactic of direct assault seemed to have been well known, especially to a military leader as astute as Philip the Good. An ambush had been laid out in anticipation that she would do just what she did:

> And as soon as she came, the enemy was pushed back and put to flight. The Maid charged forward strongly into the Burgundian army. Those in the ambush saw their soldiers who were retreating in great disarray. Then they uncovered their ambush, and, spurring their mounts on, they placed themselves between the bridge into the town and the Maid and her company.

They were trapped, and Joan herself was targeted:

> And one party among those [of the Burgundians] turned toward the Maid in such a great number that those of her company could not hope to save her. And they spoke to the Maid: 'Take pains to return to the town, or you and we will be lost!'

But Joan refused to hear this, or to retreat:

> When the Maid heard them say this, she spoke to them very angrily: 'You be quiet! Their defeat depends on you. Think only of striking at them.' Even though she said this, her men did not want to believe it, and by force they made her return directly to

the bridge. And when the Burgundians and English saw that she was trying to return to the town, with a great effort, they came to capture the bridge. And there was a great clash of arms.

Fearing the onrushing enemy troops, Guillaume de Flavy did what he thought was needed to preserve the town. He shut the gate. But in doing so, he cut off the only means that Joan had to escape into the town:

> The captain of the place, seeing the great multitude of Burgundians and English about to enter the bridge, for fear that he would lose the place, had the bridge raised and the gate shut. And thus the Maid remained closed outside and a few of her men with her. When the enemy saw this all tried hard to capture her. She resisted very strongly against them, and in the end had to be taken by five or six together, the one putting his hand on her, the others on her horse, each of them saying, 'surrender yourself to me and give me your promise [her promise not to flee].' She responded: 'I will swear and give my promise to someone other than you and I will give an oath to him.' And saying other like things, she was taken to the tent of Jean de Luxembourg [the Burgundian leader of the men who captured Joan].[62]

Georges Chastellain's Burgundian interpretation of what occurred does not mention an ambush or the shutting of gates. While fighting bravely and strongly, Joan was taken simply because she was overwhelmed by the Burgundian troops:

> The Burgundians then pushed back the French towards their lodgings, and the French, with their Maid, began to retreat very slowly, as they had found no advantage over their enemies, but only danger and harm. Accordingly, the Burgundians, seeing that, and covered with blood and not satisfied by repulsing them in defense alone, as they were able to do them no more great harm than by following them closely, struck them courageously both on foot and on horse, and did much damage to the French. Then the Maid, surpassing the nature of a woman, took on a great force, and took much pain to save her company from defeat, remaining behind as the leader and as the bravest of the troop. But there fortune permitted for the end of her glory and for the

last time that she would ever carry arms. An archer, a rough and very sour man, full of much spite because a woman, who so much had been spoken about, should have defeated so many brave men, as she had done, grabbed the edge of her cloth-of-gold doublet, and threw her from her horse flat to the ground. Never was she able to find refuge nor to receive help from her soldiers, though they tried to assist her to become remounted. But a man-at-arms named the Bastard of Wandomme, who arrived just when she fell, so pressed near her, that she gave him her promise [surrendered to him], because he said that he was a nobleman.[63]

But Joan remembered it differently, testifying that she was captured fighting in a much more bellicose manner – making a direct, confident, and aggressive assault against her enemy. She mentions no ambush and no closed gates either:

She crossed over the bridge and through the French boulevard and went with a company of soldiers manning those sections against the lord of Luxembourg's men whom she drove back twice, all the way to the Burgundian camp, and a third time half way back. And then the English who were there cut her and her men off, coming between her and the boulevard, and so her men retreated. And withdrawing into the fields on her flank, in the direction of Picardy, near the boulevard, she was captured.[64]

So Joan was taken. Asked at her trial 'whether she had a voice tell her to leave' from Compiègne, she answered that 'on that day she did not know beforehand of her capture, nor did she have any order to leave. But it always had been said to her that she would become a prisoner.'[65] But how had she actually been taken? Was she ambushed? That depends on whether one accepts Cagny's record – he was not there – or Chastellain's – also not present, but supported by Enguerrand de Monstrelet, who was present, in his belief that Joan was overwhelmed by the Burgundian troops who attacked her – or Joan's – obviously present, but perhaps not the best able to remember what had put her into the position that she was in at the time that she related the story above.

Perhaps a more important question to ask, at least a question which has been asked by Joan of Arc scholars since the middle of the fifteenth century, is: was she locked out of Compiègne on purpose? In other words, was there treason involved in her capture? Jules Michelet, Alexandre Sorel, Eug. Bourguignon, and Paul Marin are of the strong opinion that she was betrayed by Guillaume de Flavy, the military leader in charge of Compiègne.[66] While, just as strongly, Jules Quicherat, Pierre Champion, and J.-B. Mestre believe that she was not.[67]

Both the accusers and defenders must in turn either indict or vindicate the character of Compiègne's governor, Guillaume de Flavy, and the role he played in shutting off any escape possibility for Joan of Arc on that day. The question of Flavy's treason is an old one. Joan was supposed to have told her 'Burgundian' neighbor, Gérardin l'Épinal, at Châlons that 'she feared nothing except treason',[68] and as early as 1450, some authors were turning this into a prophetic remark tied to her capture at Compiègne. Within a century, that Compiègne treason was assigned to Flavy. The debate became even more intense after the mid-nineteenth-century discovery by Jules Quicherat of Perceval de Cagny's *Chronique*, and Cagny's explicit statement that it had been the 'captain of Compiègne' who 'had the bridge raised and the gate shut'.[69]

It is known that the duke of Burgundy used bribery to achieve the surrender of towns in 1430, the case of Guichard Bournel and Soissons being the perfect example. Of course, this was not the first time that such a tactic had been used in medieval conflict, nor in fact were the Burgundians the only army in the Hundred Years War to gain a town's surrender in such a way. But, if Guillaume de Flavy took such a bribe, he seems not to have done so for the surrender of the town of Compiègne, as the town did not surrender to Philip the Good on 23 May 1430, the day of the capture of Joan of Arc, or at any other time. Eventually, after waging an unsuccessful siege for the whole summer, the Burgundians were forced to retreat from Compiègne without capturing it; in fact, they were forced to withdraw in such a manner and with such speed that they lost most of their impressive gunpowder artillery train.[70] (One might even wonder if Joan's capture did not work against the duke of Burgundy, inspiring the defending troops of Compiègne to fight even harder to resist the Anglo-Burgundian efforts to make them surrender. Joan learned of the Burgundian failure to capture Compiègne while in prison, and it inspired her to stay confident during her continued imprisonment and trial.) So, if Guillaume de Flavy did take money from Philip the Good, it was only for treachery against Joan.

However, this then poses a different question: was the duke of Burgundy so fearful of the Maid that he would pay a bribe to Flavy for the capture of her alone and not for Compiègne also? Nothing in Philip the Good's character to this point would suggest as much. Certainly, she had cost him dearly as far as territory was concerned, as most of the towns that had submitted to the French on the road to Reims were his – Auxerre, Troyes, Châlons, Reims, Compiègne, Laon, and Soissons. But Joan had failed to capture his main jewel in central France, Paris, which although co-ruled with the English, had always been accepted to be Burgundy's by Philip as well as by his father, John the Fearless, who had initially captured it from the Armagnacs/French. Additionally, Philip had recently seen the return of Soissons, and Troyes was not far from returning to him as well. In May 1430, with his large army and artillery train, there was little reason to think that Compiègne would not fall shortly, followed by all of the other towns lost to the Maid the year before. So, why should he fear Joan of Arc? Of course, it would be nice to know what was said between the two when Joan was brought to meet the duke by Jean of Luxembourg a short time after her capture. But Monstrelet, who was present, writes only that 'I do not remember well' what transpired between the two enemies.[71] Ultimately, it cannot be imagined that Philip the Good, the duke of Burgundy and one of the major warlords in the Hundred Years War, would have paid a substantial bribe to Guillaume de Flavy, and that the governor would have taken it, just to capture Joan.

Coupled with the issue of why Philip the Good might have paid a bribe just to get Joan is another question: for what reason would Guillaume de Flavy take money to allow Joan's capture, but then stand in opposition to accepting a bribe for the surrender of the town? The late fifteenth-century *Diariumor Chronicle of Heinrich Token* claims that 'the captains . . . found it difficult to accept that a young girl should lead them and that the glory won by them should be attributed to her'.[72] But this cannot be seen as credible even by those who accept Guillaume de Flavy's guilt. No captain who had fought by Joan's side before had ever felt this type of jealousy, not even the duke of Alençon, the Bastard of Orléans, La Hire, or Richemont, who had seen her virtually assume their command positions. In addition, those leaders had been involved in far more successful military adventures with the Maid and seemingly received far less credit than anything which Flavy could lay claim to. He was nowhere near the engagement with Franquet d'Arras outside Lagny, and Joan had done nothing around Compiègne that could be described as the least bit successful. Her defense of Choisy had failed, and she had not even been allowed to cross the bridge over the Aisne river at Soissons. Again, simply put, what did Guillaume de Flavy have to be jealous of?

There is also the suggestion put forth by Régine Pernoud and Marie-Veronique Clin that the captain of Compiègne could have surrendered Joan because 'Guillaume de Flavy had in fact no commitment other than his personal interest, which was to build up a petty domain around Compiègne. Joan was definitely an obstacle to that ambition.'[73] Yet, if Joan was an obstacle to Guillaume de Flavy's ambition, what was Philip the Good? Why, if the object was to rule Compiègne as a small fiefdom, did Flavy not simply surrender the town to him and then rule as his governor, in similar way to what Guichard Bournel was to do for Philip at Soissons? Joan was far less of an obstacle than the duke of Burgundy, and, as it seems that Flavy intended to try to hold out against the Anglo-Burgundians, perhaps in order to preserve this personal domain, Joan's assistance would have been much more important than her removal. That could always have been arranged later.

So there seems little reason either for Philip the Good to desire treason against the Maid or for Guillaume de Flavy to perpetrate it. One further note should be entered into consideration: Joan herself did not think that there was treachery involved in her capture. In her testimony at Rouen, as seen above, she claimed that the reason that she and her men could not return to Compiègne was not that the gates into the town were closed, but that they were blocked from that retreat option by the Burgundian soldiers because those men had captured and held the bridge between herself and the town. Even if the gates had been shut and the drawbridge raised prematurely and 'treasonously', something which Joan did not seem to have noticed if it occurred, or at least she never testified that she noticed, it did not affect her capture according to her testimony.

Finally, the character of Guillaume de Flavy prior to and after the capture of the Compiègne defense should be investigated. For, in doing so, one does not see a man willing at any time to betray anyone fighting for a cause that he also believed in, even if that someone was as potentially profitable as Joan of Arc. As presented in the thorough, although biased, biography of Flavy by Pierre

Champion (who wrote the work as a means of ridding the Compiègne captain of the charge of treason), it can be seen that Flavy was a warrior of similar quality to La Hire or Ponton de Xantrailles, whose tireless loyalty to the French side and Charles VII was above reproach. The first reference to Flavy as a French soldier comes from 1417 when he fought against the English in Rouen. After that town's defeat, Flavy went to Corbeil where he participated in its successful defense against a siege by John the Fearless. In 1418–19, he appears in Paris, fighting in vain against the Burgundians; in Compiègne which he helped capture from the Burgundians; and at the relief of the siege of Saint-Martin-le-Gaillard. During this time, his family lost almost all of their land-holdings and dwellings in Picardy to those Burgundians whom he is later accused of conspiring with. During the early 1420s Guillaume de Flavy moved his fighting talents to Normandy, participating in the conflicts at Pont-Remy, Saint-Riquier, Abbeville, where he was left for dead on the battlefield, Offémont, and Meaux. And during the few years prior to Joan's involvement in French military affairs, Flavy fought against the Burgundians in the region near to her home. He was the captain of Beaumont-en-Argonne, named such by the citizens of the town, from August 1427 and through its siege by Jean de Luxembourg, which began in January 1428, until he was forced to surrender the starved town at the end of May. Allowed to leave peacefully, Flavy was then assigned almost immediately to the threatened town of La Neuville-sur-Meuse, which he fortified and held out against a Burgundian siege during the months of July and August 1428. Finally, he was present in Reims on 17 July 1429 and stood with other brave French captains at the crowning of their king, Charles VII. When Charles left the north to return to the Loire on 12 September 1429, he appointed Guillaume de Flavy as his captain in Compiègne.[74] Can there be any doubt that Flavy had earned this esteemed military position? It is true that after his successful defense of Compiègne, because of the loss of Joan during his time there, Guillaume de Flavy's career declined, never to attain even a modicum of his pre-1430 glory. The question of not having done what he could to make sure that Joan was not captured, let alone the possibility of his treason in the matter, followed Guillaume de Flavy to his grave. It was an unfortunate end for a man who had fought as hard as and far longer than Joan for the removal of the Anglo-Burgundians from the French realm.

There can be but one conclusion. The treatment of Flavy as a deviously illogical but brilliant traitor presents a far more difficult solution to what occurred at Compiègne than does the more simple and much more credible recognition that there was no treason by Guillaume de Flavy against Joan of Arc.

*   *   *

On 23 May 1430, Joan of Arc became a prisoner of war – a very famous prisoner of war. Other military leaders had been captured before during the Hundred Years War – the French at the time of Joan's capture were still holding Talbot, Suffolk, and Scales. Some of these prisoners had been of very high rank, including King John II of France, who had been taken prisoner at the battle of Poitiers in 1356. But, none, it seems, held the same attraction for their captors as the Maid did for hers. Maybe this was because she was a woman, a female military leader being rare in any military engagement at any time. However, more than likely, the gender issue was only a curiosity. Interest in Joan endured a very long time, due to the way that she fought her engagements and to Whom she gave credit for them. Her 'mission' was known to all, and the question on everyone's mind, friend or foe, was put into words by the great French author Christine de Pisan, who wrote her last work as a *Ditié* for Joan after the crowning of Charles VII. Addressing herself to the English and Burgundians opposing Joan, Christine asked what they were afraid to have answered:

> Oh, all you blind people, can you not detect God's hand in this? If you cannot you are truly stupid for how else could the Maid who strikes you all down dead have been sent to us? And you do not have sufficient strength! Do you want to fight against God?[75]

Joan became a prize of war. Like the Romans of ancient times, who dragged their captive opposing military leaders back to their capital to be displayed in triumph, Joan was paraded throughout many of the lands of France occupied by the Burgundians and then the English. She was displayed as a symbol of their victory and the French loss. She would be taken through the streets of Clairoix, Beaulieu-lès-Fontaines, Beaurevoir, Bapaume, Arras, Avesnes-le-Comte, Lucheux, Drugy, Le Crotoy, Saint-Valery-sur-Somme, Eu,

Arques, Bosc-le-Hard, and finally Rouen.[76] Only at one place did she remain for any time – at Beaurevoir Castle, where she stayed for four months with Jean of Luxembourg, his wife, Joan of Béthune, her daughter by a first marriage, Joan of Bar, and his aunt, Joan of Luxembourg, while matters concerning who would try her and where were being decided. Tradition and Joan of Arc's later testimony has it that these other Joans were very taken with her there and would have preferred her to stay with them in a sort of low-security house arrest.[77] But, eventually, she was sold to the English who wished to grant her no mercy.

Letters, too, went out to all of the occupied peoples, especially throughout that part of France which had dared to rise in opposition to this occupation. One of the first was written by Philip the Good who, as mentioned, was the first of her opponents to interview her and to glory in her imprisonment. Written within a day of her capture, the duke of Burgundy wrote:

> By the pleasure of our blessed Creator, the woman called the Maid has been taken; and from her capture will be recognized the error and mad belief of all those who became sympathetic and favorable to the deeds of this woman . . . and we write you this news hoping that you will have joy and consolation in it and that you will render homage to our Creator, who through His blessed pleasure has wished to conduct the rest of our enterprises on behalf of our lord king of England and of France and for the comfort of his good and loyal subjects.[78]

That Joan allowed herself to be made captive and would soon be lingering in a prison or worse was evidence to Philip the Good, who obviously had not read the New Testament, that she had not been directed on her mission from a divine source. She was to him a heretic.

Others also felt the same way. Within three days of her capture, the University of Paris requested that the Burgundians surrender their prize to the Inquisitor of France, Jean Graverent, to be tried for heresy. They did not, seeking a more rich reward for her capture. It finally came when the English agreed to pay the enormous sum of 10,000 *livres tournois* for Joan. The Bastard of Wandomme, who had captured her at Compiègne, received a pension of 300 *livres*, with Jean of Luxembourg receiving the rest.[79] The English promptly put her on trial for heresy, confounded her with theological questions that even the most trained doctor of theology would have been hard pressed to answer correctly, while almost completely neglecting her military career and how she might have been able to win all of those victories without the aid of deity – there are always ways of rationalizing one's own defeat in war. Found guilty of not knowing what the definition of the Church Militant was and of wearing men's clothing, Joan first abjured (confessed to heresy) under extreme pressure, and then recanted her abjuration. A little more than a year after she had been captured, on 30 May 1431, Joan of Arc was burned to death as a heretic in the marketplace of Rouen.[80] Stripped of her arms and armor, her standard torn from her hands, devoid of her troops and other generals, she may have looked like any other young woman. But this young woman relieved the siege of Orléans, conquered Jargeau, Beaugency, Meung-sur-Loire, and Saint-Pierre-le-Moutier, won the battle of Patay and numerous other skirmishes, attacked Paris and Le-Charité-sur-Loire, participated in the defense of Compiègne, saw the capitulation of too many towns to list, and stood next to King Charles VII of France as he was crowned. All of this had been accomplished in a little more than a single year. Confident she had been in battle, so too was she confident in death. She had completed her military mission and had sealed it with her blood.

9

Afterword

It would be a very fitting conclusion to the story of Joan of Arc if one could say that she was the direct cause of the end of the Hundred Years War and the expulsion of the English from most of France. Unfortunately, she was not. The fact that the war did not end until twenty-three years after her capture indicates that she did not have such an impact. Most modern historians of the conflict place far more weight on the Congress of Arras, which met in 1435, and the political turmoil and bad military leadership brought about by the weak rule of Henry VI, both during his minority and when he had reached adulthood, as causes for the war's resolution.

But, certainly Joan had an influence on both of those events. After all, had she not desired to mend the rift between Philip the Good, who switched sides from the English to the French at the Congress of Arras?[1] It could be argued that her victories influenced the peace process both because they showed the weakness of English troops and because they gave hope to the Burgundians that their French cousins were more capable warriors than they had previously believed. Yet, having established that link, it must be noted that if Joan did influence Philip to switch sides, this did not occur immediately, as the Congress did not even meet until six years after her capture. It also appears that the conference and the new alliance formed after it were prompted more by the diplomatic efforts of men like Georges de la Trémoïlle, than military efforts by generals like Joan. Finally, it must be recognized that even having both the French and Burgundians together against the undermanned English, thus turning all the resources of 'France' to the purpose of ridding the continent of English control, did not bring a quick end to the war. It was fourteen years after the Congress of Arras before Normandy was free from English control and seventeen years before Gascony was returned to the French. Not only did the Franco-Burgundian alliance not bring about a quick end to the war, but the Burgundians could not even conquer the town of Calais in the wake of the Arras congress in 1436. Besieging the English town, Philip discovered what the English had found out at Orléans, the French at Paris, and even the Burgundians at Compiègne – that well-fortified sites during the Middle Ages were difficult to defeat, even in an age of gunpowder weapons.[2]

As for Joan's influence on the turmoil of Henry VI's reign, she must be given some credit for destabilizing the English military leadership. Simply capturing and holding for ransom the likes of John Talbot, Thomas Scales, and William de la Pole, while, at the same time, discrediting John Fastolf, meant that the English had very few other military leaders to call upon. That John of Lancaster, the duke of Bedford, regent of the boy-king, and head of the English forces in France, had to take the field himself against Joan at Paris certainly indicates this. But the curious feature of medieval ransoms was that captured generals were eventually released, and, once freed, were able to continue their previous military leadership without legal or chivalric hindrance. (The French, too, had profited from such a system, with Arthur de Richemont, Jean, duke of Alençon, Jean, the Bastard of Orléans, and others able to fight beside Joan, despite previously having been captured by the English.) Thus, by the beginning of 1430 Pole had been set free, by the middle of 1430 Scales had, and by 1433 Talbot had also gained his freedom. All returned to military leadership positions, and all fought with some success against the French until the end of the war. Moreover, it does not seem that the weakness of military leadership in France solely effected the political turmoil in England, for the resulting conflict there – what would later be called the Wars of the Roses – did not begin until close to the end of the Hundred Years War. And while loss of English lands, titles, and authority in France certainly affected what occurred in England between 1450 and 1485, there is justifiable suspicion over whether Joan, who had burned nearly twenty years previously, could have, even indirectly, caused Henry VI's problems then and there.

So, if Joan did not directly influence the ending of the Hundred Years War, why is she so celebrated? No doubt the partiality of her trial and the nature of her execution had something to do with her celebrity, but other individuals, men and women, were tried and burned for supposed heresy, and not honored with sainthood, let alone with the number of statues, pieces of artwork, literature, and legends awarded to the Maid's memory. Joan's renown is attached to her military ability, to the skill she had in leading men into battle against great odds and possible death. This made the greatest influence on her time. For, not long after her death, French military leaders, some she had fought with, and some not recorded as ever participating in her engagements, began to adopt similar tactics to those that she had employed. Her policy of direct engagement/ frontal assault was a costly method of winning military contests. But, in the long run, it was more effective in wresting France from the English than any other tactic. As other French generals started to use it, they, too, began to be victorious. Even before Joan died, La Hire captured, by direct assault, the important English-held fortification of Château-Gaillard.[3] La Hire performed this tactic well, as did Ponton de Xantrailles, Arthur de Richemont, and the Bastard of Orléans. Richemont's siege of Meaux in 1439 was aided by direct engagement (while he also wisely refused to fight with Talbot's relief army).[4] So were the 1440 capture of Pontoise by the same leader, this time assisted by La Hire and Xantrailles;[5] the successful 1442 siege of La Réole by the newly ransomed Charles of Orléans and La Hire;[6] the 1449 conquest of Rouen, by Lord Dunois, formerly the Bastard of Orléans; the recapture of Harfleur in December 1449 and Honfleur in January 1450, both by Jean Bureau, a new leader who had risen through the ranks from gunner to general;[7] the reconquest of the remainder of Normandy in 1450 by Richemont, Dunois, Bureau, and others;[8] the victory of the battle of Formigny in April 1450 by Richemont;[9] the removal of the English from Gascony in 1450–3;[10] and, finally, Jean Bureau's victory in the last battle of the Hundred Years War, Castillon, in July 1453.[11] Almost all these conflicts were decided because the French military leaders followed Joan's prescribed tactics. Perhaps they, too, now believed that, should their soldiers die in battle, they would go to heaven. Or perhaps they simply reckoned that they would ultimately save more lives were they to sacrifice a few initially in acquiring a quick victory. These were not blood-thirsty individuals. Undoubtedly, all deaths in this last phase of the Hundred Years War, French or English, saddened the leaders who caused them, as much as they had saddened Joan. Yet, it may have been one of the last of these deaths which symbolized what had happened since the brief phase of the war fought by Joan of Arc. John Talbot, Joan's old adversary and later earl of Salisbury, at the advanced age of eighty, led the

English troops into defeat for the last time at the battle of Castillon, and was killed fighting among them. One wonders if among his last thoughts was the Maid, who had been his avid enemy so many years before, and who, just maybe, had ushered in his demise over twenty years later by changing French military history.

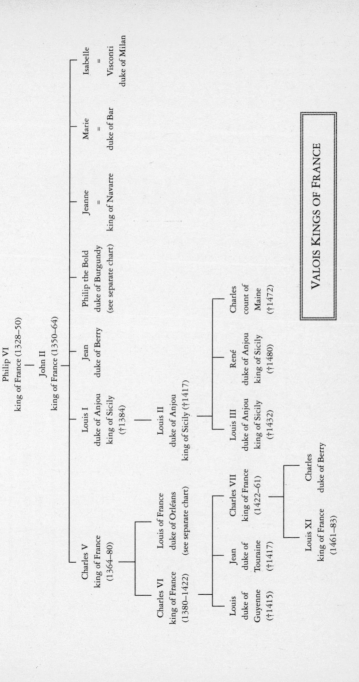

Philip VI
king of France (1328–50)

John II
king of France (1350–64)

Louis I
duke of Anjou
king of Sicily
(†1384)

Jean
duke of Berry

Philip the Bold
duke of Burgundy
(see separate chart)

Jeanne
=
king of Navarre

Marie
=
duke of Bar

Isabelle
=
Visconti
duke of Milan

Charles V
king of France
(1364–80)

Louis II
duke of Anjou
king of Sicily (†1417)

Louis of France
duke of Orléans
(see separate chart)

Charles VI
king of France
(1380–1422)

Louis III
duke of Anjou
king of Sicily
(†1432)

René
duke of Anjou
king of Sicily
(†1480)

Charles
count of
Maine
(†1472)

Louis
duke of Guyenne
(†1415)

Jean
duke of
Touraine
(†1417)

Charles VII
king of France
(1422–61)

Louis XI
king of France
(1461–83)

Charles
duke of Berry

VALOIS KINGS OF FRANCE

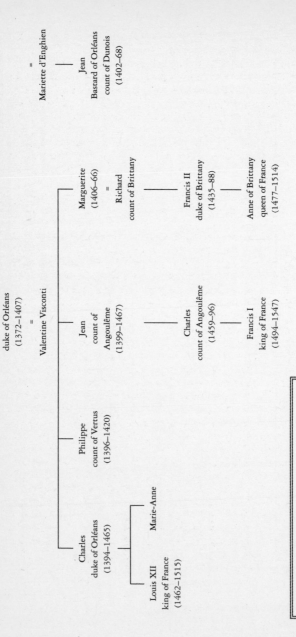

Mariette d'Enghien
=
Jean
Bastard of Orléans
count of Dunois
(1402–68)

Louis of France
duke of Orléans
(1372–1407)
=
Valentine Visconti

Marguerite
(1406–66)
=
Richard
count of Brittany

Francis II
duke of Brittany
(1435–88)

Anne of Brittany
queen of France
(1477–1514)

Jean
count of Angoulême
(1399–1467)

Charles
count of Angoulême
(1459–96)

Francis I
king of France
(1494–1547)

Philippe
count of Vertus
(1396–1420)

Charles
duke of Orléans
(1394–1465)

Marie-Anne

Louis XII
king of France
(1462–1515)

ROYAL BRANCH OF THE VALOIS-ORLÉANS
AND VALOIS-ANGOULÊME FAMILIES

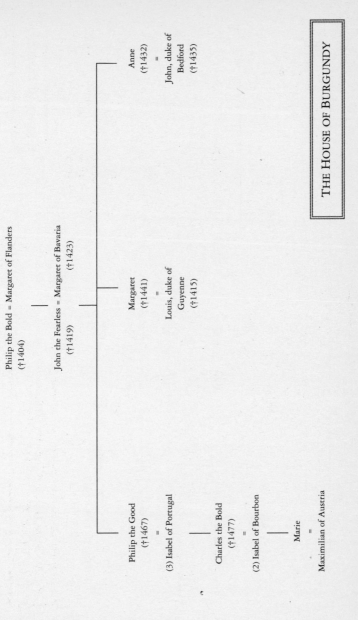

Philip the Bold = Margaret of Flanders
(†1404)

John the Fearless = Margaret of Bavaria
(†1419)   (†1423)

Margaret
(†1441)
=
Louis, duke of
Guyenne
(†1415)

Anne
(†1432)
=
John, duke of
Bedford
(†1435)

Philip the Good
(†1467)
=
(3) Isabel of Portugal

Charles the Bold
(†1477)
=
(2) Isabel of Bourbon

Marie
=
Maximilian of Austria

THE HOUSE OF BURGUNDY

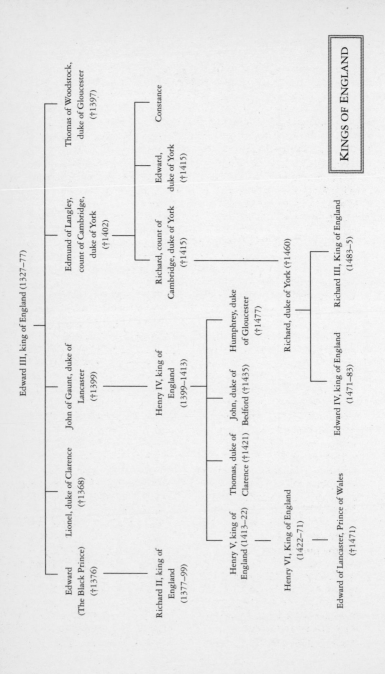

KINGS OF ENGLAND

Notes

Chapter 1: Introduction

1. This letter is found in *Procès de condamnation et de réhabilitation de Jeanne d'Arc dite La Pucelle* ed. Jules Quicherat, 5 vols (Paris, 1841–9) [hereafter Quicherat], I:489–93. The quoted portion comes from I:489–90. Unless otherwise indicated, all translations are author's. N.B. in the first volume of Jules Quicherat's work can be found an edition of the trial transcripts; the second and third volumes contain an edition of the nullification trial (or retrial) transcripts, and in the last two volumes are a collection of all contemporary sources for Joan of Arc known to this great editor. While there are in many instances better editions of the sources in question, I have used Quicherat's edition of the trial and contemporary sources and Pierre Duparc (ed.), *Procès en nullité de la condamnation de Jeanne d'Arc*, 5 vols, Société de l'histoire de France (Paris, 1977–89) [hereafter Duparc] for the nullification trial testimony.

2. A discussion of the theological questioning in Joan's Rouen trial can be found in Régine Pernoud and Marie-Véronique Clin, *Joan of Arc: Her Story*, trans. and rev. J.D. Adams (New York, 1998), pp. 103–47. These trial transcripts are found in Quicherat, I. On Joan's theological confidence and training see Régine Pernoud, *La spiritualité de Jeanne d'Arc* (Paris, 1992).

3. Joan testified to this in her trial. See Quicherat, I:106–7. See also Pernoud and Clin, pp. 79–80; W.S. Scott, *Jeanne d'Arc* (New York, 1974), p. 76; and Marina Warner, *Joan of Arc: The Image of Female Heroism* (Harmondsworth, 1981), pp. 92–4.

4. As she testified in her trial, Quicherat, I:46–7.

5. This is recorded in Quicherat, V:137–9, as decreed by Charles VII at the end of July 1429. See also Pernoud and Clin, pp. 73, 230–1 and Warner, pp. 172–3.

6. So decreed by Charles VII at the end of December 1429 as recorded in Quicherat, V:150–3.

7. Archbishop Regnault of Chartres wrote this in a letter to the people of Reims after Joan was captured at Compiègne. An edition of this is in Quicherat, V:168–9. See also Pernoud and Clin, p. 91.

8. Joan is said to have written two letters to this effect to Philip the Good; one is still extant. A facsimile of this letter can be seen in C. de Maleissye, *Les lettres de Jehanne d'Arc et la prétendue abjuration de Saint*

Ouen (Paris, 1911), p. 72; an edition of the letter is in Quicherat, V:126–7; and an edition and translation of it is in Pernoud and Clin, pp. 67–8, 253–4. Pernoud and Clin (p. 250) also record the reference to an earlier letter that she wrote to the duke of Burgundy.

9. As seen in her letter to the citizens of Tournai. See Quicherat, V:125–6, translated in Pernoud and Clin, pp. 251–2.

10. Jean, the duke of Alençon, testified at her nullification trial that at their first encounter Joan said to him, 'the more the blood of France is gathered together, the better it shall be': found in Duparc, I:381. Guillaume Gruel, Richemont's chronicler, claimed that when she first encountered the Constable, she fell on her knees to embrace him and welcome him back to the army. See Guillaume Gruel, *Chronique d'Arthur de Richemont*, in Quicherat, IV:317. This is disputed by the *Journal du siège d'Orléans* (in Quicherat, IV:175) and the *Chronique de la pucelle* (in Quicherat, IV:240), both of which claim that it was Richemont who prostrated himself in front of Joan, asking her to help him to regain his military influence and position. This will be discussed further below.

11. This happened at least twice, as found both in Dunois's testimony (Duparc, I:318–19) and in Jean d'Aulon's, her squire (Duparc, I:477).

12. In a letter Guy de Laval wrote to his grandmother, Anne de Laval, the widow of Guesclin, he claims that Joan was sending a small golden ring to her as a token of her affection for the earlier war hero's efforts against the English: found in Quicherat, V:107–8. See also Pernoud and Clin, pp. 58, 179.

13. Although Joan is never recorded as having spoken against Charles, both Perceval de Cagny (*Chronique des ducs d'Alençon* in Quicherat, IV:29–31) and Jacques Bouvier or Gilles le Bouvier, the Herald of Berry (*Chroniques du roi Charles VII* in Quicherat, IV:48–9) record her frustration with him and his counselors, in particular Georges de la Trémoille, at their military inaction after the crowning of the king. See also Pernoud and Clin, pp. 78–81.

14. Both can be found in part in Quicherat, IV. Complete editions are: *Journal du siège d'Orléans et du voyage de Reims, 1428–29*, ed. P. Charpentier and C. Cuissard (Orléans, 1896) and *Chronique de la Pucelle ou chronique de Cousinot*, ed. A. Vallet de Viriville (Paris, 1859).

15. The excellent bibliography, complete to 1988, Nadia Margolis, *Joan of Arc in History, Literature, and Film* (New York, 1990) contains an annotated list of all contemporary and near contemporary chronicles that mention Joan of Arc. The references to her in Morosini's *Diario* can be found in Antonio

Morosini, *Chronique: Extraits relatifs à l'histoire de France*, trans. and ed. L. Dorez, 4 vols (Paris, 1898–1902).

16. Editions and translations of all of these letters in found in Pernoud and Clin, pp. 247–64. Other editions are listed in Margolis, pp. 192–3. The letter to the Hussites can be found in Pernoud and Clin, pp. 258–9.

17. A list of trial transcript manuscripts, editions, and translations is found in Margolis, pp. 12–28. The most complete edition of the trial transcripts is Quicherat, I, which has been updated by Pierre Tisset and Yvonne Lanhers (eds), *Procès de condamnation de Jeanne d'Arc*, 3 vols (Paris, 1960–71).

18. A list of nullification trial transcript manuscripts, editions, and translations is also found in Margolis, pp. 12–28. The most complete edition of the nullification transcripts is Duparc, which updates Quicherat, II and III. (N.B. Although awkward, for greater accuracy when quoting from the nullification trial transcripts, I have retained the original third-person pronouns for the witnesses' testimony of their activities in relation to Joan.)

19. Complete reference is found in note 1 above.

20. Frédéric Canonge, *Jeanne d'Arc guerrièr* (Paris, 1907); Lt Col Collet, *Vie militaire de Jeanne d'Arc* (Nancy, 1919); Eug. Bourguignon, *Sainte Jeanne d'Arc (la guerrièr)* (Bruges, 1928); Frantz Funck-Brentano, *Jeanne d'Arc: Chef de guerre* (Paris, 1943); Lt Col de Lancesseur, *Jeanne d'Arc chef de guerre: Le génie militaire et politique de Jeanne d'Arc. Campagne de France, 1429–30* (Paris, 1961); and Col Ferdinand de Liocourt, *La mission de Jeanne d'Arc*, 2 vols (Paris, 1974–6). More specific studies of Joan's military activities, especially at the siege of Orléans, will be cited in their appropriate chapters below.

Chapter 2: Why Joan of Arc Was Needed

1. See note 2, Chapter 6..

2. On the Capetian Dynasty see Robert Fawtier, *The Capetian Kings of France: Monarchy and Nation, 987–1328*, trans. L. Butler and R.J. Adam (London, 1960) and Elizabeth M. Hallam, *Capetian France, 987–1328* (London, 1980). For a comparison of the French and English kings during part of this period see Charles Petit-Dutaillis, *The Feudal Monarchy in France and England from the Tenth to the Thirteenth Century* (London, 1966).

3. Malcolm Barber, *The Trial of the Templars* (Cambridge, 1978); Malcolm Barber, *The New Knighthood: A History of the Order of the Temple* (Cambridge, 1994), 280–313; and Peter Partner, *The Knights Templar and Their Myth*, second ed. (Rochester, VT, 1990), pp. 42–89.

4. On Louis IX's defeats see

William Chester Jordan, *Louis IX and the Challenge of the Crusade: A Study in Rulership* (Princeton, 1979). On the battles of Courtrai and Arques see Kelly DeVries, *Infantry Warfare in the Early Fourteenth Century: Discipline, Tactics, and Technology* (Woodbridge, 1996), pp. 9–31.

5. On the succession crisis of 1328 see Perroy, pp. 69–76; Christopher Allmand, *The Hundred Years War: England and France at War c. 1300–c. 1450* (Cambridge, 1988), pp. 10–11; and John Le Patourel, 'The Origins of the War', in Kenneth Fowler (ed.), *The Hundred Years War* (London, 1971), pp. 28–50.

6. Henry Stephen Lucas, *The Low Countries and the Hundred Years' War, 1326–1347* (Ann Arbor, 1929), pp. 240–367 and Henri Pirenne, *Histoire de Belgique*, vol. II: *Du commencement du XIVe siècle à la mort de Charles de Téméraire* (Brussels, 1903), pp. 93–115. The best biographies of Jacob van Artevelde are Hans van Werveke, *Jacques van Artevelde* (Brussels, 1948) and David Nicholas, *The Van Arteveldes of Ghent: The Varieties of Vendetta and the Hero in History* (Ithaca, 1988), pp. 1–71.

7. DeVries, *Infantry Warfare*, pp. 100–11; Pirenne, pp. 69–92; and William H. TeBrake, *A Plague of Insurrection: Popular Politics and Peasant Revolt in Flanders, 1323–28* (Philadelphia, 1993).

8. Lucas, pp. 194–223; Pirenne, pp. 112–14; and H.S. Offler, 'England and Germany at the Beginning of the Hundred Years' War', *English Historical Review* 54 (1939), 608–31.

9. Lucas, pp. 395–404; Alfred H. Burne, *The Crécy War: A Military History of the Hundred Years War from 1337 to the Peace of Bretigny, 1360* (London, 1955), pp. 51–6; and Kelly DeVries, 'God, Leadership, Flemings, and Archery: Contemporary Perceptions of Victory and Defeat at the Battle of Sluys, 1340', *American Neptune* 55 (1995), 223–42. Jonathan Sumption, *The Hundred Years War: Trial by Battle* (Philadelphia, 1991) may be used here and elsewhere, although with caution as he sometimes supplies an incomplete or inaccurate record of these events.

10. Thomas of Walsingham, *Historia Anglicana*, ed. H.T. Riley (London, 1863), I:227.

11. Lucas, pp. 404–38; Burne, *Crécy War*, pp. 56–63; Kelly DeVries, 'Contemporary Views of Edward III's Failure at the Siege of Tournai, 1340', *Nottingham Medieval Studies* 39 (1995), 70–105; and Clifford J. Rogers, 'An Unknown News Bulletin from the Siege of Tournai in 1340', *War in History* 5 (1998), 358–66.

12. Lucas, pp. 438–528 and Pirenne, pp. 116–23. Artevelde was killed in 1345. Louis of Nevers returned to govern the county, but he would be killed at the battle of Crécy the

following year and be replaced by his son, Louis of Male.

13. Perroy, pp. 114–16; Burne, *Crécy War*, pp. 66–78; DeVries, *Infantry Warfare*, pp. 137–44; and Jacques Choffel, *La guerre de succession de Bretagne* (Paris, 1975).

14. Burne, *Crécy War*, pp. 136–47; DeVries, *Infantry Warfare*, pp. 155–7; Henri Prentout, *La prise de Caen par Édouard III, 1346* (Caen, 1904); and Clifford J. Rogers, 'Edward III and the Dialectics of Strategy, 1327–1360', *Transactions of the Royal Historical Society* Sixth ser. 4 (1994), 83–102. On Edward's numbers see Andrew Ayton, 'The English Army and the Normandy Campaign of 1346', in *England and Normandy in the Middle Ages*, ed. D. Bates and A. Curry (London, 1994), pp. 253–67.

15. DeVries, *Infantry Warfare*, pp. 157–75; Burne, *Crécy War*, pp. 169–203; and Jules Viard, 'La campagne de juillet-août 1346 et la bataille de Crécy', *Moyen Age* second ser. 27 (1926), 1–84.

16. Burne, *Crécy War*, 204–3; Kelly DeVries, 'Hunger, Flemish Participation and the Flight of Philip VI: Contemporary Accounts of the Siege of Calais, 1346–47', *Studies in Medieval and Renaissance History* n.s 12 (1991), 129–81; and Jules Viard, 'Le siège de Calais, 4 septembre 1346–4 aout 1347', *Moyen Age* second ser. 30 (1929), 124–89.

17. For a discussion of the *chevauchée* as a tactic during the Hundred Years War see Allmand, *The Hundred Years War*, pp. 54–6.

18. Burne, *Crécy War*, pp. 275–321; Rogers, 'Edward III and the Dialectics of Strategy'; Richard Barber, *Edward, Prince of Wales and Aquitaine: A Biography of the Black Prince* (1978; rpt. Woodbridge, 1996), pp. 140–6; and J.-M. Tourneur-Aumont, *La bataille de Poitiers, 1356, et la construction de la France* (Paris, 1940).

19. This treaty can be found in E. Cosneau (ed.), *Les grands traités de la guerre de cent ans* (Paris, 1889). Good secondary discussions include: Perroy, pp. 138–42; Allmand, pp. 18–20; Burne, *Crécy War*, pp. 346–51; John Le Patourel, 'The Treaty of Brétigny', *Transactions of the Royal Historical Society* fifth ser. 10 (1960), 19–39; and J.J.N. Palmer, 'The War Aims of the Protagonists and the Negotiations for Peace', in Kenneth Fowler (ed.), *The Hundred Years War* (London, 1971), pp. 51–74.

20. Alfred H. Burne, *The Agincourt War: A Military History of the Latter Part of the Hundred Years War from 1369 to 1453* (London, 1956), pp. 17–32; Simeon Luce, *Histoire de Bertrand du Guesclin et son époque* (Paris, 1876); Micheline Dupuy, *Bertrand du Guesclin, captaine d'aventure, connétable de France* (Paris, 1977); and Kenneth Fowler, 'Bertrand du Guesclin – Careerist in Arms?' *History Today* 39 (June 1989), 37–43.

21. On Charles V's military advances see Perroy, pp. 144–76 and Desmond Seward, *The Hundred Years War: The English in France, 1337–1453* (New York, 1978), pp. 103–26.

22. Barber, pp. 233–7; Perroy, pp. 167–8, 178–80; and Allmand, *Hundred Years War*, p. 23.

23. Perroy, pp. 187–95; J.J.N. Palmer, *England, France and Christendom, 1377–99* (Chapel Hill, 1972); Anthony Tuck, 'Richard II and the Hundred Years War', in *Politics and Crisis in Fourteenth-Century England*, ed. J. Taylor and W. Childs (London, 1990), pp. 117–31; and Maurice Keen, 'Richard II's Ordinances of War in 1385', in *Rulers and Ruled in Late Medieval England: Essays Presented to Gerald Harriss*, ed. R.E. Archer and S. Walker (London, 1995), pp. 33–48.

24. Perroy (pp. 178–86) describes this period as 'The Exhaustion of England'.

25. Pirenne, pp. 157–207. On the Flemish rebellion of 1379–85 see Nicholas, pp. 99–159 and Maurice Vandermaesen and Marc Ryckaert, 'De Gentse opstand (1379–1385)', in ed. M. Vandermaesen, M. Ryckaerts, and M. Coornaert, *De Witte Kaproenen: De Gentse opstand (1379–1385) en de geschiedenis van de Brugse Leie* (Ghent, 1979), pp. 12–35. On the Burgundian inheritance of the county of Flanders see Richard Vaughan, *Philip the Bold: The Formation of the Burgundian State* (London, 1962).

26. Allmand, *Hundred Years War*, pp. 73–6.

27. Palmer, *England, France and Christendom*, pp. 142–51, 166–79; J.J.N. Palmer, 'The Anglo-French Peace Negotiations, 1390–1396', *Transactions of the Royal Historical Society* 16 (1966), 81–94; and Christopher Phillpotts, 'The Fate of the Truce of Paris, 1396–1415', *Journal of Medieval History* 24 (1998), 61–80.

28. Richard C. Famiglietti, *Royal Intrigue: Crisis at the Court of Charles VI, 1392–1420* (New York, 1986).

29. Palmer, *England, France and Christendom*, pp. 180–210; Aziz Suryal Atiya, *The Crusade of Nicopolis* (London, 1934); and Kelly DeVries, 'The Lack of a Western European Military Response to the Ottoman Invasions of Eastern Europe from Nicopolis (1396) to Mohács (1526)', *Journal of Military History* 63 (1999), 539–59.

30. Palmer, *England, France and Christendom*, pp. 211–26 and Caroline Barron, 'The Deposition of Richard II', in ed. J. Taylor and W. Childs, *Politics and Crisis in Fourteenth-Century England* (London, 1990), pp. 132–49.

31. Christopher Allmand, *Henry V* (Berkeley and Los Angeles, 1992), pp. 19–33 and R.R. Davies, *The Revolt of Owain Glyn Dŵr* (Oxford, 1995).

32. Allmand, *Henry V*, pp. 18–19 and A.L. Brown, 'The English Campaign in Scotland, 1400',

in ed. H. Hearder and H.R. Loyn, *British Government and Administration: Studies Presented to S. Chrimes* (Cardiff, 1974), pp. 40–54.

33. Allmand, *Henry V*, pp. 25–7; E.J. Priestly, *The Battle of Shrewsbury, 1403* (Shrewsbury, 1979); and Philip A. Haigh, *The Military Campaigns of the Wars of the Roses* (Stroud, 1995), pp. 182–8.

34. On the different popes during the fourteenth and fifteenth centuries see Guillaume Mollat, *The Popes at Avignon, 1305–1378*, trans. J. Love (London, 1963) and Yves Renouard, *The Avignon Papacy: The Popes in Exile, 1305–1403*, trans. D. Bethell (New York, 1970). On the Burgundian policy towards the Low Countries see Walter Prevenier and Wim Blockmans, *The Burgundian Netherlands* (Cambridge, 1986) and Wim Blockmans and Walter Prevenier, *In de ban van Bourgondië* (The Hague, 1988).

35. Perroy, pp. 219–26; Richard Vaughan, *John the Fearless: The Growth of Burgundian Power* (London, 1966), pp. 29–43; and Bertrand Schnerb, *Les Armagnacs et les Bourguignons: La maudite guerre* (Paris, 1988), pp. 15–77.

36. Perroy, pp. 226–7; Vaughan, *John the Fearless*, pp. 43–8; Schnerb, pp. 67–76; and Bernard Guenée, *Un meutre, une société: L'assassinat du Duc d'Orléans, 23 novembre 1407* (Paris, 1992).

37. Perroy, p. 227; Vaughan, *John*

the Fearless, pp. 46–8; and Schnerb, pp. 78–83.

38. Perroy, pp. 228–9 and Vaughan, *John the Fearless*, pp. 68–74. Part of the *Justification* is translated in Vaughan, *John the Fearless*, pp. 70–2. The full document is quoted in Engerrand de Monstrelet, *Chronique*, ed. L. Douet-d'Arcq (Paris, 1857–62), I:177–242.

39. Perroy, pp. 229–30 and Schnerb, pp. 93–7.

40. Vaughan, *John the Fearless*, pp. 49–66 and Erich Wille, *Die Schlacht von Othée, 23 septembre 1408* (Berlin, 1908).

41. Vaughan, *John the Fearless*, pp. 175–6 and Pierre Bertin, 'Le siège du chateau de Vellexon dans l'hiver 1409–1410', *Revue historique des armées* 27 (1971), 7–18.

42. Monstrelet (Douet-d'Arcq), II:172–5; *Chronique des Pays-Bas, de France, d'Angleterre et de Tournai, in Corpus chronicorum Flandriae*, 3, ed. J.J. de Smet (Brussels, 1856), p. 342; *Le livre des trahisons de France envers la maison de Bourgogne, in Chroniques relatives à l'histoire de la Belgique sous la domination des ducs de Bourgogne (textes Français)*, ed. Kervyn de Lettenhove (Brussels, 1873), p. 96; and L. de Laborde, *Les ducs de Bourgogne* (Paris, 1849), I:24.

43. Religieux de Saint-Denis, *Chronique*, ed. L. Bellaguet (Paris, 1839–52), IV:652.

44. Religieux de Saint-Denis, V:370–5; Monstrelet (Douet-d'Arcq), III:22–31; and Jean le

Fevre, *Chronique*, ed. F. Morand (Paris, 1876), I:184.

45. Perroy, pp. 230–1; Vaughan, *John the Fearless*, pp. 97–100; and Schnerb, pp. 123–43.

46. Vaughan, *John the Fearless*, pp. 91–2.

47. For references to these letters see note 8, Chapter 1.

48. The two versions of this poem can be found in W. Carew Hazlitt, *Remains of Early Popular Poetry of England* (London, 1866), II:88–108, under the title 'The Battle of Egyngecourte', and as an appendix to Monstrelet (Douet-d'Arcq), VI:549–62, under the title 'The Siege of Harflet et batayl of Agencourt'. The quote which I have used is found in Monstrelet (Douet-d'Arcq) VI:551. On the siege of Harfleur and the invasion in general see Burne, *Agincourt War*, pp. 38–75; Allmand, *Henry V*, pp. 68–82; E.F. Jacob, *Henry V and the Invasion of France* (London, 1947), pp. 60–96; P. Jubault, *D'Azincourt à Jeanne d'Arc, 1415–1430* (Amiens, 1969); and Matthew Bennett, *Agincourt 1415: Triumph Against the Odds* (London, 1991), pp. 38–44.

49. Bennett; Burne, *Agincourt War*, pp. 76–96; Allmand, *Henry V*, pp. 83–102; Jacob, *Henry V*, pp. 96–108; and Jubault, pp. 27–39.

50. For these numbers I rely on Bennett, pp. 66–73.

51. Bennett, pp. 86–8 and Jacob, *Henry V*, pp. 106–7.

52. Burne, *Agincourt War*, pp. 89–90; Allmand, *Henry V*, pp. 102–13; Jacob, *Henry V*, pp. 125–6; and Sarah Tolmie, 'Quia Hic Homo Multa Signa Facit: Henry V's Royal Entry into London, November 23, 1415', in eds M. Gosman, A. Vanderjagt, and J. Veenstra, *The Propagation of Power in the Medieval West: Selected Proceedings of the International Conference, Groningen, 20–23 November 1996* (Groningen, 1997), pp. 363–79. Henry's muster roll of troops raised in 1416–17 is found as an appendix in *Gesta Henrici quinti, Angliae regis*, ed. B. Williams (London, 1850), pp. 265–73.

53. Burne, *Agincourt War*, pp. 104–9; Allmand, *Henry V*, pp. 107–8; Jacob, *Henry V*, pp. 118–19; and E. Carleton Williams, *My Lord of Bedford, 1389–1435: Being a Life of John of Lancaster, First Duke of Bedford, Brother of Henry V and Regent of France* (London, 1963), pp. 35–40.

54. No plan as such exists in the sources, but this is certainly what Henry had in mind, judging from his maneuvers over the next few years.

55. Burne, *Agincourt War*, pp. 115–26; Jubault, pp. 45–52; Allmand, *Henry V*, pp. 116–20; Jacob, *Henry V*, pp. 125–9; and Richard Ager Newhall, *The English Conquest of Normandy, 1416–24: A Study in Fifteenth Century Warfare* (New Haven, 1924), pp. 37–91. For the siege of Caen see Léon Puiseaux, *Siège et prise de Caen par les anglais en*

1417: *Épisode de la guerre de cent ans* (Caen, 1868).

56. Burne, *Agincourt War*, pp. 126–7; Newhall, pp. 71–2, 92–7; and Jacob, *Henry V*, pp. 129–30.

57. Burne, Agincourt War, pp. 129–33; Jubault, pp. 57–64; Allmand, *Henry V*, pp. 121–8; Newhall, pp. 97–105, 110–23; Jacob, *Henry V*, pp. 130–41; and Léon Puiseaux, *Siège et prise de Rouen par les anglais (1418–1419)* (Caen 1867).

58. Burne, *Agincourt War*, pp. 133–4; Newhall, pp. 123–32; and E.F. Jacob, 'The Collapse of France, 1419–20', *Bulletin of the John Rylands Library* 26 (1941–2), 307–26.

59. Jim Bradbury, *The Medieval Siege* (Woodbridge, 1992), pp. 163–71, 282–95; Philippe Contamine, 'La guerre de siège au temps de Jeanne d'Arc', *Dossiers de archéologie* 34 (May 1979), 11–20; and Kelly DeVries, 'The Impact of Gunpowder Weaponry on Siege Warfare in the Hundred Years War', in ed. I.A. Corfis and M. Wolfe, *Medieval City Under Siege* (Woodbridge, 1995), pp. 227–44.

60. Perroy, pp. 242–3; Vaughan, *John the Fearless*, pp. 210–21; Jubault, pp. 39–46; Newhall, pp. 105–10; and Schnerb, pp. 177–80.

61. Vaughan, *John the Fearless*, pp. 221–7; Jubault, pp. 53–7; Newhall, pp. 132–9; and Schnerb, pp. 180–93.

62. Perroy, pp. 242–3; Vaughan, *John the Fearless*, 263–86; Schnerb, pp. 194–207; Jubault,

pp. 53–7; and Paul Bonenfant, *Du meurtre de Montereau au traité de Troyes* (Brussels, 1958), pp. 1–16.

63. Bonenfant; Perroy, pp. 243–4; Allmand, *Hundred Years War*, pp. 29–32; Burne, *Agincourt War*, pp. 139–44; Allmand, *Henry V*, pp. 136–50; Jacob, *Henry V*, pp. 147–59; and Palmer, 'War Aims of the Protagonist', pp. 69–73.

64. Burne, *Agincourt War*, pp. 144–80; Allmand, *Henry V*, pp. 151–82; Newhall, pp. 269–92; and Jacob, *Henry V*, pp. 160–83.

65. On the battle of Baugé see Burne, *Agincourt War*, pp. 148–63; Newhall, pp. 275–6; Allmand, *Henry V*, pp. 158–67; Jacob, *Henry V*, pp. 169–70; and Jubault, pp. 123–8. On Scots in the French army see Jubault, pp. 113–86 and Bernard Chevalier, 'Les écossais dans les armées de Charles VII jusqu'a la bataille de Verneuil', in *Jeanne d'Arc: Une époque, un rayonnement* (Paris, 1982), pp. 85–94.

66. Perroy, pp. 268–71; Allmand, *Hundred Years War*, p. 32; Allmand, *Henry V*, pp. 173–8; Jacob, *Henry V*, pp. 174–8; and Williams, pp. 74–5.

67. Allmand, *Hundred Years War*, pp. 32–3 and M.G.A. Vale, *Charles VII* (Berkeley and Los Angeles, 1974), pp. 32–3.

68. Burne, *Agincourt War*, pp. 181–95; Jubault, pp. 165–7; and Jean-Michel Dousseau, *La bataille de Cravant (1423)* (Auxerre, 1987).

69. Burne, *Agincourt War*,

pp. 196–215; Jubault,
pp. 172–84; and Williams,
pp. 106–17.

70. Burne, *Agincourt War*, pp.
216–24; Jubault, pp. 187–202,
210–12; Williams, pp. 127–36,
148–59; and Amicie de Villaret,
*Campagnes des Anglais dans
l'Orléanais, la Beauce Chartrain et
le Gatinais (1421–1428):
L'armée sous Warwick et Suffolk
au siège de Montargis. Campagnes
de Jeanne d'Arc sur la Loire
postérierures au siège d'Orléans*
(Orléans, 1893).

71. Burne, *Agincourt War*,
pp. 220–1; Jubault, pp. 202–4;
Vale, pp. 35–41; and Jean-Paul
Etcheverry, *Arthur de Richemont
le justicier, précurseur, compagnon
et successeur de Jeanne d'Arc ou
l'honneur d'être Français* (Paris,
1983).

72. Burne, pp. 225–49 and
Jubault, pp. 216–19. This will
be discussed further below.

73. On the destruction of France
during the Hundred Years War
see Nicholas Wright, *Knights
and Peasants: The Hundred Years
War in the French Countryside*
(Woodbridge, 1998) and Alain
Girardot, 'La guerre au XIVe
siècle: La dévastation, ses
modes et ses degrés', *Bulletin de
la sociétés d'histoire et
d'archéologie de la Meuse* 30–1
(1994–5), 1–32.

74. On why her men followed Joan,
see Kelly DeVries, 'A Woman as
Leader of Men: A Reassessment
of Joan of Arc's Military
Career', in ed. C. Wood and
B. Wheeler, *Fresh Verdicts on
Joan of Arc* (New York, 1996),
pp. 3–18.

Chapter 3: A Military Mission?

1. On the history of Joan's
iconography, with a reference
to this early artistic endeavor,
see Pernoud and Clin,
pp. 240–3.

2. In the *Guardian*, 13 May 1998,
an article, '"Only Portrait" of
Joan of Arc Found', announced
the discovery in the Notre
Dame de Beamont chapel at
Joan's birthplace, Domrémy, of
a fresco possibly dating from
her time or slightly after. It
purports to be a 'mainly ochre-
coloured portrait [which]
shows a pretty teenager with
round cheeks, a mass of blonde
hair piled under a peasant
headdress and piercing blue
eyes kneeling calmly between
the arms of another local saint,
Thiáut of Provins'. Nothing
further is known about this
fresco, nor, so far as I know,
has it ever been shown or
photographed. Considering the
date and the lack of publicity
surrounding this 'only
portrait', one can only assume
that it has now been
discredited.

3. Pernoud and Clin, p. 256.
4. Aulon, in Duparc, I:486.
5. Alençon, in Duparc, I:387. See
also the retrial testimony of
Bertrand de Poulengy in
Duparc, I:306.
6. Thibaut, in Duparc, I:370. See
also Régine Pernoud, *Joan of
Arc by Herself and Her
Witnesses*, trans. E. Hyams
(New York, 1964), pp. 64–5.
7. Dunois, in Duparc, I:325.
8. Joan, in Quicherat, I:46. (N.B.
Because the record of Joan's

trial is in the third person, I have continued to use a third person grammatical format in my translations.) This was also testified to at the nullification trial by Jean Moreau (in Duparc, I:252), Béatrice (in Duparc, I:257), Dominique Jacob (in Duparc, I:256), and Hauviette (in Duparc, I:275), and repeated verbatim in the *Chronique de la Pucelle, in Quicherat*, IV:204–5. See also Pernoud, *Joan of Arc*, pp. 15–16. It seems curious that they never asked Joan when she was born, or how old she was. Perhaps everyone knew, or perhaps she did not know. Unfortunately, without a definite response to such a question, Joan's age during the events of 1429–30 cannot be known for sure. Some believe, on no good evidence, that Joan was born in 1412, making her seventeen years old when she began her military career. Other guesses are 1414 or 1410, making her fifteen or nineteen. But, as none of these are based on the least amount of original source evidence, scholars, such as Régine Pernoud and Jules Quicherat, have simply not discussed her age. In agreeing with their wisdom, I, too, will not ponder on such an unanswerable question.

9.   There are a few French fanatics, though, who persist in this claim, lost perhaps in the false notion of a fifteenth-century world where no peasant girl could rise to the station that she did without having some noble blood flowing inside her. See Pernoud and Clin, p. 222, and Pernoud, *Joan of Arc*, pp. 24–9. (While Régine Pernoud was alive – she died in 1998 – she tirelessly fought against this notion and the one that claimed that Joan had escaped the pyre and her persecutors. In almost every one of her books, she waged a crusade against the largely French scholars who wished to alter history. Pernoud was a French patriot, and she saw Joan as the quintessential example of loyalty to her country, but she would not go so far as to change history to make the story of Joan's life 'better'.)

10.   For an investigation of Joan's house and life in Domrémy, the best work is Siméon Luce, *Jeanne d'Arc à Domrémy: recherches critiques sur les origines de la mission de la Pucelle*, 2 vols (Paris, 1886).

11.   Pernoud and Clin, p. 221, and Pierre Champion, *Jeanne d'Arc* (Paris, 1933), p. 4.

12.   On this see the nullification testimonies of Jean Moreau (in Duparc, I:253), Hauviette (in Duparc, I:275), and Bertrand de Poulengy (in Duparc, I:304–5).

13.   Laxart, in Duparc, I:295–6. See also the testimonies of Jean Moreau (in Duparc, I:253), Béatrice (in Duparc, I:258), Colin (in Duparc, I:288), Hauviette (in Duparc, I:275), Mengette (in Duparc, I:284–5), and Isabellette (in Duparc, I:282).

14. Béatrice (in Duparc, I:258), Jean Moreau (in Duparc, I:253), and Colin (in Duparc, I:287). See also the testimonies of Etienne de Sionne, Dominqiue Jacob, Henri Arnoul, Perrin Drappier, Simonin Musnier, Hauviette, Mengette, Michel Lebuin, Isabellette, Durand Laxart, Jean Waterin, Jean Colin, Jean le Fumeux, and Nicolas Bailly (in Duparc, I:255–310).

15. Waterin, in Duparc, I:277.

16. Joan, in Quicherat, I:51–2. See also Pernoud, *Joan of Arc*, p. 30.

17. Joan, in Quicherat, I:52–3. See also Pernoud, *Joan of Arc*, pp. 30–1, and Champion, *Jeanne d'Arc* pp. 10–11. Domrémy was in the castellany of Vaucouleurs. Vaucouleurs was also, in Champion's words, 'the last shred of France on the eastern extreme of the realm'. On the persistence of Vaucouleurs to remain this 'last shred of France' in the wake of constant English and Burgundian military engagement see Henri Bataille, 'Vaucouleurs ou l'énigma d'un siège', *Dossiers de archéologie* 34 (May 1979), 56–63.

18. Joan, in Quicherat, I:171. See also Pernoud, *Joan of Arc*, pp. 30–1. On the significance of Saint Michael in late medieval France see Colette Beaune, *The Birth of an Ideology: Myths and Symbols of Nation in Late-Medieval France*, trans. Susan Ross Huston, ed. Fredric L. Cheyette (Berkeley and Los Angeles, 1991), pp. 152–71.

19. Épinal, in Duparc, I:279. On the idea that Joan was to be married while still in Domrémy see Pernoud, *Joan of Arc*, pp. 23–4.

20. Lebuin, in Duparc, I:293.

21. Laxart, in Duparc, I:296. Joan repeated the same prophecy to Catherine Royer (in Duparc, I:298). See also Pernoud and Clin, pp. 19–20, and Pernoud, *Joan of Arc*, pp. 31–3.

22. On Isabeau's reputation as a villain during Joan's time see Rachel Gibbons, 'Isabeau of Bavaria, Queen of France (1385–1422): The Creation of an Historical Villainess', *Transactions of the Royal Historical Society*, sixth ser., 6 (1996), 51–73. Gibbons' attempt to rehabilitate Isabeau's reputation is, however, unconvincing.

23. So Joan had told Seguin Seguin, as testified to in the nullification trial, in Duparc, I:472. A description of Vaucouleurs and its fortifications in Joan's day is found in Bataille, 'Vaucouleurs ou l'énigma d'un siège' and Henri Bataille, *Vaucouleurs: Les remparts qui ont sauvé Jeanne-d'Arc* (Vosges, n.d.). On her visits with Robert de Baudricourt see Paul Gache, *Sainte Jeanne d'Arc à Vaucouleurs* (Vailly-sur-Sauldre, 1982).

24. Laxart, in Duparc, I:296. The Latin 'alapas' means 'to beat or slap'. Baudricourt's 'mockery and derision' is emphasized in *Chronique de la Pucelle*, in Quicherat, IV:205. See also Pernoud, *Joan of Arc*, p. 33.

25. Jean de Metz, in Duparc,

I:289–90. There are several different spellings of Jean's surname. Novelompont is found in Quicherat's edition.

26. Laxart, in Duparc, I:296. See also Pernoud, *Joan of Arc*, p. 36.

27. There is also a possibility that Joan's mission had nothing to do with Philip's decision to send troops into Domrémy. The duke had for the last few years been occupied with the acquisition of the counties of Hainault, Holland, and Zeeland, all controlled by his cousin, the countess Jacqueline of Bavaria, and her husband, Humphrey of Gloucester. With this acquisition completed a short time before the attack on Domrémy, it could be that Philip was simply returning his attention to matters closer to home and sought to punish a village that held out for the dauphin against the duke's wishes. For a detailed discussion of this history, see Vaughan, *Philip the Bold*, pp. 29–50. Witnesses recalling this attack at the nullification trial include: Jean Moreau, Dominique Jacob, Hauviette, and Isabellette (all in Duparc, I:252–84). On the attack of Joan's village see Funck-Brentano, pp. 32–3.

28. There might have been no second meeting with Robert de Baudricourt. It is only in the nullification trial testimony of Marguerite la Touroulde (in Duparc, I:378) that such can be said, and then only because she claims it was the duke of Lorraine who sent to Robert de Baudricourt to ask for a visit from Joan because 'he was ill'. Of course, this might present yet another reason, a less military one, for the second meeting between Robert and Joan.

29. Laxart, in Duparc, I:296. Also mentioning the visit with the duke of Lorraine is Jean Moreau (in Duparc, I:255), Jean de Metz (in Duparc, I:290), and Bertrand de Poulengy (in Duparc, I:306).

30. Touroulde, in Duparc, I:378. See also Pernoud and Clin, pp. 18–19, and Pernoud, *Joan of Arc*, p. 38.

31. Joan, in Quicherat, I:53–4. See also Pernoud and Clin, pp. 18–19, and Pernoud, *Joan of Arc*, p. 38.

32. On this visit see Bertrand de Poulengy, in Duparc, I:306; Pernoud and Clin, p. 19; and Champion, *Jeanne d'Arc*, p. 20.

33. Royer, in Duparc, I:298. See also Pernoud and Clin, p. 20, and Pernoud, *Joan of Arc*, p. 38.

34. On the presentation of men's clothing to Joan, see Durand Laxart (in Duparc, I:296), Jean de Metz (in Duparc, I:290), and Bertrand de Poulengy (in Duparc, I:306). Metz later recalled that he had asked her if she wished to travel in these clothes and that she agreed, apparently thinking that nothing was wrong with doing so.

35. Laxart, in Duparc, I:296.

36. Poulengy, in Duparc, I:306. See also René Olivier, 'La lance, l'épée et la hache (les armes de la Pucelle)', *Les amis de Jeanne d'Arc* 42.3 (1995), 18–19.

37. The names of Joan's
    companions on this journey
    are included in the nullification
    trial testimonies of Bertrand de
    Poulengy and Jean de Metz (in
    Duparc, I:306, 290). See also
    Pernoud and Clin, pp. 19–21,
    and Champion, *Jeanne d'Arc*,
    p. 21.
38. Jean de Metz (in Duparc,
    I:290–1) and Bertrand de
    Poulengy (in Duparc, I:306). A
    possible route is described in
    Champion, *Jeanne d'Arc*,
    pp. 20–4.
39. Royer, in Duparc, I:299.
40. Poulengy, in Duparc, I:306–7.
41. Metz, in Duparc, I:291.
42. Seguin Seguin and Husson
    Lemaitre, in Duparc, I:471,
    467–8.
43. Bertrand de Poulengy (in
    Duparc, I:306–7) and Jean de
    Metz (in Duparc, I:291).
44. On the importance of this
    shrine see Beaune, pp. 127–32.
45. Joan, in Quicherat, I:75–6. See
    also Pernoud and Clin,
    pp. 15–16; Pernoud, *Joan of
    Arc*, p. 46; and Champion,
    Jeanne d'Arc, pp. 23–4.
46. Barbin, in Duparc, I:375.
47. Simon Charles, in Duparc,
    I:400. See also Pernoud and
    Clin, pp. 21–2, and Pernoud,
    Joan of Arc, p. 49.
48. On Chinon Castle see Vicomte
    du Motey, *Jeanne d'Arc à Chinon
    et Robert de Rouvres* (Paris,
    1927), pp. 15–18 and Armand
    Durlewanger, *The Royal Chateau
    of Chinon*, trans. Stan and Rita
    Morton (Colmar, 1982).
49. Simon Charles, in Duparc,
    I:400. Simon Charles may not
    have been present, as he

reported that he had been
attending to the dauphin's
business in Italy when Joan
arrived at Chinon. Whether he
had returned or not before her
meeting with the dauphin
cannot be determined from his
testimony.
50. Gaucourt, in Duparc, I:326.
51. Pasquerel, in Duparc, I:389–90.
    See also Pernoud and Clin, pp.
    23–5; Pernoud, *Joan of Arc*, pp.
    53–4, 66; Warner, pp. 75–6;
    Vale, pp. 51–3; Motey, pp. 30–1;
    Claude Desana, 'La première
    entrevue de Jeanne d'Arc et de
    Charles VII à Chinon (Mars
    1429)', *Analecta Bollandiana* 84
    (1966), 113–26. Jules
    Quicherat, *New Aspects of the
    Case History of Jeanne d'Arc*,
    trans. H.G. Francq (Brandon,
    1971), pp. 28–30; Antoine
    Thomas, 'Le "signe royal" et le
    secret de Jeanne d'Arc', *Revue
    historique* 103 (1910), 278–82;
    and Dom Charles Poulet,
    'Jeanne d'Arc à Chinon. Les
    causes naturelles et
    surnaturelles de l'acceptation
    royale,' *Historisch tijdschrift* 1
    (1923), 13–21. Some have
    argued that this certainly could
    not have been the 'secret'
    message 'known only to God'
    which Charles received from
    Joan; that it must have been
    something more than a simple
    confirmation of his royalty. I
    am inclined to agree. Later
    traditions have Charles VII
    uttering a prayer before Joan's
    arrival and having Joan repeat
    that prayer to him. See
    Quicherat, *New Aspects*, p. 30
    and Vale, pp. 52–3.

52. Alain Chartier, in Quicherat,
     V:133. See also Quicherat, *New
     Aspects*, p. 28.

53. Alençon, in Duparc, I:381;
     Pernoud and Clin, pp. 26–7;
     and Pernoud, *Joan of Arc*, pp.
     50–1. On her freedom within
     Chinon Castle see the retrial
     testimony of her page, Louis de
     Coutes, in Duparc, I:362.

54. Simon Charles, in Duparc,
     I:399–400.

55. Seguin, in Duparc, I:472–3.
     This interview took place in
     Poitiers. See also Alençon's
     testimony, in Duparc, I:382.

56. The names of these are
     included in Champion, *Jeanne
     d'Arc*, p. 31.

57. Charles T. Wood, for one,
     believes that the loss of this
     interrogation transcript is
     suspicious. It is known to have
     existed during Joan's lifetime,
     for she refers to it frequently at
     her trial in Rouen, calling it the
     'book (or register) of Poitiers'.
     Wood believes, on very little
     evidence it must be admitted,
     that its destruction was
     probably by Charles VII or
     someone of his circle, perhaps
     Regnault de Chartres, the
     archbishop of Reims, who never
     liked Joan or the way she
     conducted her warfare. See
     Charles T. Wood, 'Joan of Arc's
     Mission and the Lost Record of
     Her Interrogation at Poitiers', in
     ed. B. Wheeler and C.T. Wood,
     Fresh Verdicts on Joan of Arc
     (New York, 1996), pp. 19–20.
     See also Pernoud, *Joan of Arc*,
     pp. 58, 67–8, and Quicherat,
     New Aspects, p. 2.

58. All of this is according to

     Seguin Seguin (in Duparc,
     I:472), the only Poitiers
     interrogator who testified about
     this examination at the
     nullification trial. See also
     Pernoud and Clin, pp. 25–30;
     Pernoud, *Joan of Arc*, pp. 54–8,
     66–7; Champion, *Jeanne d'Arc*,
     p. 32; and Motey, pp. 37–42.

59. Seguin, in Duparc, I:472–3.
     See also Simon Charles, Raoul
     de Gaucourt, and Jean d'Aulon,
     in Duparc, I:399–400, 326–7,
     475–6. See also Pernoud, *Joan
     of Arc*, pp. 56–7.

60. Aulon, in Duparc, I:476. See
     also Jean Pasquerel, in Duparc,
     I:389; Pernoud and Clin, pp.
     30–1; and Pernoud, *Joan of Arc*,
     pp. 58–9.

61. See Aulon, in Duparc, I:476–7.

62. Dunois, in Duparc, I:317;
     Champion, *Jeanne d'Arc*, pp.
     35–6; and Pernoud, *Joan of Arc*,
     pp. 60–1. See also the accounts
     of Hémon Raguier, in
     Quicherat, V:258.

63. Aulon, in Duparc, I:477. See
     also the accounts of Charles's
     treasurer, Hémon Raguier, 10
     March 1429, in Quicherat,
     V:258; the retrial testimonies of
     Louis de Coutes and the Duke
     d'Alençon, in Duparc, I :363
     and I:382; Pernoud, *Joan of
     Arc*, p. 59; Champion, *Jeanne
     d'Arc*, p. 35; and Charles
     ffoulkes, 'The Armour of
     Jeanne d'Arc', *The Burlington
     Magazine* 16 (Dec 1909),
     141–6.

64. On the sword of Saint-
     Catherine-de-Fierbois see
     Pernoud and Clin, p. 16;
     Pernoud, *Joan of Arc*, pp. 61–2;
     Champion, *Jeanne d'Arc*, p. 23;

Quicherat, *New Aspects*, pp. 30–1; Olivier, p. 19; and Bonnie Wheeler, 'Joan of Arc's Sword in the Stone', in ed. C. Wood and B. Wheeler, *Fresh Verdicts on Joan of Arc* (New York, 1996), pp. xi–xvi. On the importance of Saint-Catherine-de-Fierbois as a shrine in late medieval France see Beaune, pp. 127–32.

65. On these see Olivier, pp. 17–20.
66. She testified of this at her trial, in Quicherat, I:236. See also Pernoud, *Joan of Arc*, p. 62.
67. Quicherat, *New Aspects*, p. 31; Olivier, p. 18; and Wheeler, p. xv.
68. As found in the anonymous *Le mystère du siège d'Orléans*, eds F. Guessard and E. de Certain (Paris, 1862), ll. 412–15. See also Beaune, p. 131.
69. Pernoud and Clin, p. 16.
70. Joan, in Quicherat, I:235–6.
71. *Journal du siège d'Orléans*, in Quicherat IV:129.
72. Champion, *Jeanne d'Arc*, p. 34.
73. See Dunois's nullification trial testimony, in Duparc, I:317.
74. Poulengy, in Duparc, I:306.
75. This is Champion's estimate (*Jeanne d'Arc*, pp. 25–6).
76. Seguin, in Duparc, I:473.

Chapter 4: Relieving the Siege of Orléans

1. See Luce, *Histoire de Bertrand du Guesclin*; Fowler, 'Bertand du Guesclin;' and Dupuy.
2. See Kelly DeVries, 'Robert Knolles', in ed. W.W. Kibler and G.A. Zinn, *Medieval France: An Encyclopedia* (New York, 1995), p. 341.
3. Alençon, in Duparc, I:381.
4. Touroulde, in Duparc, I:378.
5. Alençon, in Duparc, I:387–8.
6. Pius II, *Commentarii rerum memorabilium quae temporibus suis contingerunt* in Quicherat, IV:510.
7. Some of these studies include: Canonge, pp. 9–31; Collet, pp. 60–101; Bourguignon, pp. 7–103; Funck-Brentano, pp. 61–79; Lancesseur, pp. 45–71; Jules Quicherat, *Histoire du siège d'Orléans et des honneurs rendus à la Pucelle* (Paris, 1854); Régine Pernoud, *La libération d'Orléans, 8 mai 1429* (Paris, 1969); Armand Bouvier, *Orléans, cœur de la France et Jeanne la libératrice* (Orléans, 1929); Edouard Bruley, *Jeanne d'Arc à Orléans* (Orléans, 1929); and Henri Baraude, 'Le siège d'Orléans et Jeanne d'Arc, 1428–1429,' *Revue des questions historiques* 80–1 (1906–7), 31–65, 74–112, 395–424. See also Pernoud and Clin, pp. 33–51; Pernoud, *Joan of Arc*, pp. 70–107; and Champion, *Jeanne d'Arc*, pp. 39–51. Original sources on this conflict are: *Journal du siège d'Orléans*, in Quicherat, IV:151–65; *Chronique de la Pucelle* in Quicherat, IV:221–32; Perceval de Cagny, *Chroniques*, in Quicherat, IV:5–11; Jean Chartier, *Chronique de Charles VII*, in Quicherat, IV:56–64; Jacques Bouvier or Gilles le [Herald of Berry], *Chroniques du roi Charles VII*, in Quicherat, IV:42–4; Guillaume Giraut *Note sur la levée du siège d'Orléans*, in

Quicherat, IV:282–3; *Chronique de Lorraine*, in Quicherat, IV:332–4; the Continuator of Guillaume de Nangis, *Chronique Parisienne*, in Quicherat, IV:313; Engerrand de Monstrelet, *Chroniques*, in Quicherat, IV:363–8; Jean de Wavrin, *Recueil de chroniques et anchiennes istoires de la Grant Bretaigne a present nommee Engleterre*, in Quicherat, IV:408–11; Jean Lefèvre de Saint-Rémy, *Chronique*, in Quicherat, IV:430–1; and Eberhard von Windecken, *Denkwürdigkeiten zur Geschichte des Zeitalters Kaiser Sigismund*, in Quicherat, IV:486–96.

8. Jean Chartier, in Quicherat, IV:70.

9. M. Boucher de Molandon and Adalbert de Beaucorps, *L'armée anglaise vaincue par Jeanne d'Arc sous les murs d'Orléans* (Orléans, 1892), especially pp. 134–9, and Louis Jarry, *Le compte de L'armée anglaise au siège d'Orléans, 1428–1429* (Orléans, 1892), especially pp. 58–65. See also Burne, *Agincourt War*, pp. 228–9.

10. Burne, *Agincourt War*, p. 229.

11. The *Journal du siège de Orléans* (in Quicherat, IV:105–6) comments on how few English fortifications and men there were. Jacques Bouvier (in Quicherat, IV:42) notes that Joan knew this too, as she reconnoitered these positions while staying in Orléans. On the distances of the boulevards from the walls of Orléans see Philippe Contamine, 'Les armées française et anglaise à l'époque de Jeanne d'Arc', *Revue des sociétés savantes de haute-normandie. Lettres et sciences humaines* 57 (1970), 5–6.

12. Descriptions of the bridge and the Tourelles can be found in Burne, *Agincourt War*, p. 229; M. Vergnaud-Romangnesi, *Notice historique sur le fort des Tourelles de l'ancien pont de la ville d'Orléans, où Jeanne d'Arc combattit et fut blessée, sur la découverte de ses restes en juillet 1831* (Paris, 1832); M. Collin, *La casemate du bont du pont des Tourelles à Orléans du coté de la Sologne* (Paris, 1867); and M. Collin, *Les derniers jours du pont des Tourelles à Orléans* (Orléans, 1875).

13. *Journal du siège d'Orléans*, in Quicherat, IV:97. On the use of gunpowder weapons during this period, and in particular during the engagements participated in by Joan of Arc, see Kelly DeVries, 'The Use of Gunpowder Weaponry By and Against Joan of Arc During the Hundred Years War', *War and Society* 14 (1996), 1–16.

14. The best source for this is the *Journal du siège d'Orléans*, in Quicherat, IV:98–9. See also Burne, *Agincourt War*, pp. 229–30.

15. See, for example, Burne, *Agincourt War*, p. 230.

16. Monstrelet, ed. L. Douet-d'Arcq, IV:299–300; *Journal d'un siège de Orléans*, in Quicherat, IV:100–2; *The Brut, or the Chronicles of England*, ed. F.W.D. Brie (London, 1906),

I:434–5; and a poem, 'De par Orliens', found in L. Jarry, ed., 'Deux chansons normandes sur le siège d'Orléans et la mort de Salisbury', *Bulletin de la société archéologique et historique de l'Orléannais* 10 (1893), 366–7 and Siméon Luce, ed., 'Une pièce de vers sur le siège d'Orléans', in *La France pendant la guerre de cent ans: Épisodes historiques et vie privée aux XIVe et XVe siècles*, second edn (Paris, 1893), pp. 207–14. See also Pernoud, *Joan of Arc*, pp. 74–5; Pernoud, *Libération d'Orléans*, pp. 7–10; Burne, *Agincourt War*, pp. 230–1; Liocourt, II:81; and Kelly DeVries, 'Military Surgical Practice and the Advent of Gunpowder Weaponry', *Canadian Bulletin of Medical History* 7 (1990), 136.

17. *Journal d'un siège d'Orléans*, in Quicherat, IV:103–4 and Cagny, in Quicherat, IV:8. See also Liocourt, II:81.

18. The extraordinary exchange of gunfire by both sides at the siege of Orléans is one of its most interesting aspects and well deserving of more study. For a brief discussion see DeVries, 'The Use of Gunpowder Weaponry'; Pernoud, *Libération d'Orléans*, pp. 124–5; and Liocourt, I:76. 79–80.

19. The only exception to this is an episode recorded in the *Journal d'un siège d'Orléans* (in Quicherat, IV:104) which occurred on 7 December 1428, when troops from the Tourelles attempted to capture the

Orléanais stronghold at the end of their side of the broken bridge known as Belle-Croix.

20. Jacques Debal, 'Les fortifications et le pont d'Orléans au temps de Jeanne d'Arc', *Dossiers d'archéologie* 34 (May 1979), 88–90 and Jacques Debal, 'La topographie de l'enceinte fortifiée d'Orléans au temps de Jeanne d'Arc', in *Jeanne d'Arc: une époque, un rayonment* (Paris, 1982), pp. 25–6.

21. On boulevards see DeVries, 'Impact of Gunpowder Weaponry on Siege Warfare', pp. 237–9, and Kelly DeVries, 'Facing the New Military Technology: Non-Trace Italienne Anti-Gunpowder Weaponry Defenses, 1350–1550', forthcoming in eds B.S. Hall and B. Steele, *Colonels and Quartermasters: War and Technology in the Old Regime* (Cambridge, 2000). On the English construction of boulevards at Orléans see *Journal du siège d'Orléans*, in Quicherat, IV:109, and Pernoud, *Libération d'Orléans*, pp. 92–3.

22. Pernoud, *Libération d'Orléans*, p. 83. On whose calculations she bases these figures is unknown.

23. On the Tourelles boulevard see DeVries, 'Impact of Gunpowder Weaponry on Siege Warfare', p. 238; Debal, 'Les fortifications et le pont d'Orléans,' pp. 88–90; and Debal, 'La topographie de l'enceinte fortifiée d'Orléans', pp. 25–6. This boulevard remained in place until at least 1676, as a drawing from that

time (reproduced in Debal, 'Les fortifications et le pont d'Orléans', p. 89, and Debal, 'La topographie de l'enciente fortifiée d'Orléans,' p. 37) shows it still in place. But this illustration shows the boulevard to be of stone construction, thus different from the boulevard that was constructed by the English in 1428. (This has led some to believe that the original boulevard was also in stone – including those who constructed the model in the Musée de Jeanne d'Arc in Orléans – but this was clearly not the case when evidence is considered, either from the original sources or from traditional fifteenth-century boulevard construction techniques.)

24. *Journal du siège d'Orléans*, in Quicherat, IV:98. A general statement of the valiance of the Orléanais is found in the *Journal du siège d'Orléans*, in Quicherat, IV:102–3, and in the nullification trial testimony of Jean Lullier, in Duparc, I:331.

25. *Journal du siège d'Orléans*, in Quicherat, IV:105. See also Pernoud, *Joan of Arc*, pp. 75–6, and Pernoud *Libération d'Orléans*, pp. 95–6.

26. See the *Journal du siège d'Orléans*, in Quicherat, IV:150, and Pernoud, *Libération d'Orléans*, p. 114.

27. See Gibbons.

28. Most of this and what follows comes from Pernoud and Clin, pp. 180–1, and Jean Thibault, 'Un prince territorial au XVe

siècle: Dunois, Bâtard d'Orléans', *Bulletin de la sociétés archéologique et historique de l'Orléanais* n.s. 14 (1997), 3–46.

29. See, for example, Burne, *Agincourt War*, pp. 148–63, and James Hamilton Wylie and W.T. Waugh, *The Reign of Henry the Fifth* (Cambridge, 1929), III:305–15.

30. On the Bastard of Orléans' role in the siege of Montargis see Burne, *Agincourt War*, pp. 221–2.

31. For an alternative view see Régine Pernoud (ed.) *The Retrial of Joan of Arc: The Evidence at the Trial for Her Rehabilitation*, trans. J.M. Cohen (London, 1955), p. 101 n.1, who defends the Bastard's military leadership at Orléans.

32. *Journal du siège d'Orléans*, in Quicherat, IV:106.

33. *Journal du siège d'Orléans*, in Quicherat, IV:110, and Pernoud, *Joan of Arc*, p. 76.

34. *Journal du siège d'Orléans*, in Quicherat, IV:107, 114, 116, 117.

35. The best source on the battle of the Herrings is: *Journal du siège d'Orléans*, in Quicherat, IV:120–6, or *Journal du siège d'Orléans*, ed. Charpentier and Cuissard, pp. 38–52. Secondary accounts include Burne, *Agincourt War*, pp. 234–6; Pernoud, *Libération d'Orléans*, pp. 99–103; Charles Oman, *A History of the Art of War in the Middle Ages* (London, 1924), II:392; and Ferdinand Lot, *L'art militaire et les armées au moyen âge en*

Europe et dans le Proche Orient (Paris, 1946), II:47–53.

36. *Journal du siège d'Orléans*, in Quicherat, IV:121. Pernoud, *Libération d'Orléans*, pp. 99–100, only uses the 4,000 number.

37. Monstrelet (Douet–d'Arcq) IV:313. See also the *Journal du siège d'Orléans*, in Quicherat, IV:126.

38. On this, for example, see DeVries, *Infantry Warfare in the Early Fourteenth Century*.

39. *Journal du siège d'Orléans*, in Quicherat, IV:124.

40. *Journal du siège d'Orléans*, in Quicherat, IV:122–3.

41. Dunois, in Quicherat, IV:317. See also Pernoud, *Libération d'Orléans*, p. 107. Joan's trial results at Poitiers had even reached Bruges by 10 May 1429, according to a letter recorded in Morosini, III:53. See also Liocourt, II:71.

42. *Journal du siège d'Orléans*, in Quicherat, IV:130–1, and Pernoud, *Libération d'Orléans*, pp. 104–5.

43. On this and what follows see Pierre Duparc, 'La délivrance d'Orléans et la mission de Jeanne d'Arc', in *Jeanne d'Arc: Une époque, un rayonnement* (Paris, 1982), pp. 153–8.

44. There is an indication that Joan may have gone on a pilgrimage to Puy with Pasquerel on 25 March, the day of the Annunciation. Régine Pernoud wonders if it is on or at least because of this journey that Joan decides to write this letter. See Pernoud, *Libération d'Orléans*, p. 113.

45. Although the original letter has long disappeared, there were several copies of it made, many of which survive. The French text can be found edited in Pernoud and Clin, pp. 249–50, and Quicherat, V:95–8. I have used the English translation in Pernoud and Clin, pp. 33–4.

46. On the requirements for a 'just war', including the declaration of war see Frederick H. Russell, *The Just War in the Middle Ages* (Cambridge, 1975) and Kelly DeVries, 'Medieval Declarations of War: An Example from 1212', *Scintilla* 4 (1987), 20–37.

47. Mention of the letter appears in several nullification trial testimonies and contemporary chronicles; for these references see Pernoud and Clin, p. 249.

48. Pernoud and Clin, pp. 247–9.

49. Lullier, in Duparc, I:331. See also Dunois, in Duparc, I:319–20.

50. Aulon, in Duparc, I:477. Aulon also claims that the Bastard traveled to Blois by boat and that he actually met Joan along the Loire river but outside of Blois. Whether this is to indicate that she had ventured towards Orléans on her own and had become lost – hence the reason for the Bastard's attempts to find her – is not in any contemporary source. However, because Dunois does not refer to this in his retrial testimony, and because Aulon seems to confuse this arrival in Blois with Joan's arrival in Orléans,

some might question this incident.

51. Dunois, in Duparc, I:317–18.
52. Alençon, in Duparc, I:381. See also Jean de Metz, in Duparc, II:289–90.
53. Monstrelet, in Quicherat, IV:364, and Joan, in Quicherat, I:78.
54. Dunois, in Duparc, I:317; Jean Chartier, in Quicherat, IV:54; *Chronique de la Pucelle*, in Quicherat, IV:217; Eberhard de Windecken, in Quicherat, IV:491; and Liocourt, II:90.
55. See Alençon's testimony at the nullification trial, in Duparc, I:382.
56. Pasquerel, in Duparc, I:391. See also Pernoud and Clin, p. 37.
57. See Dunois and Aulon's nullification trial testimonies, in Duparc, I:318, 477.
58. This date is disputed. Only Pasquerel gives a time when Joan and the army left Blois, and then only to say that it took them three days to reach Orléans. See Pasquerel, in Duparc, I:391–2.
59. Pasquerel, in Duparc, I:391–2.
60. Dunois, in Duparc, I:319.
61. Pasquerel, in Duparc, I:391–2.
62. Dunois testifies (in Duparc, I:319) that the army was split and that only Joan and a very few of the leaders crossed over the Loire and entered Orléans. Other sources indicate the same by their leaving the main French force always on the southern side of the Loire river. Liocourt (II:92) gives a count of 2,000 men-at-arms for this expedition, but he cites no reference for this tally.

63. Dunois, in Duparc, I:319. See also Pasquerel, in Duparc, I:392.
64. See Pasquerel, in Duparc, I:391–2, and Monstrelet, in Quicherat, IV:364.
65. *Chronique de la Pucelle*, in Quicherat, IV:218.
66. See Duparc, I:391 n.1.
67. *Journal du siège d'Orléans*, in Quicherat, IV:151–2.
68. *Journal du siège d'Orléans*, in Quicherat, IV:153. See also Pernoud and Clin, pp. 40–1.
69. Jacques l'Esbahy, in Duparc, I:333.
70. Louis de Coutes, in Duparc, I:363. See also *Chronique de la Pucelle*, in Quicherat, IV:219–20.
71. Dunois, in Duparc, I:318. The *Chronique de la Pucelle* (in Quicherat, IV:218–19) contains the same speech. See also Pernoud, *Libération d'Orléans*, pp. 117–18, and Liocourt, II:91. On the constant discord between Joan and the Bastard see Jean Chartier, in Quicherat, IV:59.
72. Coutes, in Duparc, I:363. It is possible that Coutes and Dunois were testifying of the same event, but confusing the day. Yet, Coutes does seem quite confident on his dating, and it certainly fits with what Joan does during the rest of 30 April.
73. *Journal du siège d'Orléans*, in Quicherat, IV:154.
74. Louis de Coutes, in Duparc, I:363–4. (The translation of 'maquereaulx mescréans' as 'unbelieving pimps' is Pernoud, *Retrial*, p. 136.)

75. *Journal du siège d'Orléans*, in Quicherat, IV:155. See also Pernoud, *Libération d'Orléans*, p. 123 and Liocourt, II:97.

76. *Journal du siège d'Orléans*, in Quicherat, IV:154. See also the *Chronique de la Pucelle*, in Quicherat, IV:220–1.

77. See the testimony of Jean d'Aulon, in Duparc, I:477, and the *Journal du siège d'Orléans*, in Quicherat, IV:155.

78. See *Journal du siège d'Orléans*, in Quicherat, IV:155; Pernoud, *Joan of Arc*, p. 85; and Pernoud, *Libération d'Orléans*, p. 128.

79. *Journal du siège d'Orléans*, in Quicherat, IV:156 and Jacques Bouvier, in Quicherat, IV:42; Pernoud, *Libération d'Orléans*, p. 128.

80. Alençon, in Duparc, I:383. Alençon was not present in Orléans at this time, but took this position after examining the English defenses once the siege had been lifted. He preceded this nullification trial comment by saying that he believed that the English fortifications were captured by 'miracle'. See also the *Journal du siège d'Orléans*, in Quicherat IV: 158.

81. *Journal du siège d'Orléans*, in Quicherat, IV:156.

82. This is recorded as an entry in the Orléans treasurer's rolls for 3 May (edited in an appendix found in Pernoud, *Libération d'Orléans*, p. 212). See Pernoud, *Joan of Arc*, p. 85 and Pernoud, *Libération d'Orléans*, p. 128.

83. Aulon, in Duparc, I:478. See also the *Chronique de la Pucelle*, in Quicherat, IV:222, and

Pernoud, *Libération d'Orléans*, pp. 128–9.

84. According to an inventory of Hémon Ragiuer, the Bastard had brought with him 532 more soldiers (see Liocourt, II:98); perhaps he believed that even with this number the French army was too small to face the English.

85. Aulon, in Duparc, I:478–9. See also *Chronique de la Pucelle*, in Quicherat, IV:218–19 and Pernoud, *Libération d'Orléans*, p. 129.

86. Aulon, Coutes, and Pasquerel, in Duparc, I:479–80; 364; and 392. Coutes' testimony is confused here and seems to combine all of the next few days' activities after this specific remembrance. See also Liocourt, II:99–100.

87. *Journal du siège d'Orléans*, in Quicherat, IV:157. See also the *Chronique de la Pucelle*, in Quicherat, IV:222–4, and Jean Chartier, in Quicherat, IV:57.

88. *Journal du siège d'Orléans*, in Quicherat, IV:157–8. See also Aulon, in Duparc, I:480; Coutes, in Duparc, I:364; and Pasquerel, in Duparc, IV:392. Perceval de Cagny (in Quicherat, IV:7) claims that all prisoners were put to death, but there is no corroborating evidence for this.

89. *Chronique de la Pucelle*, in Quicherat, IV:224, and Monstrelet, in Quicherat, IV:365.

90. Pasquerel, in Duparc, I:392–3.

91. Pasquerel, in Duparc, I:393–4. See also the *Chronique de la Pucelle*, in

Quicherat, IV:225; Pernoud, *Libération d'Orléans*, pp. 131–2; and Liocourt, II:103. There is a problem here, however, as the *Journal du siège d'Orléans* (in Quicherat, IV:154), as mentioned above, indicated that all heralds had been returned previously.

92. The quote is from Aulon, in Duparc, I:480. See also Coutes, in Duparc, I:364; the *Journal du siège d'Orléans*, in Quicherat, IV:158–9; the *Chronique de la Pucelle*, in Quicherat, IV:224; and Jean Chartier, in Quicherat, IV:57, 59. Both Pernoud, *Joan of Arc*, pp. 86–7, and Pernoud and Clin, p. 44, accept without comment Pasquerel's assertion that Joan did not fight on the day of Ascension. (Liocourt, II:101–3, simply notes the confusion among the sources.) Equally without comment or justification, Pernoud (*Joan of Arc*, pp. 88–9), redates the attack on the boulevard of Saint Jean le Blanc to the following day, before the French assault on the boulevard of the Augustins, despite all contemporary dating to the contrary. It is possible that Jean Pasquerel did not know of her expedition against the boulevard of Saint Jean le Blanc, but it definitely seems to have taken place. On the other hand, there was no actual combat between the two armies, so perhaps Pasquerel is taking this into consideration in his claims

that Joan did not fight on Ascension Day. On the need for boats each time the French crossed the Loire to attack an English boulevard there see Jean Chartier, in Quicherat, IV:60.

93. While others testify that no fighting was done with troops in the boulevard itself, Jean d'Aulon testified (in Duparc, I:430–1) that an attack was made by the English from the boulevard of the Augustins against the retiring French. This attack was only halted when Joan of Arc and La Hire charged on their horses 'with lances couched' against the English and 'drove them back into the boulevard of the Augustins'.

94. Simon Charles, in Duparc, I:401.

95. See *Journal du siège d'Orléans*, in Quicherat, IV:158.

96. Pasquerel, in Duparc, I:394.

97. *Journal du siège d'Orléans*, in Quicherat, IV:158–9. See also Pernoud, *Libération d'Orléans*, p. 133.

98. Aulon, in Duparc, I:481–2. See also Liocourt, II:104–5.

99. Pasquerel, in Duparc, I:394–5. See also Coutes, in Duparc, I:365, and Liocourt, II:106. Joan also testified (in Quicherat, I:79) that she knew that she would be wounded in the attack on the Tourelles.

100. See Cagny, in Quicherat, IV:8.

101. *Journal du siège d'Orléans*, in Quicherat, IV:159. See also Pernoud, *Joan of Arc*, p. 89, and Pernoud, *Libération d'Orléans*, p. 134.

102. See Pasquerel, in Duparc, I:395.

103. John Bliese has made a number of studies of earlier battlefield orations and has some interesting theses on what was recorded and what might actually have been said. The studies that apply here are: 'Rhetoric and Morale: A Study of Battle Orations from the Central Middle Ages', *Journal of Medieval History* 15 (1989), 201–26 and 'When Knightly Courage May Fail: Battle Orations in Medieval Europe', *Historian* 53 (1991), 489–504. That Joan is not reported to have given any battlefield oration puts her in the minority, although it may have been that she did not think that such a speech was hers to give, that either the Bastard of Orléans, one of the other generals, or the priests attending to the army should be encouraging them to fight. She may also have had the confidence that her troops would fight for her whether she made a speech to them or not.

104. Cagny, in Quicherat, IV:8.

105. *Journal du siège d'Orléans*, in Quicherat, IV:159–60. See also the nullification testimonies of Louis de Coutes and Jean Lullier, in Duparc, I:165 and I:331–2. Cagny (in Quicherat, IV:8) reports that three or four assaults were made against the Tourelles.

106. Dunois, in Duparc, I:320. See also Lullier and Coutes, in Duparc, I:332 and I:365; the *Chronique de la Pucelle*, in Quicherat, IV:228; and Pernoud, *Libération d'Orléans*, p. 138.

107. Pasquerel, in Duparc, I:395. See also Liocourt, II:109. In her own testimony (in Quicherat, I:79), Joan recalled her wounding at the Tourelles, and said that St Catherine helped her not to give in to her pain, but to keep fighting until the Tourelles had fallen.

108. Dunois, in Duparc, I:320–1. Cagny (in Quicherat, IV:8) reports that the small gunpowder weapons known as couleuvrines supported the final assault made against the Tourelles. See also the *Chronique de la Pucelle*, in Quicherat, IV:228–30.

109. Joan, in Quicherat, I:79. See also Pernoud, *Joan of Arc*, p. 93.

110. Reimbursement of this barge and a description of its use on that day is recorded in the Orléans' account books (Pernoud, *Libération d'Orléans*, p. 219). See also Pernoud and Clin, p. 47. It must be doubted that such a fire would have seriously damaged the Tourelles fortifications or even the bridge spans on which it was built. But, once again, this shows the determination of the citizens of Orléans to assist in whatever way possible with the defense of their city.

111. Aulon, in Duparc, I:483–4. See also Liocourt, II:110. A *target* was a small French shield generally held by one hand to ward off missile fire. It should

also be noted that, as frequent reference is made to a boulevard at the Tourelles, there is a possibility that the English had also built an earthen rampart around this fortification to increase its defensability.

112. Pasquerel, in Duparc, I:395. See also the *Chronique de la Pucelle*, in Quicherat, IV:230; Cagny, in Quicherat, IV:9; Pernoud, *Libération d'Orléans*, pp. 141–2; and Liocourt, II:111.

113. Pasquerel, in Duparc, I:395. Bouvier puts the number of English dead at 400–500 (in Quicherat, IV:44).

114. *Journal du siège d'Orléans*, in Quicherat, IV:163. See also *Chronique de la Pucelle*, in Quicherat, IV:231; Cagny, in Quicherat, IV:9; Pernoud, *Joan of Arc*, p. 92; Pernoud and Clin, p. 48; and Pernoud, *Libération d'Orléans*, p. 142.

115. Aulon, in Duparc, I:484.

116. Lullier, in Duparc, I:332. See also Dunois, Aulon, Coutes, and Pasquerel, in Duparc, I:321, 484, 365–6, and 395. Almost all of these say the same thing.

117. *Journal du siège d'Orléans*, in Quicherat, IV:163–4. See also *Chronique de la Pucelle*, in Quicherat, IV:231–2; Cagny, in Quicherat, IV:10; Bouvier, in Quicherat, IV:44; Jean Chartier, in Quicherat, IV:62–3; Pernoud, *Joan of Arc*, pp. 92–3; Pernoud and Clin, pp. 50–1; and Pernoud, *Libération d'Orléans*, pp. 142–3.

118. Cagny, in Quicherat, IV:9. But Liocourt (II:114) tallies the number of English soldiers only at 2,000, a much smaller number of troops than could be put against them by the French.

119. These two reasons are given by Monstrelet (in Quicherat, IV:360) to explain the English retreat on 8 May.

120. *Journal du siège d'Orléans*, in Quicherat, IV:164–5.

121. In Quicherat, V:100–4. See also Pernoud, *Joan of Arc*, pp. 96–97, and Pernoud and Clin, pp. 50–1.

122. See, for example, Pernoud, *Joan of Arc*, p. 97.

123. The order for these clothes is found in Quicherat, V:113. See also Pernoud, *Joan of Arc*, p. 99.

124. This letter is found in Quicherat, V:131–6. See also Pernoud, *Joan of Arc*, pp. 97–8.

125. See also the letter from the dauphin's counselor and Seneschal of Berry, Perceval de Bouainvilliers, to the Duke of Milan, Philippe Maria Visconti, in Quicherat, V:114–21, and Christine de Pisan, *Ditié de Jehanne d'Arc*, ed. A.J. Kennedy and K. Varty (Oxford, 1977).

126. For the Holy Roman Empire see Eberhard von Windecken, in Quicherat, V:498, and for the southern Low Countries and Italy see Antonio Morosini, III:53–4.

127. Clément de Fauquembergue, in Quicherat, IV:451. See also Monstrelet, in Quicherat, IV:363–8, and Pernoud and Clin, p. 51.

128. In Quicherat, V:136–7. See

also Pernoud, *Joan of Arc*, pp. 100–1. Quicherat dates this letter to the end of July 1429, but Pernoud dates it, in my opinion more accurately, to 1434. If this is correct, it is a particularly interesting document in that it reveals that Bedford, the leader of the English forces in France during this time, believed that the relief of the siege of Orléans was the turning point of this phase of the Hundred Years War. On the effect of the liberation of Orléans on the English leadership over other parts of occupied France see Anne E. Curry, 'L'effet de la libération sur l'armée anglaise: Les problèmes de l'organisation militaire en Normandie, de 1429 à 1435', in *Jeanne d'Arc: Une époque, un rayonnement* (Paris, 1982), pp. 95–106.

129. See Pernoud and Clin, pp. 221–2.

130. This has come down to us as *Le Mystère du siège d'Orléans*. See Pernoud and Clin, pp. 243–5.

131. See Pernoud and Clin, p. 245.

132. Lullier, in Duparc, I:332.

Chapter 5: Cleaning Up the Loire

1. See note 90 in the last chapter.

2. Liocourt, II:133. However, Villaret (pp. 74–5) claims a total of 8,000 in the French army. While Liocourt's number may be too small, Villaret's is certainly too large.

3. Dunois, in Duparc, I:321. See also Jean Chartier, in Quicherat, IV:64, and Villaret, pp. 72–3.

4. *Chronique de la Pucelle*, in Quicherat, IV:234.

5. Alençon, in Duparc, I:383. Perceval de Cagny's figure of 2,000–3,000 (Perceval de Cagny, *Chronique des ducs d'Alençon*, in Quicherat, IV:12) includes all of the troops in the French army at Jargeau and might be a more accurate depiction of the total force available to Joan there.

6. For Fastolf's itinerary see Liocourt, II:140.

7. See Bourgeois of Paris, *Journal*, in Quicherat, IV:462–3.

8. Both of these points are recorded in the *Chronique de la Pucelle*, in Quicherat, IV:233, and by Enguerrand de Monstrelet, in Quicherat, IV:368–9.

9. On Fastolf's military career and the profits he made from it see K.B. McFarlane, 'The Investment of Sir John Fastolf's Profits of War', in *England in the Fifteenth Century: Collected Essays* (London, 1981), pp. 175–98.

10. Liocourt, II:140. On Fastolf's numbers see Liocourt, II:133, 140.

11. *Journal du siège d'Orléans*, in Quicherat, IV:168–9. Virtually the same scene is reported by Dunois in his nullification trial testimony (in Duparc, I:322–3).

12. *Journal du siège d'Orléans*, in Quicherat, IV:167. See also Perceval de Cagny, in Quicherat, IV:12, and Monstrelet, in Quicherat, IV:368.

13. Jean Chartier, in Quicherat, IV:64.

14. See *Chronique de la Pucelle*, in Quicherat, IV:234, and Jean Chartier, in Quicherat, IV:64. Despite the duke of Alençon claiming that the Bastard of Orléans and Florent d'Illiers were in charge of the 'king's men' at Jargeau (in Duparc, I:383), which might give the impression that they commanded the forces there, other sources seem to indicate that these men were in charge only of some of the soldiers and not of the whole French army.

15. On the duke of Alençon's relationship with the dauphin, Charles, see his short biography in Pernoud and Clin, pp. 172–3.

16. Alençon, in Duparc, I:381.

17. See Alençon, in Duparc, I:381–2.

18. See Alençon, in Duparc, I:385, for her promise to his wife and mother. See Pernoud and Clin, p. 172, for dates on which she stayed at Saint-Laurent.

19. Alençon, in Duparc, I:384–5. See also Pernoud and Clin, pp. 59–60, and Pernoud, *Joan of Arc*, p. 114.

20. The description of the town's fortifications and numbers of soldiers are Liocourt's (II:133). See also Villaret, pp. 80–1.

21. Alençon, in Duparc, I:383. See also Liocourt, II:134.

22. The quote comes from Alençon's nullification testimony (in Duparc, I:384). See also the *Journal du siège d'Orléans*, in Quicherat, IV:167; Cagny, in Quicherat, IV:12;

Jean Chartier, in Quicherat, IV:65; Pernoud and Clin, p. 59; and Pernoud, *Joan of Arc*, p. 113.

23. Cagny, in Quicherat, IV:12. See also Liocourt, II:134.

24. Several contemporary sources mention this bombardment including: Alençon, in Duparc, I:384; *Journal du siège d'Orléans*, in Quicherat, IV:170–2; *Chronique de la Pucelle*, in Quicherat, IV:234; Cagny, in Quicherat, IV:12; and Jean Chartier, in Quicherat, IV:65. See also Liocourt, II:135; Villaret, pp. 77–8; Canonge, pp. 36–9; Collet, pp. 106–15; Bourguignon, pp. 123–31; Funck-Brentano, pp. 85–6; Lancesseur, pp. 72–4; and Contamine, 'La guerre de siège', pp. 11–12. There are indications in the Orléans comptes that all of the gunpowder weapons which had been used in defending that city, as well as the guns captured from the English there, were sent with the French army to Jargeau. These included 'cannon, couleuvrines, and a great bombard which needed 22 horses to transport and whose balls were not able to be lifted by two people'. Also in the artillery train were gunpowder, projectiles, masons, carpenters, and cannoniers. See Villaret, p. 77.

25. *Journal du siège d'Orléans*, in Quicherat, IV:171. See also Villaret, p. 83.

26. Alençon, in Duparc, I:384. See also Liocourt, II:135.

27. Joan, in Quicherat, I:79–80.

28. Alençon, in Duparc, I:384. See
    also Pernoud and Clin, p. 59,
    and Pernoud, *Joan of Arc*,
    pp. 113–14.

29. Monstrelet, in Quicherat,
    IV:369.

30. *Journal du siège d'Orléans*, in
    Quicherat, IV:171–2. See also
    the *Chronique de la Pucelle*, in
    Quicherat, IV:237, and
    Liocourt, II:136.

31. Cagny, in Quicherat, IV:12–13.
    See also *Journal du siège
    d'Orléans*, in Quicherat, IV:172.

32. Alençon, in Duparc, I:385. See
    also Pernoud and Clin, p. 60,
    and Pernoud, *Joan of Arc*, p. 114.

33. This was testified to by
    Alençon, in Duparc, I:385. See
    also Villaret, p. 84.

34. Alençon, in Duparc, I:385. On
    Joan's wounding and her
    encouragement of her soldiers
    see also the *Journal du siège
    d'Orléans*, in Quicherat, IV:172,
    and Villaret, pp. 83–4. On the
    French breaking through the
    French walls see *Journal du
    siège d'Orléans*, in Quicherat,
    IV:172; Cagny, in Quicherat,
    IV:13; and Jean Chartier, in
    Quicherat, IV:65. Villaret (p.
    84) claims that the French
    broke through the walls at the
    breach made by the *Bergière*'s
    felling of a tower, but there is
    nothing in the contemporary
    sources to indicate the
    accuracy of this claim.

35. See Bouvier, in Quicherat,
    IV:45; *Journal du siège d'Orléans*,
    in Quicherat, IV:173; and
    Chronique de la Pucelle, in
    Quicherat, IV:237–8.

36. Jean Chartier, in Quicherat,
    IV:65 and *Chronique de la*

Pucelle, in Quicherat, IV:238.
See also Liocourt, II:137 and
Villaret, pp. 84–5. The *Journal
du siège d'Orléans* (in
Quicherat, IV:173) indicates
also that the church of
Jargeau and several of the
houses were pillaged.

37. This is the total given by
    Alençon (in Duparc, I:385).
    Other tallies include: 300
    (Monstrelet, in Quicherat,
    IV:369) and 300–400 (Jean
    Chartier, in Quicherat, IV:65).
    Most others simply express the
    total killed in general terms:
    Journal du siège d'Orléans, in
    Quicherat, IV:173; *Chronique de
    la Pucelle*, in Quicherat, IV:238;
    Cagny, in Quicherat, IV:13; and
    Bouvier, in Quicherat, IV:45.
    Liocourt (II:137) has a figure
    of 700 English dead but does
    not indicate how he arrived at
    that number, while Villaret
    (p. 85) agrees with Chartier's
    300–400 number.

38. Except for Perceval de Cagny's
    total of eighteen or twenty
    killed (in Quicherat, IV:13)
    which probably should not be
    taken seriously.

39. See the *Journal du siège
    d'Orléans*, in Quicherat, IV:173;
    the *Chronique de la Pucelle*, in
    Quicherat, IV:234–5; Cagny, in
    Quicherat, IV:13; and Jean
    Chartier, in Quicherat, IV:65.
    The Orléans comptes record a
    town present to Joan and the
    other French military leaders of
    six barrels of wine in gratitude
    for the victory. See Villaret,
    p. 86.

40. See Villaret, p. 86. This is also
    recorded in the Orléans

comptes. The same preacher said Mass on 10 May 1429, during one of the celebrations for the relief of the siege of Orléans.

41. See Jean de Waurin (in Quicherat, IV:414).

42. Cagny, in Quicherat, IV:13.

43. See the *Journal du siège d'Orléans*, in Quicherat, IV:173–4; the *Chronique de la Pucelle*, in Quicherat, IV:238–9; Cagny, in Quicherat, IV:13; and Liocourt, II:138.

44. *Journal du siège d'Orléans*, in Quicherat, IV:174. See also the *Chronique de la Pucelle*, in Quicherat, IV:239–40; Cagny, in Quicherat, IV:13; Jean Chartier, in Quicherat, IV:65; and Villaret, p. 87.

45. Jean Chartier, in Quicherat, IV:65.

46. *Journal du siège d'Orléans*, in Quicherat, IV:173–4. See also Villaret, p. 87.

47. For this and the rest of my brief biography of Richemont see Pernoud and Clin, pp. 198–200 and Etcheverry.

48. Burne, *Agincourt War*, pp. 220–1, for one, is not too impressed by Richemont's military capabilities.

49. Perceval de Cagny (in Quicherat, IV:14) claims that Richemont, while on his march to meet with Joan, had been filled in on the details of the capture of Jargeau.

50. Alençon, in Duparc, I:385–6. See also the *Chronique de la Pucelle*, in Quicherat, IV:238; Pernoud, *Joan of Arc*, pp. 115–16; and Villaret, pp. 89–90.

51. See Alençon's nullification trial testimony, in Duparc, I:386; Dunois, in Duparc, I:322; Waurin, in Quicherat, IV:416–17; and the *Chronique de la Pucelle*, in Quicherat, IV:239.

52. Waurin, in Quicherat, IV:413.

53. Colonel Liocourt (II:139) does this, although the reason is not revealed.

54. *Chronique de la Pucelle*, in Quicherat, IV:240–1.

55. Alençon, in Duparc, I:386. See also Villaret, pp. 90–1; Etcheverry, pp. 144–5; and E. Fonssagrives, 'Jeanne d'Arc et Richemont', *Bulletin de la société polymathique du Morbihan* (1920), 8–11. On the numbers in Richemont's force see Jean Chartier, in Quicherat, IV:66.

56. Guillaume Gruel, *Chronique d'Arthur de Richemont* in Quicherat, IV:317. See also Pernoud, *Joan of Arc*, p. 116, and Villaret, pp. 91–2.

57. According to Gruel (in Quicherat, IV:316), Charles had discovered the Constable's march to Beaugency and had sent messengers telling him that he was forbidden to go there.

58. Waurin, in Quicherat, IV:416–17. See also Pernoud and Clin, pp. 60–1, and Pernoud, *Joan of Arc*, pp. 116–17.

59. Gruel, in Quicherat, IV:318.

60. See Alençon's testimony, in Duparc, I:385; the *Chronique de la Pucelle*, in Quicherat, IV:240; and Cagny, in Quicherat, IV:14.

61. Liocourt, II:138–9. For a

description of the castle and medieval town see Daniel Vannier, *Beaugency* (Beaugency, 1991). A schematic drawing of the keep can be found in Jean Mesqui, *Châteaux et enceintes de la France médiévale: De la défense à la résidence* (Paris, 1991), II:213.

62. See the *Journal du siège d'Orléans*, in Quicherat, IV:173–4.

63. See the *Journal du siège d'Orléans*, in Quicherat, IV:175; the *Chronique de la Pucelle*, in Quicherat, IV:240; Cagny, in Quicherat, IV:14; and Jean Chartier, in Quicherat, IV:66.

64. See the *Comptes de forteresse*, in Quicherat, V:263, and Liocourt, II:142.

65. The quote is from the *Journal du siège d'Orléans*, in Quicherat, IV:175, which also contains the fullest account of the terms of surrender. See also the testimony of Alençon, in Duparc, I:385; the *Chronique de la Pucelle*, in Quicherat, IV:241–2; Gruel, in Quicherat, IV:318; Cagny, in Quicherat, IV:14–15; and Jean Chartier, in Quicherat, IV:66–7.

66. *Journal du siège d'Orléans*, in Quicherat, IV:176. See also the *Chronique de la Pucelle*, in Quicherat, IV:242.

67. *Journal du siège d'Orléans*, in Quicherat, IV:176. See also the *Chronique de la Pucelle*, in Quicherat, IV:242; Gruel, in Quicherat, IV:318; Waurin, in Quicherat, IV:417; and Bouvier, in Quicherat, IV:45.

68. Alençon, in Duparc, I:386. See also the testimony of Dunois, in Duparc, I:322; the *Chronique de la Pucelle*, in Quicherat, IV:242–3; the *Journal du siège d'Orléans*, in Quicherat, IV:177; Monstrelet, in Quicherat, IV:371–2; Pernoud, *Joan of Arc*, p. 117; and Liocourt, II:144.

69. On the recognition by the French leadership that speed was an important tactic at the battle of Patay see Jean Chartier, in Quicherat, IV:67–8; the *Chronique de la Pucelle*, in Quicherat, IV:242; the *Journal du siège d'Orléans*, in Quicherat, IV:176; and Liocourt, II:144. On the English attempting to reach Janville see the *Journal du siège d'Orléans*, in Quicherat, IV:176; Cagny, in Quicherat, IV:15; and Bouvier, in Quicherat, IV:45. Jean Waurin (in Quicherat, IV:418) claims that the English were trying to march to Paris.

70. Waurin, in Quicherat, IV:421. See also Pernoud, *Joan of Arc*, p. 118, and Liocourt, II:145.

71. The *Journal du siège d'Orléans* (in Quicherat, IV:177) has only 4,000 in the English army, but as that is the number which had arrived with Fastolf, who had not lost anyone in combat, I have added another thousand English troops to indicate those who had been already on the Loire before Fastolf's army arrived.

72. Gruel, in Quicherat, IV:318–19. See also the *Chronique de la Pucelle*, in Quicherat, IV:243, and Liocourt, II:144.

73. *Journal du siège d'Orléans*, in Quicherat, IV:177.

74. Waurin, in Quicherat, IV:421. See also Monstrelet, in Quicherat, IV:372, and Liocourt, II:145.
75. Monstrelet, in Quicherat, IV:374. See also Liocourt, II:148.
76. See the *Chronique de la Pucelle*, in Quicherat, IV:242.
77. See, for example, Burne, *Agincourt War*, p. 268 note 1.
78. Burne, *Agincourt War*, pp. 268-9.
79. Michel de Lombarès, 'Patay, 18 juin 1429', *Revue historique de l'armée* 22 (1966), 5-16.
80. Liocourt, II:148-9. Unfortunately, Liocourt's plan of the battle is found on p. 111 and is thus extremely difficult to follow in connection with his discussion more than thirty-five pages later. Nevertheless, I believe that Liocourt is probably correct in his findings.
81. The quotes all come from Waurin (in Quicherat, IV:421-2). See also Cagny, in Quicherat, IV:14; Liocourt, II:145; and Lombarès, pp. 12-13. That they were located near Saint-Sigismond comes from a letter written by a battle participant, Jacques de Bourbon ('Lettre de Jacques de Bourbon', *Revue bleue* (13 Feb 1892), 203).
82. Waurin, in Quicherat, IV:422. See also Monstrelet, in Quicherat, IV:372; Jean Chartier, in Quicherat, IV:68; Pernoud and Clin, p. 61; and Pernoud, *Joan of Arc*, p. 118. Burne, *Agincourt War*, Villaret, and Lombarès all diminish the role of the stag in this battle, believing that it was the French surprise that carried the day. In ignoring the eye-witness and best source on the battle, however, they weaken their credibility.

83. Gruel (in Quicherat, IV:319) claims that this ultimately is what causes Fastolf's defeat. See also Pernoud and Clin, pp. 61-2; Pernoud, *Joan of Arc*, p. 119; Liocourt, II:146; and Lombarès, pp. 13-14.
84. Waurin, in Quicherat, IV:423.
85. See Waurin, in Quicherat, IV:423; Bourbon, p. 203; and Liocourt, II:145.
86. See Monstrelet, in Quicherat, IV:373, and Jean Chartier, in Quicherat, IV:68. Waurin does not record this part of the battle, having already fled, it seems, by the time that this occurred.
87. So timed by the author of the *Chronique de la Pucelle* (in Quicherat, IV:243).
88. This number of English casualties is given by Gruel (in Quicherat, IV:319) and Bouvier (in Quicherat, IV:45). Waurin (in Quicherat, IV:423) claims a death toll of 2,000, with 200 more captured, and Monstrelet's figures (in Quicherat, IV:373-4) are 1,800 dead and 100-120 captured. Finally, Cagny (in Quicherat, IV:15-16) and Jean Chartier (in Quicherat, IV:68) claim that there were 2,000-3,000 dead English soldiers with, according to Cagny alone, another 400-500 made prisoners. On the French dead, Thibault d'Armagnac testified (in Duparc, I:404) that

the French had lost only one.

89. See the *Journal du siège d'Orléans*,
in Quicherat, IV:177; the
Chronique de la Pucelle, in
Quicherat, IV:244; and
Monstrelet, in Quicherat, IV:374.

90. See Waurin, in Quicherat,
IV:424; Monstrelet, in
Quicherat, IV:371; the *Journal
du siège d'Orléans*, in Quicherat,
IV:178; and Cagny, in
Quicherat, IV:15.

91. Coutes, in Duparc, I:366.

92. See the *Journal du siège
d'Orléans*, in Quicherat, IV:178,
and Cagny, in Quicherat, IV:16.

Chapter 6: The Road to Reims

1. Bouvier, in Quicherat, IV:45–6,
and the *Chronique de la Pucelle*,
in Quicherat, IV:244.

2. Edouard Perroy's tallies of
10–12 million French
inhabitants and 3½ English
inhabitants (pp. 36, 50–1) are
pre-Black Death numbers
(1328). However, there is no
indication in his work, or in
anyone else's, that the
population disparity one
hundred years later was any
different.

3. Anne Curry, 'English Armies in
the Fifteenth Century', ed. A.
Curry and M. Hughes, in *Arms,
Armies and Fortifications in the
Hundred Years War* (Woodbridge,
1994), p. 45. This citation refers
to a chart that lists the numbers
of troops sent each year to
France between 1415 and
1450. Curry's entire article
(pp. 39–68) is devoted to the
calculation of English soldiers
serving in France during the
fifteenth century.

4. See, for example, Guy
Llewelyn Thompson, *Paris
and its People under English
Rule: The Anglo-Burgundian
Regime, 1420–1436* (Oxford,
1991).

5. There may have been such a
pro-French group operating in
Troyes, as their sheltering of
Friar Richard, who had been
driven from Paris for
treasonous preaching earlier in
the year, might be evidence
that a group of French
sympathizers existed there. (For
a short biography of Friar
Richard see Pernoud and Clin,
p. 198.) It is also possible that
these sympathizers were
instrumental in surrendering
the town to Joan on 9 July.

6. See note 7 in chapter 1.

7. For editions of this letter see
Quicherat, V:125–6, and
Pernoud and Clin, p. 251. I
have used the Pernoud and
Clin translation (p. 252). The
letter itself no longer exists, but
it was recorded in the city
registers. Why Joan claimed to
have captured Fastolf, when
she had not, is a mystery. It is
known that she wrote also to
Duke Philip the Good of
Burgundy at this time, but this
letter no longer survives in any
form. See Pernoud and Clin,
p. 62, and Pernoud, *Joan of Arc*,
p. 120.

8. For a short biography of La
Trémoïlle see Pernoud and
Clin, p. 190.

9. Both the *Journal du siège
d'Orléans* (in Quicherat,
IV:178–81) and the *Chronique
de la Pucelle* (in Quicherat,

IV:246–50), the two narrative sources that speak most positively about Joan, decry at length La Trémoïlle's opposition to her. See also Liocourt, II:157–65.

10. Dunois, in Duparc, I:323. See also the *Chronique de la Pucelle*, in Quicherat, IV:246–8, and Jean Chartier, in Quicherat, IV:69.

11. Cosne and La Charité were held not by the English themselves but by a mercenary leader, Perrinet Gressart, and his forces. Both would become targets for Joan in 1430.

12. See the *Journal du siège d'Orléans*, in Quicherat, IV:178–80; the *Chronique de la Pucelle*, in Quicherat, IV:246–7; and Jean Chartier, in Quicherat, IV:69. Although La Trémoïlle is not specifically identified as the proponent of these alternate proposals, and Regnault of Chartres, the archbishop of Reims and a later opponent of Joan's, was also present, La Trémoïlle's blame can be inferred from these sources.

13. These numbers are given by Pernoud and Clin (p. 62) without substantiation.

14. On this phenomenon see DeVries, 'A Woman As Leader of Men'.

15. Cagny, in Quicherat, IV:16–17. On the army's travel to Gien see the *Journal du siège d'Orléans*, in Quicherat, IV:179, Cagny, in Quicherat, IV:16–17; and Jean Chartier, in Quicherat, IV:71.

16. Cagny, in Quicherat, IV:17–18.

17. See Burne, *Agincourt War*, p. 169.

18. See Jean Chartier, in Quicherat, IV:72; Monstrelet, in Quicherat, IV:377–8; and Pernoud, *Joan of Arc*, pp. 120–1.

19. See Jean Chartier, in Quicherat, IV:72; Cagny, in Quicherat, IV:18; *Chronique de la Pucelle*, in Quicherat, IV:251; and C.-R. Pernin, *Jeanne d'Arc à Troyes* (Paris, 1894), p. 9.

20. See note 63 in chapter two for references to this treaty.

21. This letter also no longer exists, but a transcription of it has survived in the seventeenth-century register of Jean Rogier. Editions of the letter are in Quicherat, IV:284–8, and Pernoud and Clin, pp. 252–3. I have used the Pernoud and Clin translation (p. 253).

22. Pernin, p. 12. See also the *Journal du siège d'Orléans*, in Quicherat, IV:181.

23. The *Journal du siège d'Orléans* (in Quicherat, IV:181) and Jean Chartier (in Quicherat, IV:72) are the only sources that mention this garrison and its ill-advised sortie.

24. See Jean Chartier, in Quicherat, IV:72–3, and Monstrelet, in Quicherat, IV:378.

25. Joan, in Quicherat, I:100. See also Monstrelet, in Quicherat, IV:3; Pernoud and Clin, p. 63; Pernoud, *Joan of Arc*, pp. 121–2; and Pernin, pp. 18–20.

'By my Martin' appears to have been Joan's particular oath. According to many witnesses, she expressed it on numerous occasions, mostly in private conversations.

26. See the *Journal du siège d'Orléans*, in Quicherat, IV:182; Jean Chartier, in Quicherat, IV:73; and Pernoud, *Joan of Arc*, p. 122. However, Pernoud wonders whether this could have been the case at a time of harvest.

27. Dunois, in Duparc, I:324. See also the *Journal du siège d'Orléans*, in Quicherat, IV:182–3; Jean Chartier, in Quicherat, IV:73–5; Pernoud, *Joan of Arc*, pp. 122–3; and Pernin, pp. 20–1, 25–7.

28. See the *Journal du siège d'Orléans*, in Quicherat, IV:183, and Jean Chartier, in Quicherat, IV:76.

29. See Simon Charles's nullification trial testimony, in Duparc, I:401–2; Pernoud and Clin, p. 63; and Pernoud, *Joan of Arc*, p. 123.

30. Simon Charles, in Duparc, I:401–2. See also Dunois's nullification trial testimony, in Duparc, I:324; the *Journal du siège d'Orléans*, in Quicherat, IV:183–4; Jean Chartier, in Quicherat, IV:76; Monstrelet, in Quicherat, IV:378; Pernoud and Clin, p. 63, Pernoud, *Joan of Arc*, p. 123; and Pernin, pp. 27–31.

31. Cagny, in Quicherat, IV:18–19.

32. See the *Journal du siège d'Orléans*, in Quicherat, IV:184–5; Jean de Chartier, in Quicherat, IV:76–7; Cagny, in Quicherat, IV:18; and Pernoud and Clin, p. 64.

33. Épinal, in Duparc, I:279. On the visit with some of her former friends and acquaintances see Pernoud and Clin, p. 64, and Pernoud, *Joan of Arc*, pp. 123–4.

34. Simon Charles, in Duparc, I:402. See also Pernoud, *Joan of Arc*, p. 124.

35. Joan, in Quicherat, I:187. See also Pernoud, *Joan of Arc*, p. 125.

36. *Journal du siège d'Orléans*, in Quicherat, IV:186. For an account of the crowning see the *Journal du siège d'Orléans*, in Quicherat, IV:185–6; Cagny, in Quicherat, IV:19–20; Jean Chartier, in Quicherat, IV:77–8; Bouvier, in Quicherat, IV:46; Monstrelet, in Quicherat, IV:378–81; Fauquembergue, in Quicherat, IV:453; Pernoud and Clin, pp. 64–8; and Pernoud, *Joan of Arc*, pp. 124–6.

Chapter 7: The Decline of a Military Leader

1. Monstrelet, in Quicherat, IV:380.

2. See Thompson.

3. This is found in the Archives Nationales, X.12.4796, fols. 239–41.

4. Bourgeois of Paris, in Quicherat, IV:463–4. See also Pernoud and Clin, p. 73, and Liocourt, II:219.

5. Gruel, in Quicherat, IV:320. See also Pernoud and Clin, p. 76.

6. This letter is found in Monstrelet, in Quicherat, IV:382–6. See also Pernoud, *Joan of Arc*, pp. 131–2, and Liocourt, II:211–12.

7. For a short biography of Bedford see Pernoud and Clin, pp. 176–7. A longer one can be found in Williams.

8. See Jean Chartier, in Quicherat, IV:78.

9. See Pernoud and Clin, p. 72.
10. This letter is preserved in the Archives du Nord in Lille. It is edited in Quicherat V:126–7 and Pernoud and Clin, pp. 253–4. I have used the translation found in Pernoud and Clin, pp. 67–8. See also Pernoud, *Joan of Arc*, p. 128, and Liocourt, II:198.
11. See Liocourt, II:199.
12. This letter is also still extant and located in the Archive Municipales in Reims. It is edited in Quicherat, IV:139–40, and Pernoud and Clin, p. 254. I have used the Pernoud and Clin translation (p. 255). See also Liocourt, II:210.
13. Greffier de la Rochelle, as quoted in Liocourt, II:199.
14. Alençon, in Duparc, I:472–3, and Seguin, in Duparc I:382.
15. Joan, in Quicherat, I:146–7. See also Pernoud, *Joan of Arc*, p. 134, and Liocourt, II:218. Both of these modern commentators, and others, accept this statement without question. But it is a confusing thing for Joan to say, as there is no record either in her trial testimony or anywhere else that mentions who these 'noblemen' might be.
16. See Pernoud and Clin, pp. 69–70, and Liocourt, II:205.
17. See the *Journal du siège d'Orléans*, in Quicherat, IV:178; Cagny, in Quicherat, IV:20; Bouvier, in Quicherat, IV:46; Jean Chartier, in Quicherat, IV:78; and Liocourt, II:205.
18. Cagny, in Quicherat, IV:20. See also Bouvier, in Quicherat, IV:46, Jean Chartier, in Quicherat, IV:78; and Liocourt, II:206–7.
19. See Pernoud and Clin, pp. 73, 230–1, and Liocourt, II:207.
20. See Cagny, in Quicherat, IV:20.
21. Cagny, in Quicherat, IV:21. See also Bouvier, in Quicherat, IV:46, and Jean Chartier, in Quicherat, IV:78. The fortifications of Provins have received excellent modern study. See Jean Mesqui, *Provins: La fortification d'une ville au moyen âge* (Paris, 1979).
22. Luce, *Jean d'Arc à Domrémy*, II:250, and Liocourt, II:208. On Joan's visit to the duke of Lorraine see note 29 in Chapter 3 above.
23. *Journal du siège d'Orléans*, in Quicherat, IV:189. See also Liocourt, II:213.
24. See the *Journal du siège d'Orléans*, in Quicherat, IV:188–9; Cagny, in Quicherat, IV:21; Bouvier, in Quicherat, IV:46, and Jean Chartier, in Quicherat, IV:78. At Crépy-en-Valois, the king received the surrender of Compiègne.
25. Cagny, in Quicherat, IV:21–3. The engagement at Montépilloy is one of the best described military encounters of the Hundred Years War. Other sources include: Jean Chartier, in Quicherat, IV:80–4; Monstrelet, in Quicherat, IV:386–9; Saint-Rémy, in Quicherat, IV:433–5; the *Journal du siège d'Orléans*, in Quicherat, IV:189–90; and Bouvier, in Quicherat, IV:47. See also Pernoud and Clin,

pp. 73–4; Pernoud, *Joan of Arc*, pp. 132–3; and Liocourt, II:214–17.

26. Monstrelet, in Quicherat, IV:388.

27. Monstrelet, in Quicherat, IV:387. Monstrelet also includes the English formation and command structure. Most sources identify these soldiers as coming from the Burgundian-controlled region of Picardy. See also Liocourt, II:215.

28. Liocourt's battle plan (II:215) is confusing and does not attend to the sources. It should be disregarded.

29. Jean Chartier (in Quicherat, IV:82–3) includes the French command structure and formations; Joan of Arc, the Bastard of Orléans, and La Hire all took up positions in the vanguard. See also Liocourt, II:214–15.

30. Jean Chartier (in Quicherat, IV:83) writes that the English had spent all night setting up this fortification.

31. Bouvier, in Quicherat, IV:47. Jean Chartier (in Quicherat, IV:83–4) sees a similar distance, claiming that the two lines were only the space of two crossbow shots apart.

32. Jean Chartier, in Quicherat, IV:84.

33. Jean Chartier (in Quicherat, IV:84) maintains that some combat did take place when Joan moved forward, resulting in deaths on both sides, before she returned to her earlier position. Even if that did occur, the fuller warfare which

she sought by this tactic failed to take place. See Liocourt, II:215.

34. Cagny, in Quicherat, IV:23. See also Liocourt, II:215.

35. See Jean Chartier, in Quicherat, IV:85; Monstrelet, in Quicherat, IV:391; Pernoud, *Joan of Arc*, p. 134; and Liocourt, II:217.

36. See Monstrelet, in Quicherat, IV:391, and Jean Chartier, in Quicherat, IV:85. Paul Marin, *La génie militaire de Jeanne Darc (siège de Paris, 1429)* (Paris, 1889), p. 146, claims that Bedford had moved to Rouen because he felt that Paris was on the verge of falling. But, as Bedford returned to Paris before that happened, Marin is simply wrong here. More than likely, Bedford's move to Rouen had to do with Richemont's attacks on western Normandy and their effect on Normans who wished to join the French rather than remain with the English.

37. Cagny, in Quicherat, IV:24. See also Pernoud and Clin, p. 76, and Liocourt, II:218.

38. Dean of the Collegiate Church of St Thibaud of Metz, *Chroniques de la noble ville et cité de Metz* in Quicherat, IV:321.

39. See Jean Chartier, in Quicherat, IV:86; the *Journal du siège d'Orléans*, in Quicherat, IV:197; and Liocourt, II:218.

40. See Cagny, in Quicherat, IV:24. Paul Marin (p. 140) has a French army size of 6,000 men, but he does not reveal how he calculates this number. I believe that such a figure is far too large.

41. See Cagny, in Quicherat,

IV:24–5; Jean Chartier, in Quicherat, IV:86; and Bouvier, in Quicherat, IV:47.

42. See Monstrelet (ed. Douet-d'Arcq), II:348–9, and Liocourt, II:207–9, 218.

43. See Pernoud and Clin, pp. 75–6.

44. Monstrelet, in Quicherat, IV:388.

45. See Henri Couget, *Jeanne d'Arc devant Paris* (Paris, 1925), pp. 21–3, 76–7, and Liocourt, II:221, 223–4. Liocourt's idea that there were two moats, one dry and the other filled with water, is not supported by archaeological or written evidence. Sixteenth-century maps of the Saint-Honoré gate (found detailed in Couget, pp. 139, 149, 159) clearly show only one moat, but that it was only filled with water in the middle. Hence, it is entirely possible that Joan could have stepped off the edge of the higher ground on to the dry moat, and then later have needed bundles of sticks, etc., a common moat filler during sieges, to be placed in the wet part of the moat.

46. Jean Chartier, in Quicherat, IV:87.

47. For references see note 61 in chapter 2.

48. See Bourgeois of Paris, *Journal d'un bourgeois de Paris, 1405–49*, ed. A. Teutey (Paris, 1881), pp. 243, 245. See also Liocourt, II:220. Couget (pp. 15–16), on the other hand, contends that there were many who would have joined Joan if she had been able to get through the walls.

49. Cagny, in Quicherat, IV:25. See also Jean Chartier, in Quicherat, IV:86; the *Journal du siège d'Orléans*, in Quicherat, IV:197; Pernoud, *Joan of Arc*, pp. 136–7; Liocourt, II:220–1; and Couget, pp. 13–14.

50. Jean Chartier, in Quicherat, IV:86–7.

51. Cagny, in Quicherat, IV:24–5.

52. Cagny, being Alençon's chronicler, is naturally the most detailed contemporary reporter of this part of the story (in Quicherat, IV:25–6). See also Pernoud, *Joan of Arc*, p. 137, and Couget, pp. 16–17. Joan may have planned to carry out an attack on 7 September as well, but that one, for whatever reason, does not seem to have taken place. See Liocourt, II:222, and Couget, pp. 18–20.

53. Cagny, in Quicherat, IV:26–7. See also Liocourt, II:223–4, and Couget, pp. 25–30. During this initial attack, the boulevard in front of Saint-Honoré gate, if there was in fact one there, must have been overrun. That no contemporary source says so, indicates that perhaps a boulevard had not been constructed there.

54. Fauquembergue, in Quicherat, IV:457. Several contemporary chroniclers agree with Cagny that no French were killed or wounded; others agree with Fauquembergue that many were killed or wounded. See Couget, pp. 39–43.

55. Cagny, in Quicherat, IV:26–7. See also the *Journal du siège*

d'Orléans, in Quicherat,
IV:198–9; Jean Chartier, in
Quicherat, IV:87–8; Monstrelet,
in Quicherat, IV:392–3; the
Bourgeois de Paris, in
Quicherat, IV:464–6;
Fauquembergue, in Quicherat,
IV:457; Liocourt, II:224–5; and
Couget, pp. 35–7.

56. Bourgeois de Paris, in
Quicherat, IV:464–6. See also
Couget, pp. 33–4.

57. Cagny, in Quicherat, IV:27. See
also Couget, p. 43.

58. See Cagny, in Quicherat,
IV:27–8; Liocourt, II:225; and
Couget, pp. 43–4.

59. Germain Lefèvre-Pontalis
confirmed this part of Cagny's
chronicle when he discovered a
letter written by Henry VI in
1431 reminding a citizen of
Denisot Doe, one of the villages
surrounding Paris, of the
bridge's existence during the
time of Joan's attacks. See
Germain Lefèvre-Pontalis, 'Un
détail du siège de Paris par
Jeanne d'Arc', *Bibliothèque de
l'écoles des chartes* 46 (1885),
5–15. He (pp. 5–6), Paul Marin
(pp. 142–5), and Ferdinand de
Liocourt (II:225), all maintain
that the bridge was to be used
by Joan that day, 9 September,
when the king called off the
attacks, but there is no
contemporary evidence to
support that theory.

60. Cagny, in Quicherat, IV:27–8.
See also Pernoud, *Joan of Arc*, p.
138, and Couget, pp. 44–5.

61. Bouvier, in Quicherat, IV:48.

62. Saint-Rémy, in Quicherat,
IV:436.

63. See the *Journal de siège*

d'Orléans, in Quicherat, IV:201;
Jean Chartier, in Quicherat,
IV:88–9; and Liocourt, II:226.

64. Monstrelet, in Quicherat,
IV:394.

65. See the *Journal du siège
d'Orléans*, in Quicherat,
IV:201–2; Cagny, in Quicherat,
IV:29; Pernoud and Clin, pp.
79–80; and Pernoud, *Joan of
Arc*, p. 29.

66. Cagny, in Quicherat, IV:30. See
also Bouvier, in Quicherat,
IV:48–9, and Pernoud, *Joan of
Arc*, pp. 141–2.

67. Cagny, in Quicherat, IV:29.

68. Joan, in Duparc, I:179. See also
Liocourt, II:226.

69. Jean Chartier, in Quicherat,
IV:89. For stories that the armor
remained in Saint-Denis after
the Hundred Years War see, for
example, Liocourt (II:226), who,
using a basilica treasury report
from 1626, believes that the
armor was still there in the
seventeenth century, and
Pernoud (*Joan of Arc*, p. 139),
who holds that the armor
currently resides in the Musée
de la armée in Paris. What is
claimed to have been her armor
appears to have been something
later placed in the basilica if
Jean Chartier is correct.

70. *Journal du siège d'Orléans*, in
Quicherat, IV:199–200.

71. Alençon, in Duparc, I:387.

72. Most military historians see
Joan's attack on Paris as an
impressive military feat. See
Liocourt, II:218–25; Canogne,
pp. 56–67; Collet, pp.
199–250; Bourguignon, pp.
212–33; Funck-Brentano, pp.
120–5; Lancesseur, pp.

96–111; Marin, pp. 140–60; and Contamine, 'Guerre de siège', pp. 12–13. Yet, Couget (pp. 20–1) maintains that the attack of 8 September 'was not sufficiently prepared, nor sustained'.

Chapter 8: The End of a Military Leader

1. See Liocourt, II:227.
2. See Liocourt, II:252; Villaret, p. 109; and André Bossuat, *Perrinet Gressart et François de Surienne: Agents de l'Angleterre. Contribution à l'étude des relations de l'Angleterre et de la Bourgogne avec la France, sous le règne de Charles VII* (Paris, 1936).
3. For a biography of Perrinet Gressart see Pernoud and Clin, pp. 185–7, and Bossuat. Much of the following about Gressart's life comes from these sources.
4. On Bertrand du Guesclin's free company experience see the references in note 20 in Chapter 2.
5. On mercenaries and mercenary captains during the Hundred Years War see Allmand, *Hundred Years War*, pp. 73–6; Philippe Contamine, *War in the Middle Ages*, trans. M. Jones (Oxford, 1984), pp. 99–101, 150–65; and M.G.A.Vale, *War and Chivalry: Warfare and Aristocratic Culture in England, France and Burgundy at the End of the Middle Ages* (London, 1981), pp 151–7.
6. See Pernoud and Clin, p. 186; Bossuat, p. 112; and Calemard, 'La chevauchée de Jeanne d'Arc et son appel aux habitants de Riom', *Revue politique et parlementaire* 140 (1929), 435.
7. Aulon, in Duparc, I:484. See also Pernoud, *Joan of Arc*, p. 143, and Bossuat, pp. 111–12.
8. Aulon, in Duparc, I:484, and J.-L. Jaladon de la Barre, *Jeanne d'Arc à Saint-Pierre-le-Moutier et deux juges nivernais à Rouen* (Nevers, 1868), pp. 25–6.
9. See Pernoud and Clin, p. 80; Villaret, p. 108; and Bossuat, pp. 113–14.
10. See Liocourt, II:249.
11. Liocourt, II:249, and Jaladon de la Barre, pp. 18–19.
12. Aulon, in Duparc, I:484. In comparison to the French army, which does not seem to have been very large at all, the number of soldiers in Saint-Pierre-le-Moutier may have appeared to be 'a large number' to Jean d'Aulon, and he can be excused for exaggerating the opposing numbers. But the small size of the place, even today, means that the number there can have been nothing in comparison to some of the towns which Joan had previously encountered.
13. Aulon, in Duparc, I:484–5. See also Pernoud and Clin, pp. 80–1; Pernoud, *Joan of Arc*, pp. 143–4; Villaret, p. 109; Bossuat, p. 115; Jaladon de la Barre, pp. 28–30; and Calemard, pp. 436–7.
14. Thierry, in Duparc, I:330. See also Villaret, p. 109; Jaladon de la Barre, pp. 32–3; and Calemard, p. 437.
15. This can be found in the

Archives Communales de Riom, AA.33. It is edited in Quicherat, V:147–8, and Pernoud and Clin, p. 257. I have used my own translation. See also Calemard; Bossuat, pp. 115–16; and Jaladon de la Barre, pp. 35–6.

16. A transcription of Albret's letter to the citizens of Riom is found in Calemard, pp. 438–40.

17. On the gunpowder weapons sent to the French besieging La Charité see Liocourt, II:250–1; Bossuat, pp. 116–17; and Villaret, pp. 159–65. In Villaret is a transcription of the gunpowder weapons inventory. On the money sent by the inhabitants of Orléans and Bourges see Villaret, p. 111.

18. Bouvier, in Quicherat, IV:49. See also Pernoud and Clin, p. 81; Pernoud, *Joan of Arc*, p. 145; Liocourt, II:251; and Villaret, p. 111.

19. See Liocourt, II:251–2.

20. See Jean Chartier, in Quicherat, IV:91; Cagny, in Quicherat, IV:31; and Bouvier, in Quicherat, IV:49. (The quotes are from Chartier and Cagny respectively.) See also Pernoud and Clin, p. 81; Pernoud, *Joan of Arc*, p. 145; Liocourt, II:252; and Bossuat, p. 118. The exact date of departure from La Charité is not known, but it was probably sometime between 22 and 24 December.

21. Cagny, in Quicherat, IV:31. See also Villaret, p. 111, and Jaladon de la Barre, p. 40.

22. Joan, in Quicherat, I:109. See also Villaret, p. 111, and Bossuat, p. 118.

23. See Pernoud and Clin, p. 81, and Bossuat, p. 118.

24. The document ennobling them is edited in Quicherat V:150–3. See also Pernoud and Clin, p. 81, and Pernoud, *Joan of Arc*, pp. 145–6.

25. Pernoud and Clin (p. 82) have Joan spending much of her time at La Trémoïlle's castle in Sully-sur-Loire. But there is very little evidence beyond the letters written there in March to indicate that this was her winter residence for all of January, February, and March.

26. The original of this letter still exists and is held privately. Editions can be found in Quicherat, V:160, and Pernoud and Clin, p. 258. The partial translation which I have quoted is from Pernoud and Clin, p. 83.

27. This letter, too, is still extant; it too is privately held. Editions are in Quicherat, V:161, and Pernoud and Clin, pp. 259–60. I have used a translation of Pernoud and Clin, p. 260.

28. This letter, originally written in Latin, is most found in a German translation in the Vienna *Reichsregister* D. f. 236 r. I have used the translation in Pernoud and Clin, p. 259.

29. Pernoud and Clin (pp. 158–9) are direct in their opinion that Joan did not write this letter: 'This letter was not dictated by Joan; it is the work of Pasquerel, her confessor.' Liocourt (II:267) accepts the letter as hers.

30. See Pernoud and Clin, p. 82,

and Pernoud, *Joan of Arc*, pp. 146–7.

31. See Pernoud and Clin, p. 84, and Pernoud, *Joan of Arc*, p. 146.

32. On the Burgundian attempts to take Compiègne see Pernoud and Clin, p. 83; Richard Vaughan, *Philip the Good: The Apogee of Burgundy* (London, 1970), pp. 17–25; Pierre Champion, *Guillaume de Flavy: Captaine de Compiègne: Contribution à l'histoire de Jeanne d'Arc et à l'étude de la vie militaire et privée au XVe siècle* (Paris, 1906); and Louis Carolus-Barre, 'Compiègne et la guerre, 1414–1430', in *111e Congres national des Sociétés savantes, Poitiers, 1986, Histoire médiévale, T. I: 'La France Anglaise'*, pp. 383–92.

33. Cagny, in Quicherat, IV:32. See also Pernoud, *Joan of Arc*, p. 147, and Pernoud and Clin, pp. 84–5. Pernoud and Clin do not accept that the king would have kept her from travelling to help the Compiègnoise.

34. Joan testified of this in her own trial (in Quicherat, I:105). See also Pernoud and Clin, p. 85, and Liocourt, II:272.

35. She also testified of this (in Quicherat, I:115). See also Pernoud and Clin, p. 85, and Liocourt, II:272–3.

36. See Pernoud and Clin, p. 85, and Pernoud, *Joan of Arc*, p. 149.

37. On the battle of Lagny see Cagny, in Quicherat, IV:32; Jean Chartier, in Quicherat, IV:91–2; Monstrelet, in Quicherat, IV:399–400;

Georges Chastellain, *Chronique de ducs de Bourgogne*, in Quicherat, IV:441–3; Pernoud and Clin, p. 85; Liocourt, II:273; and Alexandre Sorel, *La prise de Jeanne d'Arc devant Compiègne et l'histoire des sièges de la même ville sous Charles VI et Charles VII* (Paris, 1889), pp. 143–4.

38. Chastellain, in Quicherat, IV:442.

39. Chastellain, in Quicherat, IV:442; Monstrelet, in Quicherat, IV:399; and Jean Chartier, in Quicherat, IV:91.

40. Monstrelet, in Quicherat, IV:399.

41. On this sword see Olivier, pp. 19–20.

42. See Pernoud and Clin, p. 85, and Liocourt, p. 273.

43. Article XXXIX, in Quicherat, I:264.

44. See Pernoud and Clin, pp. 85–6. This Louis of Bourbon, the count of Vendôme, was not the same as the Louis of Bourbon, count of Montpensier, who was with Joan on the upper Loire late in 1429. The Bourbon family was large, with at least two Louis, it appears, and all of them titled. Regnault of Chartres would write one of the most heinous and disloyal letters after Joan's capture condemning her activities as independent and 'full of pride' (see Pernoud and Clin, p. 91).

45. See Chastellain, in Quicherat, IV:444–5. On the siège of Compiègne see Burne, *The Agincourt War*, pp. 264–7; Canogne, pp. 74–85; Collet,

pp. 272–97; Bourguignon,
pp. 264–73; Funck-Brentano,
pp. 141–6; Lancesseur,
pp. 123–37; Sorel; Champion,
Guillaume de Flavy; Vaughan,
Philip the Good, pp. 17–25; and
Paul Marin, *Jeanne d'Arc
tacticien et stratégiste: L'art
militaire dans la première moitié
du XVe siècle*, 4 vols (Paris,
1889–90) [all four volumes
discuss this siege exclusively].

46. See Vaughan, *Philip the Good*,
p. 17.

47. See Kelly DeVries and Robert
D. Smith, *The Artillery of the
Dukes of Burgundy*
(forthcoming), and Joseph
Garnier, *L'artillerie des ducs de
Bourgogne d'après les documents
conservés aux archives de la
Côte-d'Or* (Paris, 1895).

48. Jean de Waurin, *Récueil des
croniques et anchiennes istories de
la Grant Bretaigne*, ed. W. and
E.L.C.P. Hardy (London,
1864–91), III:362; Monstrelet
(ed. Douet-d'Arcq), IV:418–19;
Morosini, III:319–23; and
Georges Chastellain, *Oeuvres*,
ed. Kervyn de Lettenhove
(Brussels, 1863–6), II:53.
See also Liocourt, II:279–80
and DeVries, 'The Use of
Gunpowder Weaponry', pp.
15–16.

49. Contamine, 'Guerre de siège',
p. 16.

50. As transcribed in Champion,
Guillaume de Flavy, pp. 174–83.
See also Alain Salamagne,
'L'attaque des places-fortes au
XVe siècle à travers l'exemple des
guerres anglo et franco-
bourguignonnes', *Revue
historique* 289 (1993), 78–9.

51. See Pernoud and Clin, p. 232,
and Sorel, pp. 161–7.

52. Champion, *Guillaume de Flavy*,
p. 48.

53. Quoted in Champion, *Guillaume
de Flavy*, p. 49 n.10.

54. Jean Chartier, in Quicherat,
IV:92.

55. See Saint-Rémy, in Quicherat,
IV:436; Bouvier, in Quicherat,
IV:49; Pernoud and Clin, p. 86;
Liocourt, II:281–2; and Sorel,
pp. 150–9.

56. Bouvier, in Quicherat,
IV:49–50. See also Pernoud
and Clin, p. 86, and Liocourt,
II:282–3.

57. The selling of the town comes
from Bouvier, in Quicherat,
IV:50. The price comes from the
third compte of Jean Abonnel,
Archives du Nord, B 1492 f. 64,
transcribed in Champion,
Guillaume de Flavy, p. 168. See
also Liocourt, II:283, and
Pernoud and Clin, p. 86.

58. Cagny, in Quicherat, IV:32–3.
See also Pernoud and Clin,
p. 86; Pernoud, *Joan of Arc*,
p. 150; Liocourt, II:283; and
Sorel, pp. 171–3.

59. See Cagny, in Quicherat, IV:33.

60. Cagny, in Quicherat, IV:33. See
also Pernoud and Clin, p. 86;
Pernoud, *Joan of Arc*, p. 150;
and Liocourt, II:283.

61. Chastellain, in Quicherat,
IV:444–5. See also Pernoud
and Clin, p. 86.

62. Cagny, in Quicherat, IV:34. See
also Pernoud, *Joan of Arc*, p. 150.

63. Chastellain, in Quicherat,
IV:446–7. See also Monstrelet,
in Quicherat, IV:401–2;
Pernoud, *Joan of Arc*, p. 151;
and Sorel, pp. 183–4.

64. Joan, in Quicherat, I:207–8. See also Pernoud, *Joan of Arc*, pp. 149–50.

65. Joan, in Quicherat, I:207.

66. Jules Michelet, *Joan of Arc*, trans. A. Guérard (Ann Arbor, 1957), pp. 50–3; Sorel, pp. 287–300; Bourguignon, pp. 264–73; and Marin, *Jeanne d'Arc tacticien et stratégiste*. See also Pernoud and Clin, pp. 231–3, who suggest that the treason of Flavy was 'at least plausible'.

67. Quicherat, *New Aspects*, pp. 35–8; Champion, *Guillaume de Flavy*; and J.-B. Mestre, *Guillaume de Flavy n'a pas trahi Jeanne d'Arc* (Paris, 1934).

68. Épinal, in Duparc, I:279. On Joan's visit with some of her former friends and acquaintances see Pernoud and Clin, p. 64, and Pernoud, *Joan of Arc*, pp. 123–4.

69. See note 63 above.

70. Sorel, pp. 225–70; Vaughan, *Philip the Good*, pp. 24–5; Carolus-Barre, pp. 386–7; and DeVries, 'The Use of Gunpowder Weapons', pp. 15–16.

71. Monstrelet, in Quicherat, IV:402.

72. As quoted in Pernoud and Clin, p. 233.

73. Pernoud and Clin, p. 233.

74. Guillaume de Flavy's military biography is found in Champion, *Guillaume de Flavy*, pp. 5–61.

75. Christine de Pisan, p. 48.

76. In setting this itinerary, I have followed the route set by Pierre Rocolle, *Un prisonnier de guerre nommé Jeanne d'Arc* (Paris, 1982).

77. See Pernoud and Clin, pp. 92–4.

78. As translated in Pernoud and Clin, p. 90.

79. See Pernoud and Clin, pp. 95–8.

80. So many books have been written about Joan's trial and execution that it would be folly to try to list them all. Concise descriptions of what occurred can be found in Pernoud and Clin, pp. 103–38, and Pernoud, *Joan of Arc*, pp. 165–254.

Chapter 9: Afterword

1. On the Congress of Arras see Joyceline Gledhill Dickinson, *The Congress of Arras, 1435: A Study in Medieval Diplomacy* (Oxford, 1955).

2. See Burne, *Agincourt War*, pp. 279–81.

3. Burne, *Agincourt War*, p. 272, and Allmand, *Hundred Years War*, p. 76. The French held the important castle for less than a month before it was recaptured by the English. As was Joan's experience, after defeating the English, La Hire found himself unsupported by men, arms, and supplies.

4. Burne, *Agincourt War*, pp. 287–9.

5. Burne, *Agincourt War*, pp. 293–302.

6. Burne, *Agincourt War*, p. 302.

7. Burne, *Agincourt War*, p. 313.

8. Burne, *Agincourt War*, pp. 313–15.

9. Burne, *Agincourt War*, pp. 315–24.

10. Burne, *Agincourt War*, pp. 331–5.

11. Burne, *Agincourt War*, pp. 335–45.

Bibliography

PRIMARY SOURCES

Bourbon, Jacques, 'Lettre de Jacques de Bourbon', *Revue bleue* (13 Feb 1892), 203.

Bourgeois of Paris, *Journal*, in *Procès de condamnation et de réhabilitation de Jeanne d'Arc dite la Pucelle*, ed. Jules Quicherat, Société de l'histoire de France, Paris, 1841–9 [hereafter Quicherat], IV:461–74.

——, *Journal d'un bourgeois de Paris, 1405–49*, ed. A. Teutey, Paris, 1881.

Bouvier, Jacques, or Gilles le [Herald of Berry], *Chroniques du roi Charles VII*, in Quicherat, IV:40–50.

Brut, or the Chronicles of England, The, ed. F.W.D. Brie, 2 vols, London, 1906.

Cagny, Perceval de, *Chronique des ducs d'Alençon*, in Quicherat, IV:1–37.

Chartier, Jean, *Chronique de Charles VII*, in Quicherat, IV:51–94.

Chastellain, Georges, *Chronique de ducs de Bourgogne*, in Quicherat, IV:440–7.

——, *Oeuvres*, ed. Kervyn de Lettenhove, 3 vols, Brussels, 1863–6.

Chronique de la Pucelle, in Quicherat, IV:203–53.

Chronique de la Pucelle ou chronique de Cousinot, ed. A. Vallet de Viriville, Paris, 1859.

Chronique des Pays-Bas, de France, d'Angleterre et de Tournai, in *Corpus chronicorum Flandriae*, 3, ed. J.J. de Smet, Brussels, 1856.

Chronique de Lorraine, in Quicherat, IV:329–38.

Continuator of Guillaume de Nangis, *Chronique Parisienne*, in Quicherat, IV:313–14.

Cosneau, E., ed., *Les grands traités de la guerre de cent ans*, Paris, 1889.

Dean of the Collegiate Church of St Thibaud of Metz, *Chroniques de la noble ville et cité de Metz*, in Quicherat, IV.

Duparc, Pierre, ed., *Procès en nullité de la condamnation de Jeanne d'Arc*, 5 vols, Société de l'histoire de France, Paris, 1977–89.

Fauquembergue, Clément de, *Journal, 1417–30*, in Quicherat, IV:450–60.

Fevre, Jean le, *Chronique*, ed. F. Morand, Paris, 1876.

Gesta Henrici quinti, Angliae regis, ed. B. Williams, London, 1850.

Giraut, Guillaume, *Note sur la levée du siège d'Orléans*, in Quicherat, IV:282–3.

Gruel, Guillaume, *Chronique d'Arthur de Richemont*, in Quicherat, IV:315–20.

Hazlitt, W. Carew, ed., *Remains of Early Popular Poetry of England*, 2 vols, London, 1866.

Jarry, L., ed., 'Deux chansons normandes sur le siège d'Orléans et la mort de Salisbury', *Bulletin de la société archéologique et historique de l'Orléannais* 10 (1893), 359–70.

Journal du siège d'Orléans, in Quicherat, IV:95–202.

Journal du siège d'Orléans et du voyage de Reims, 1428–29, ed. P. Charpentier and C. Cuissard, Orléans, 1896.

Livre des trahisons de France envers la maison de Bourgogne, Le, in *Chroniques relatives à l'histoire de la Belgique sous la domination des ducs de Bourgogne (textes Français)*, ed. Kervyn de Lettenhove, Brussels, 1873.

Luce, Siméon, ed., 'Une pièce de vers sur le siège d'Orléans', in *La France pendant la guerre de cent ans: Épisodes historiques et vie privée aux XIVe et XVe siècles*, second edn, Paris, 1893, pp. 207–14.

Monstrelet, Engerrand de, *Chroniques*, in Quicherat, IV:360–404.

——, *Chronique*, ed. L. Douet-d'Arcq, Société de l'histoire de France, 6 vols, Paris, 1857–62.

Morosini, Antonio, *Chronique: Extraits relatifs à l'histoire de France*, trans. and ed. L. Dorez. 4 vols, Société de l'histoire de France, Paris, 1898–1902.

Mystère du siège d'Orléans, Le, eds. F. Guessard and E. de Certain, Paris, 1862.

Pernoud, Régine, ed., *The Retrial of Joan of Arc: The Evidence at the Trial for Her Rehabilitation*, trans. J.M. Cohen, London, 1955.

Pisan, Christine de, *Ditié de Jehanne d'Arc*, ed. A.J. Kennedy and K. Varty, Oxford, 1977.

Pius II, *Commentarii rerum memorabilium quae temporibus suis contingerunt*, in Quicherat, IV.

Quicherat, Jules, ed., *Procès de condamnation et de réhabilitation de Jeanne d'Arc dite la Pucelle*, Société de l'histoire de France, Paris, 1841–9.

Religieux de Saint-Denis, *Chronique*, ed. L. Bellaguet, Paris, 1839–52.

Saint-Rémy, Jean Lefèvre de, *Chronique*, in Quicherat, IV:429–39.

Tisset, Pierre, and Yvonne Lanhers, eds., *Procès de condamnation de Jeanne d'Arc*, 3 vols, Société de l'histoire de France, Paris, 1960–71.

Walsingham, Thomas of, *Historia Anglicana*, ed. H.T. Riley, 2 vols, Rolls Series, London, 1863.

Waurin, Jean de, *Recueil de chroniques et anchiennes istoires de la Grant Bretaigne a present nommée Engleterre*, in Quicherat, IV:405–24.

——, *Récueil des croniques et anchiennes istories de la Grant Bretaigne*, ed. W. and E.L.C.P. Hardy, 5 vols, London, 1864–91.

Windecken, Eberhard von, *Denkwürdigkeiten zur Geschichte des Zeitalters Kaiser Sigismund*, in Quicherat, IV:485–502.

SECONDARY SOURCES

Allmand, Christopher, *Henry V*, Berkeley and Los Angeles, 1992.

——, *The Hundred Years War: England and France at War* c. *1300*–c. *1450*, Cambridge, 1988.

Atiya, Aziz Suryal, *The Crusade of Nicopolis*, London, 1934.

Ayton, Andrew, 'The English Army and the Normandy Campaign of 1346', in *England and Normandy in the Middle Ages*, ed. D. Bates and A. Curry, London, 1994, pp. 253–67.

Baraude, Henri, 'Le siège d'Orléans et Jeanne d'Arc, 1428–1429', *Revue des questions historiques* 80–81 (1906–7), 31–65, 74–112, 395–424.

Barber, Malcolm, *The New Knighthood: A History of the Order of the Temple*, Cambridge,1994.

——, *The Trial of the Templars*, Cambridge, 1978.

Barber, Richard, *Edward, Prince of Wales and Aquitaine: A Biography of the Black Prince*, 1978; rpt. Woodbridge, 1996.

Barron, Caroline, 'The Deposition of Richard II', in *Politics and Crisis in Fourteenth-Century England*, ed. J. Taylor and W. Childs, London, 1990, pp. 132–49.

Bataille, Henri, *Vaucouleurs: Les remparts qui ont sauvé Jeanne-d'Arc*, Vosges, n.d.

——, 'Vaucouleurs ou l'énigma d'un siège', *Dossiers de archéologie* 34 (May 1979), 56–63.

Beaune, Colette, *The Birth of an Ideology: Myths and Symbols of Nation in Late-Medieval France*, trans. Susan Ross Huston, ed. Fredric L. Cheyette, Berkeley and Los Angeles, 1991.

Bennett, Matthew, *Agincourt 1415: Triumph Against the Odds*, London, 1991.

Bertin, Pierre, 'Le siège du chateau de Vellexon dans l'hiver 1409–1410', *Revue historique des armées* 27 (1971), 7–18.

Blockmans, Wim and Walter Prevenier, *In de ban van Bourgondië*, The Hague, 1988.

Bonenfant, Paul, *Du meurtre de Montereau au traité de Troyes*, Brussels, 1958.

Bossuat, André, *Perrinet Gressart et François de Surienne: Agents de l'Angleterre. Contribution à l'étude des relations de l'Angleterre et de la Bourgogne avec la France, sous le règne de Charles VII*, Paris, 1936.

Boucher de Molandon, M. and Adalbert de Beaucorps, *L'armée anglaise vaincue par Jeanne d'Arc sous les murs d'Orléans*, Orléans, 1892.

Bourguignon, Eug., *Sainte Jeanne d'Arc (la guerrière)*, Bruges, 1928.

Bouvier, Armand, *Orléans, coeur de la France et Jeanne la libératrice*, Orléans, 1929.

Bradbury, Jim, *The Medieval Siege*, Woodbridge, 1992.

Brown, A.L., 'The English Campaign in Scotland, 1400', in *British Government and Administration: Studies Presented to S. Chrimes*, ed. H. Hearder and H.R. Loyn, Cardiff, 1974, pp. 40–54.

Bruley, Edouard, *Jeanne d'Arc à Orléans*, Orléans, 1929.

Burne, Alfred H., *The Agincourt War: A Military History of the Latter Part of the Hundred Years War from 1369 to 1453*, London, 1956.

——, *The Crécy War: A Military History of the Hundred Years War from 1337 to the Peace of Bretigny, 1360*, London, 1955.

Calemard, 'La chevauchée de Jeanne d'Arc et son appel aux habitants de Riom', *Revue politique et parlementaire* 140 (1929), 433–47.

Canonge, Général Frédéric, *Jeanne d'Arc guerrière*, Paris, 1907.

Carolus-Barre, Louis, 'Compiègne et la guerre, 1414–1430', in *111e Congres national des Sociétés savantes, Poitiers, 1986, Histoire médiévale, T. I: 'La France Anglaise'*, pp. 383–92.

Champion, Pierre, *Guillaume de Flavy: Captaine de Compiègne: Contribution à l'histoire de Jeanne d'Arc et à l'étude de la vie militaire et privée au XVe siècle*, Paris, 1906.

——, *Jeanne d'Arc*, Paris, 1933.

Charpentier, Paul, *Histoire du siège d'Orléans, 1428–1429*, Orléans, 1894.

Chevalier, Bernard, 'Les écossais dans les armées de Charles VII jusqu'a la bataille de Verneuil', in *Jeanne d'Arc: Une époque, un rayonnement*, Paris, 1982, pp. 85–94.

Choffel, Jacques, *La guerre de succession de Bretagne*, Paris, 1975.

Collet, Lieutenant-Colonel, *Vie militaire de Jeanne d'Arc*, Nancy, 1919.

Collin, M., *La casemate du bont du pont des Tourelles à Orléans du coté de la Sologne*, Paris, 1867.

——, *Les derniers jours du pont des Tourelles à Orléans*, Orléans, 1875.

Contamine, Philippe, 'Les armées française et anglaise à l'époque de Jeanne d'Arc', *Revue des sociétés savantes de haute-normandie. Lettres et sciences humaines* 57 (1970), 5–33.

——, 'La guerre de siège au temps de Jeanne d'Arc', *Dossiers de archéologie* 34 (May 1979), 11–20.

——, *War in the Middle Ages*, trans. M. Jones, Oxford, 1984.

Couget, Henri, *Jeanne d'Arc devant Paris*, Paris, 1925.

Curry, Anne E., 'L'effet de la libération sur l'armée anglaise: Les problèmes de l'organisation militaire en Normandie, de 1429 à 1435', in *Jeanne d'Arc: Une époque, un rayonnement*, Paris, 1982, pp. 95–106.

——, 'English Armies in the Fifteenth Century', in *Arms, Armies and Fortifications in the Hundred Years War*, ed. A. Curry and M. Hughes, Woodbridge, 1994, pp. 39–68.

Davies, R.R., *The Revolt of Owain Glyn Dŵr*, Oxford, 1995.

Debal, Jacques, 'Les fortifications et le pont d'Orléans au temps de Jeanne d'Arc', *Dossiers d'archéologie* 34 (May 1979), 77–92.

——, 'La topographie de l'enceinte fortifiée d'Orléans au temps de Jeanne d'Arc', in *Jeanne d'Arc: une époque, un rayonment*, Colloque d'histoire médiévale, Orléans, Octobre 1979, Paris, 1982, pp. 23–41.

Desana, Claude, 'La première entrevue de Jeanne d'Arc et de Charles VII à Chinon (Mars 1429)', *Analecta Bollandiana* 84 (1966), 113–26.

DeVries, Kelly, 'Contemporary Views of Edward III's Failure at the Siege of Tournai, 1340', *Nottingham Medieval Studies* 39 (1995), 70–105.

——, 'Facing the New Military Technology: Non-Trace Italienne Anti-Gunpowder Weaponry Defenses, 1350–1550', forthcoming in *Colonels and Quartermasters: War and Technology in the Old Regime*, eds. B.S. Hall and B. Steele, Cambridge, 2000.

——, 'God, Leadership, Flemings, and Archery: Contemporary Perceptions of Victory and Defeat at the Battle of Sluys, 1340', *American Neptune* 55 (1995), 223–42.

——, 'Hunger, Flemish Participation and the Flight of Philip VI: Contemporary Accounts of the Siege of Calais, 1346–47', *Studies in Medieval and Renaissance History* n.s 12 (1991), 129–81.

——, 'The Impact of Gunpowder Weaponry on Siege Warfare in the

Hundred Years War', in *Medieval City Under Siege*, ed. I.A. Corfis and M. Wolfe, Woodbridge, 1995, pp. 227–44.

——, *Infantry Warfare in the Early Fourteenth Century: Discipline, Tactics, and Technology*, Woodbridge, 1996.

——, 'The Lack of a Western European Military Response to the Ottoman Invasions of Eastern Europe from Nicopolis (1396) to Mohács (1526)', *Journal of Military History* 63 (1999).

——, 'Medieval Declarations of War: An Example from 1212', *Scintilla* 4 (1987), 20–37.

——, 'Military Surgical Practice and the Advent of Gunpowder Weaponry', *Canadian Bulletin of Medical History* 7 (1990), 131–46.

——, 'Robert Knolles', in *Medieval France: An Encyclopedia*, ed. W.W. Kibler and G.A. Zinn, New York, 1995, p. 341.

——, 'The Use of Gunpowder Weaponry By and Against Joan of Arc During the Hundred Years War', *War and Society* 14 (1996), 1–16.

——, 'A Woman as Leader of Men: A Reassessment of Joan of Arc's Military Career', in *Fresh Verdicts on Joan of Arc*, ed. C. Wood and B. Wheeler, New York, 1996, pp. 3–18.

—— and Robert D. Smith, *The Artillery of the Dukes of Burgundy* (forthcoming).

Dickinson, Joyceline Gledhill, *The Congress of Arras, 1435: A Study in Medieval Diplomacy*, Oxford, 1955.

Dousseau, Jean-Michel, *La bataille de Cravant (1423)*, Auxerre, 1987.

Duparc, Pierre, 'La délivrance d'Orléans et la mission de Jeanne d'Arc', in *Jeanne d'Arc: Une époque, un rayonnement*, Paris, 1982, pp. 153–8.

Dupuy, Micheline, *Bertrand du Guesclin, captaine d'aventure, connétable de France*, Paris, 1977.

Durlewanger, Armand, *The Royal Chateau of Chinon*, trans. Stan and Rita Morton, Colmar, 1982.

Etcheverry, Jean-Paul, *Arthur de Richemont le justicier, précurseur, compagnon et successeur de Jeanne d'Arc ou l'honneur d'être Français*, Paris, 1983.

Famiglietti, Richard C., *Royal Intrigue: Crisis at the Court of Charles VI, 1392–1420*, New York, 1986.

Fawtier, Robert, *The Capetian Kings of France: Monarchy and Nation, 987–1328*, trans. L. Butler and R.J. Adam, London, 1960.

ffoulkes, Charles, 'The Armour of Jeanne d'Arc', *The Burlington Magazine* 16 (Dec 1909), 141–6.

Fonssagrives, E., 'Jeanne d'Arc et Richemont', *Bulletin de la société polymathique du Morbihan* (1920), 3–20.

Fowler, Kenneth, 'Bertrand du Guesclin – Careerist in Arms?' *History Today* 39 (June 1989), 37–43.

——, ed. *The Hundred Years War*, London, 1971.

Funck-Brentano, Frantz, *Jeanne d'Arc chef de guerre*, Paris, 1943.

Gache, Paul, *Sainte Jeanne d'Arc à Vaucouleurs*, Vailly-sur-Sauldre, 1982.

Garnier, Joseph, *L'artillerie des ducs de Bourgogne d'après les documents conservés aux archives de la Côte-d'Or*, Paris, 1895.

Gibbons, Rachel, 'Isabeau of Bavaria, Queen of France (1385–1422): The Creation of an Historical Villainess', *Transactions of the Royal Historical Society*, sixth ser. 6 (1996), 51–73.

Girardot, Alain, 'La guerre au XIVe siècle: La dévastation, ses modes et ses degrés', *Bulletin de la sociétés d'histoire et d'archéologie de la Meuse* 30–31 (1994–5), 1–32.

Guenée, Bernard, *Un meutre, une société: L'assassinat du Duc d'Orléans, 23 novembre 1407*, Paris, 1992.

Haigh, Philip A., *The Military Campaigns of the Wars of the Roses*, Stroud, 1995.

Hallam, Elizabeth M., *Capetian France, 987–1328*, London, 1980.

Jacob, E.F., 'The Collapse of France, 1419–20', *Bulletin of the John Rylands Library* 26 (1941–2), 307–26.

——, *Henry V and the Invasion of France*, London, 1947.

Jaladon de la Barre, J.-L., *Jeanne d'Arc à Saint-Pierre-le-Moutier et deux juges nivernais à Rouen*, Nevers, 1868.

Jarry, Louis, *Le compte de L'armée anglaise au siège d'Orléans, 1428–1429*, Orléans, 1892.

Jordan, William Chester, *Louis IX and the Challenge of the Crusade: A Study in Rulership*, Princeton, 1979.

Jubault, P., *D'Azincourt à Jeanne d'Arc, 1415–1430*, Amiens, 1969.

Keen, Maurice, 'Richard II's Ordinances of War in 1385', in *Rulers and Ruled in Late Medieval England: Essays Presented to Gerald Harriss*, ed. R.E. Archer and S. Walker, London, 1995, pp. 33–48.

Laborde, L. de, *Les ducs de Bourgogne*, Paris, 1849.

Lancesseur, Lt-Colonel de, *Jeanne d'Arc, chef de guerre: Le génie militaire et politique de Jeanne d'Arc, campagne de France, 1429–1430*, Paris, 1961.

Lefèvre-Pontalis, Germain, 'Un détail du siège de Paris par Jeanne d'Arc', *Bibliothèque de l'écoles des chartes* 46 (1885), 5–15.

Le Patourel, John, 'The Origins of the War', in Kenneth Fowler, ed., *The Hundred Years War*, London, 1971, pp. 28–50.

——, 'The Treaty of Brétigny', *Transactions of the Royal Historical Society* fifth ser. 10 (1960), 19–39.

Liocourt, Ferdinand de, *La mission de Jeanne d'Arc*, 2 vols, Paris, 1974–6.

Lombarès, Michel de, 'Patay, 18 juin 1429', *Revue historique de l'armée* 22 (1966), 5–16.

Lot, Ferdinand, *L'art militaire et les armées au moyen âge en Europe et dans le Proche Orient*, 2 vols, Paris, 1946.

Lucas, Henry Stephen, *The Low Countries and the Hundred Years' War, 1326–1347*, Ann Arbor, 1929.

Luce, Siméon, *Histoire de Bertrand du Guesclin et son époque*, Paris, 1876.

——, *Jeanne d'Arc à Domrémy: recherches critiques sur les origines de la mission de la Pucelle*, 2 vols, Paris, 1886.

Marin, Paul, *La génie militaire de Jeanne Darc (siège de Paris, 1429)*, Paris, 1889.

——, *Jeanne d'Arc tacticien et stratégiste: L'art militaire dans la première moitié du XVe siècle*, 4 vols, Paris, 1889–90.

McFarlane, K.B., 'The Investment of Sir John Fastolf's Profits of War', in *England in the Fifteenth Century: Collected Essays*, London, 1981, pp. 175–98.

Mesqui, Jean, *Châteaux et enceintes de la France médiévale: De la défense à la résidence*, 2 vols, Paris, 1991.

——, *Provins: La fortification d'une ville au moyen âge*, Bibliothèque de la société Française d'archéologie, 11, Paris, 1979.

Mestre, J.-B., *Guillaume de Flavy n'a pas trahi Jeanne d'Arc*, Paris, 1934.

Michelet, Jules, *Joan of Arc*, trans. A. Guérard, Ann Arbor, 1957.

Mollat, Guillaume, *The Popes at Avignon, 1305–1378*, trans. J. Love, London, 1963.

Motey, Vicomte du, *Jeanne d'Arc à Chinon et Robert de Rouvres*, Paris, 1927.

Newhall, Richard Ager, *The English Conquest of Normandy, 1416–24: A Study in Fifteenth Century Warfare*, New Haven, 1924.

Nicholas, David, *The Van Arteveldes of Ghent: The Varieties of Vendetta and the Hero in History*, Ithaca, 1988.

Offler, H.S., 'England and Germany at the Beginning of the Hundred Years' War', *English Historical Review* 54 (1939), 608–31.

Olivier, René, 'La lance, l'épée et la hache (les armes de la Pucelle)', *Les amis de Jeanne d'Arc* 42.3 (1995), 14–21.

Oman, Charles, *A History of the Art of War in the Middle Ages*, 2 vols, London, 1924.

Palmer, J.J.N., 'The Anglo-French Peace Negotiations, 1390–1396', *Transactions of the Royal Historical Society* 16 (1966), 81–94.

——, *England, France and Christendom, 1377–99*, Chapel Hill, 1972.

——, 'The War Aims of the Protagonists and the Negotiations for Peace', in Kenneth Fowler, ed., *The Hundred Years War*, London, 1971, pp. 51–74.

Partner, Peter, *The Knights Templar and Their Myth*, second edn, Rochester, VT, 1990.

Pernin, C.-R., *Jeanne d'Arc à Troyes*, Paris, 1894.

Pernoud, Régine, *Joan of Arc by Herself and Her Witnesses*, trans. E. Hyams, New York, 1964.

——, *La libération d'Orléans, 8 mai 1429*, Paris, 1969.

——, *La spiritualité de Jeanne d'Arc*, Paris, 1992.

—— and Marie-Véronique Clin, *Joan of Arc: Her Story*, trans. and rev. J.D. Adams, New York, 1998.

Perroy, Edouard, *The Hundred Years War*, trans. W.B. Wells, New York, 1951.

Petit-Dutaillis, Charles, *The Feudal Monarchy in France and England from the Tenth to the Thirteenth Century*, London, 1966.

Phillpotts, Christopher, 'The Fate of the Truce of Paris, 1396–1415', *Journal of Medieval History* 24 (1998), 61–80.

Pirenne, Henri, *Histoire de Belgique*, Vol. II: *Du commencement du XIVe siècle à la mort de Charles de Téméraire*, Brussels, 1903.

Poulet, Dom Charles, 'Jeanne d'Arc à Chinon. Les causes naturelles et surnaturelles de l'acceptation royale', *Historisch tijdschrift* 1 (1923), 13–21.

Prentout, Henri, *La prise de Caen par Édouard III, 1346*, Caen, 1904.

Prevenier, Walter and Wim Blockmans, *The Burgundian Netherlands*, Cambridge, 1986.

Priestly, E.J., *The Battle of Shrewsbury, 1403*, Shrewsbury, 1979.

Puiseux, Léon, *Siège et prise de Caen par les anglais en 1417: Épisode de la guerre de cent ans*, Caen, 1868.

——, *Siège et prise de Rouen par les anglais (1418–1419)*, Caen, 1867.

Quicherat, Jules, *Histoire du siège d'Orléans et des honneurs rendus à la Pucelle*, Paris, 1854.

——, *New Aspects of the Case History of Jeanne d'Arc*, trans. H.G. Francq, Brandon, 1971.

Renouard, Yves, *The Avignon Papacy: The Popes in Exile, 1305–1403*, trans. D. Bethell, New York, 1970.

Rocolle, Pierre, *Un prisonnier de guerre nommé Jeanne d'Arc*, Paris, 1982.

Rogers, Clifford J., 'Edward III and the Dialectics of Strategy, 1327–1360', *Transactions of the Royal Historical Society* sixth ser. 4 (1994), 83–102.

——, 'An Unknown News Bulletin from the Siege of Tournai in 1340', *War in History* 5 (1998), 358–66.

Russell, Frederick H., *The Just War in the Middle Ages*, Cambridge, 1975.

Salamagne, Alain, 'L'attaque des places-fortes au XVe siècle à travers l'exemple des guerres anglo et franco-bourguignonnes', *Revue historique* 289 (1993), 65–113.

Schnerb, Bertrand, *Les Armagnacs et les Bourguignons: La maudite guerre*, Paris, 1988.

Scott, W.S., *Jeanne d'Arc*, New York, 1974.

Seward, Desmond, *The Hundred Years War: The English in France, 1337–1453*, New York, 1978.

Sorel, Alexandre, *La prise de Jeanne d'Arc devant Compiègne et l'histoire des sièges de la même ville sous Charles VI et Charles VII*, Paris, 1889.

Sumption, Jonathan, *The Hundred Years War: Trial by Battle*, Philadelphia, 1991.

TeBrake, William H., *A Plague of Insurrection: Popular Politics and Peasant Revolt in Flanders, 1323–28*, Philadelphia, 1993.

Thibault, Jean, 'Un prince territorial au XVe siècle: Dunois, Bâtard d'Orléans', *Bulletin de la sociétés archéologique et historique de l'Orléanais* n.s. 14 (1997), 3–46.

Thomas, Antoine, 'Le "signe royal" et le secret de Jeanne d'Arc', *Revue historique* 103 (1910), 278–82.

Thompson, Guy Llewelyn, *Paris and its People under English Rule: The Anglo-Burgundian Regime, 1420–1436*, Oxford, 1991.

Tolmie, Sarah, '*Quia Hic Homo Multa Signa Facit:* Henry V's Royal Entry into London, November 23, 1415', in *The Propagation of Power in the Medieval West: Selected Proceedings of the International Conference, Groningen, 20–23 November 1996*, eds. M. Gosman, A. Vanderjagt, and J. Veenstra, Groningen, 1997, pp. 363–79.

Tourneur-Aumont, J.-M., *La bataille de Poitiers, 1356, et la construction de la France*, Paris, 1940.

Tuck, Anthony, 'Richard II and the Hundred Years War', in *Politics and Crisis in Fourteenth-Century England*, ed. J. Taylor and W. Childs, London, 1990, pp. 117–31.

Vale, M.G.A., *Charles VII*, Berkeley and Los Angeles, 1974.

——, *War and Chivalry: Warfare and Aristocratic Culture in England, France and Burgundy at the End of the Middle Ages*, London, 1981.

Vandermaesen, Maurice and Marc Ryckaert, 'De Gentse opstand (1379–1385)', in *De Witte Kaproenen: De Gentse opstand (1379–1385) en de geschiedenis van de Brugse Leie*, ed. M. Vandermaesen, M. Ryckaerts, and M. Coornaert, Ghent, 1979, pp. 12–35.

Vannier, Daniel, *Beaugency*, Beaugency, 1991.

Vaughan, Richard, *John the Fearless: The Growth of Burgundian Power*, London, 1966.

——, *Philip the Bold: The Formation of the Burgundian State*, London, 1962.

——, *Philip the Good: The Apogee of Burgundy*, London, 1970.

Vergnaud-Romangnesi, M., *Notice historique sur le fort des Tourelles de l'ancien pont de la ville d'Orléans, où Jeanne d'Arc combattit et fut blessée, sur la découverte de ses restes en juillet 1831*, Paris, 1832.

Viard, Jules, 'La campagne de juillet–aôut 1346 et la bataille de Crécy', *Moyen Age* second ser. 27 (1926), 1–84.

——, 'Le siège de Calais, 4 septembre 1346–4 aôut 1347', *Moyen Age* second ser. 30 (1929), 124–89.

Villaret, Amicie de, *Campagnes des Anglais dans l'Orléanais, la Beauce Chartrain et le Gatinais (1421–1428): L'armée sous Warwick et Suffolk au siège de Montargis. Campagnes de Jeanne d'Arc sur la Loire postérierures au siège d'Orléans*, Orléans, 1893.

Warner, Marina, *Joan of Arc: The Image of Female Heroism*, Harmondsworth, 1981.

Werveke, Hans van, *Jacques van Artevelde*, Brussels, 1948.

Wheeler, Bonnie, 'Joan of Arc's Sword in the Stone', in *Fresh Verdicts on Joan of Arc*, ed. C. Wood and B. Wheeler, New York, 1996, pp. xi–xvi.

Wille, Erich, *Die Schlacht von Othée, 23 septembre 1408*, Berlin, 1908.

Williams, E. Carleton, *My Lord of Bedford, 1389–1435: Being a Life of John of Lancaster, First Duke of Bedford, Brother of Henry V and Regent of France*, London, 1963.

Wright, Nicholas, *Knights and Peasants: The Hundred Years War in the French Countryside*, Woodbridge, 1998.

Wylie, James Hamilton and W.T. Waugh, *The Reign of Henry the Fifth*, 3 vols, Cambridge, 1929.

Index